Second Class Citizens

The treatment of disabled people in austerity Britain

STEF BENSTEAD

Second Class Citizens

The treatment of disabled people in austerity Britain

STEF BENSTEAD

First published in September 2019 by the
Centre for Welfare Reform, Sheffield, UK

www.centreforwelfarereform.org

Copyright © Stef Benstead 2019

Typeset in Goudy Old Style by Henry Iles

288 pp

ISBN: 978-1-912712-18-2

All rights reserved. No part of this book may be
reproduced in any form without permission
from the publisher except for the quotation
of brief passages in reviews.

*Dedicated to
Reverend Mark Glew
with thanks*

Contents

Chapters

1. A breach of human rights?...9
2. Who are the disabled?...25
3. Disabled people in history..36
4. The dawn of welfare..45
5. The campaign for inclusion..58
6. Moving away from the welfare state...........................72
7. The ongoing welfare dependency narrative................86
8. The austerity programme...102
9. Employment and Support Allowance........................122
10. Employment Support..140
11. Personal Independence Payment...............................163
12. Social Care and the Independent Living Fund.........182
13. General benefits...202
14. Disability and access...226
15. Disability and poverty..243
16. A breach of rights...262
17. Epilogue: Moving forward...270

Figures

Figure 1. Cumulative impact of austerity policies...21
Figure 2. Complexity of disability...33
Figure 3. Housebuilding over time...80
Figure 4. Trend in social security for working age adults...103
Figure 5. UK social spending compared to OECD average...103
Figure 6. Debt as a percentage of GDP before and after 2007/08...105
Figure 7. History of UK debt and GDP...109
Figure 8. UK recovery from recessions...110
Figure 9. The inadequacy of Universal Credit...247

Boxes

Box 1. Disability data...27
Box 2. Mental illness data...32
Box 3. How the welfare state combats the five giants...48
Box 4. Principles of the welfare state...52
Box 5. ESA data...131
Box 6. Harms caused by ESA...132
Box 7. Outcomes of the Work Programme...146
Box 8. PIP & DLA award rate data...168
Box 9. Impact of cuts on adult social care...183
Box 10. On-going institutionalisation...193
Box 11. Failing housing policy...204
Box 12. Austerity's impact on housing...205
Box 13. Poverty in the UK...245
Box 14. Austerity's impact on poverty...251
Box 15. CHORUS principles...276

About the Author...286
Acknowledgements...287

1

A breach of human rights?

In 2016 the United Nations made an extraordinary announcement: that the United Kingdom, a rich and developed country, was violating basic human rights.[1] In particular, the UK was breaching disabled citizens' rights. This was not entirely unexpected. As early as 2012, less than two years into a new Conservative-Liberal Democrat Coalition Government, a committee made up of members of both the House of Commons and the House of Lords had concluded that the largely as-yet unimplemented plans for austerity measures were likely to be retrogressive.[2] The UK Independence Mechanism, responsible for independent monitoring of disabled people's rights in the UK, and Just Fair, a charity set up to examine the implementation of people's economic, social and cultural rights, had also supplied evidence of retrogression.[3]

The UN came to its conclusion following two extensive investigations. One was a routine investigation by the Committee on Economic, Social and Cultural Rights (CESCR), as part of a series of reviews of countries conducted by the UN on a rolling basis.[4] The second, specifically on disabled people's rights, was launched in response to evidence submitted to the UN that the UK was breaching disabled people's rights.[5] It was the first time that a country had been investigated specifically by the Committee on the Rights of Persons with Disabilities (CRPD) since its introduction in 2007. These additional investigations, carried out under the name of Optional Protocols, only happen upon receipt of a request to the UN to investigate alongside reliable evidence of serious, grave or systematic violations of rights.

The CESCR report, to which they invited the UK Government to respond, concluded that the cuts in and changes to public spending that were initiated since 2010 were sufficiently grave and insufficiently necessary that they were a breach of rights. The UN's expression of being "seriously concerned" by the disproportionate impact of spending cuts on poor and disadvantaged people and "deeply concerned" about the cuts introduced by the Welfare Reform Act 2012 and Welfare Reform and Work Act 2016 is not typical. These are unusually high warnings for a body that mostly restricts itself to merely expressing 'concern' about the grave and systematic violations of rights on which it reports.

As well as the two committee-based investigations, the UK has also been visited by nine UN Special Rapporteurs between 2010 and 2018. Special Rapporteurs are unpaid experts appointed by the UN to investigate either specific countries, such as Eritrea and Syria, or specific themes, such as education, toxic waste and indigenous peoples. Unlike the Optional Protocols, which require reliable evidence of actual grave or systematic violations, these Special Procedures can be carried out where there is as-yet only a high risk of violation, including general trends and draft policy.[6] Special Rapporteurs make their own decisions regarding whether to investigate a country, but won't investigate if a request for investigation is clearly politically motivated. These reports contribute to the Universal Periodic Reviews that the UN carries out into every country on a four to five year rolling basis.

Perhaps the two most significant visits since 2010 have been the 2013 visit of Raquel Rolnik on the role of housing in the right to an adequate standard of living ("Outrage as 'loopy' UN investigator lectures Britain"[7]), and the 2018 visit of Philip Alston on extreme poverty ("some good outcomes have certainly been achieved, but great misery has also been inflicted unnecessarily"[8]). Both found violations of human rights and received high media attention. Other visits under the Special Procedures, such as on freedom of assembly (the anti-terrorism strategy, Prevent, "is having the opposite of its intended effect: by dividing, stigmatising and alienating segments of the population"[9]), racism ("alarming increase in hate crime and a normalisation of hateful discourse"[10]) and privacy ("the UK can now justifiably reclaim its leadership role"[11]) did not receive the same media or political attention.

1. A BREACH OF HUMAN RIGHTS?

The UK Government strongly disagreed with the findings of the various UN investigations, with one MP even calling the CESCR's report a "grotesque misrepresentation."[12] The government pointed to the amount of money it spends on sick and disabled people each year and reiterated its own conclusion that it is a world leader in providing for disabled people. It claimed that the use of personal budgets in social care have increased people's choice and control; that housing and transport has been made more accessible; that there is a wide range of work-related support available to disabled people; and that disability-related benefits have been exempt from the wider benefit freezes.[13] It also pointed to its intentions for integrating work and healthcare as another example of increasing inclusion for disabled people. The government did agree that it is right that it be committed to implementing the various rights as laid out in the UN Conventions, but believed that it was adequately meeting these requirements.

The UK Government is exceptional in its assessment of its provision of disabled people's rights. All other bodies, whether user-led disabled people's organisations, charities, independent monitors, parliamentary committees or international overseers, consider that the UK Government has breached disabled people's rights since the election, in 2010, of a coalition government committed to austerity and reducing the role of the government in public life (typically by deregulation and contracting out public services to the private sector). Many of the points raised by the UK Government in its defence against the CRPD report are matters of contention, with the reality behind the government's words being quite different from the alleged intent.

This book sets out what has actually happened to disabled people's lives in the UK since 2010, and to some extent why, so that we can understand whether there is a problem that needs rectifying and to what extent there has been a breach of rights. First, however, we need to understand what our human rights are and what it means to be in breach of them.

Basic rights

After the horrors of World War II, there was widespread international consensus that a new framework for international law was needed. Countries wanted to make sure that the social conditions that eventually resulted in the Holocaust could not happen again. Humanity needed a common standard of fundamental rights that, universally applied, would prevent a repeat of the barbarous atrocity of the Holocaust. The declaration of these basic human rights was to remind us that we all, whatever ability or lifestyle or race, have a minimum level of humanity that merits a minimum decency of treatment.[14]

Drafted by the representatives of multiple countries, the UN Declaration of Human Rights had to achieve consensus amongst people from a wide range of legal and cultural backgrounds. It had to sift out which rights were basic across all peoples and societies, and which were not. The result was a comprehensive document of 30 Articles, or statements, regarding the basic rights of all people that applied across all times, places and cultures. These ranged from the right to freedom from slavery and torture, through equal recognition before the law, to the right to personal development.

Whilst careful not to declare as a fundamental right anything that was culturally-bound, the agreed-upon minimum included not just surviving at the physical level but also the right to live in an environment that promotes thriving at the social and cultural level.

Article 25 declares:

> *"Everyone has the right to a standard of living adequate for the health and well-being of himself and of his family, including food, clothing, housing and medical care and necessary social services."*

This is expanded upon in Article 22, which includes social and cultural rights and lays responsibility at the door of the State, to ensure that:

> *"Everyone, as a member of society, has the right to social security and is entitled to realisation, through national effort and international co-operation and in accordance with the organisation and resources of each State, of the economic, social and cultural rights indispensable for his dignity and the free development of his personality."*

Generally speaking, people achieve much of their economic, social and cultural rights through their right to decent work with just and favourable pay (Article 23). By being in paid employment, individuals can earn money to purchase the goods, services and access to society that they need to meet their physical, social and cultural needs. Paid work itself can contribute to social and cultural needs – if it is decent work.

1. A BREACH OF HUMAN RIGHTS?

Not everyone is able to engage in (sufficient) paid work to meet their physical, social and cultural needs. But everyone still has the right to fulfilment of these needs, as stated in Article 25:

> *"[Everyone has...] the right to security in the event of unemployment, sickness, disability, widowhood, old age or other lack of livelihood in circumstances beyond his control."*

At these points in a person's life, when illness or old age or recession mean a person cannot work, it becomes incumbent upon the State to step up. Savings don't last forever without replenishment, and the families of those unable to work may not earn enough to support another adult. Governments have a responsibility to ensure that, through whatever mechanisms they judge best, no-one is left unable to participate fully in society or thrive socially and culturally, let alone unable to meet basic physical needs such as food and housing.

Whilst citizens also bear responsibility, in particular to engage in remunerative work to provide for themselves, a person cannot have a responsibility to work if work is not available to them. To blame and penalise a person in such a situation is manifestly unfair. Such a person may be sick or disabled; over-burdened with caring duties; or living in an area of deprivation where there aren't enough jobs for every jobseeker. Whatever the reason, the State has a duty to its citizens to provide the opportunity to succeed in work for those who can work and to provide alternative means to access basic rights for those who can't work.

The UK has agreed that these are basic human rights which the government is under an obligation to make available to all of its citizens. It has formally ratified the UN Declaration of Human Rights, International Covenant on Economic, Social and Cultural Rights and Convention on the Rights of Persons with Disabilities. It has issued standing invitations to the UN to allow any Special Rapporteur to visit under the Special Procedures mechanism, rather than deciding which Rapporteurs can come on a case-by-case basis; and has additionally signed the Optional Protocols, which allow the UN to receive complaints regarding rights violations and investigate those which the appropriate Committee considers to contain reliable evidence of grave and systematic violations. The UK has thereby given Special Rapporteurs and UN Committees the right to investigate and comment on the UK's provision of human rights.

Progressive realisation

The UN recognises that achieving human rights takes time and resources; basic rights simply can't be achieved overnight even if a country had all the resources necessary. The UN therefore only asks that countries firstly meet a minimum core of rights, and secondly work towards the provision of full human rights. The minimum rights are the rights to essential food, essential primary healthcare, basic shelter and housing and a basic education. Any country in which a significant number of individuals do not have access to one or more of these is, prima facie, breaching human rights.[15]

The minimum core is not an indicator of success in achieving human rights, but rather is one of two sufficient conditions for being in breach of human rights. A country that is succeeding on the basic core must then also meet the second condition, which is that it actively works to progress access to human rights. The UN requires that a State that has ratified a given UN Convention must, and without delay, take intentional, real steps to improve human rights. This means that the government must be continuously and explicitly working to improve the living standards and access to human rights of its citizens, and enacting policies that make concrete improvements to people's lives. Countries that have established the absolute bare minimum but are failing to progress are in breach of human rights as well as countries that are not providing the bare minimum.

For example, if the benefits available to sick and disabled people have never been adequate for a decent standard of living, then it is not acceptable merely to increase benefits in line with inflation each year, and thus preserve their real value. This would be a breach of rights, by failing to improve the lot of people who are in need. To not be guilty of breaching rights, the government must be doing all that it can to increase the real value of benefits for people too sick or disabled to work. A regression in rights or failure to progress when progression was possible are both breaches of rights.

A breach in rights doesn't necessarily mean a deliberate choice to cut goods or services. It might be the consequence of other policies or actions that impact on the provision of, access to and enjoyment of our human rights. For example, a programme of house destruction that didn't first ensure that the people made homeless had a suitable property to go to could be a breach of human rights. This has happened in Nigeria, where the clearing of informal fishing settlements such as Otodo-Gbame has been ruled a breach of rights, because there were no resettlement plans for the evicted people.[16]

1. A BREACH OF HUMAN RIGHTS?

It was not the clearing of the slum so much as the failure to provide for those affected that was the problem.

Similarly in London, some residents of the Heygate and Sutton estates feel that they have been treated the same way. When the Heygate estate was knocked down, residents were promised a new development of desirable and affordable homes. But owners had been served compulsory purchase orders at levels around only 25% of what one of the new, 'affordable' homes would cost.[17] In Sutton, there are plans to demolish 462 social flats and replace them with 237 social and 106 private flats, which could not possibly accommodate all of those made to leave their homes.[18]

Reducing financial support to people in need can also be a breach of rights, if it means people are less able to achieve independence or basic standards of living. Of course, it would not be a breach of rights if people had enough resources after the reduction to achieve basic living standards. Reducing child benefit to better-off parents, therefore, was not a breach of rights – these parents can afford the necessities and even some luxuries without state aid. However, if financial support for a particular group of people – such as the long-term sick and disabled – was only just enough to afford them an adequate standard of living, then a cut in this support could be a breach of rights. Such reductions in the level of support is one of the things that the UN Committees were looking for as they investigated the UK.

Maximum resources

The UN accepts that a country may, at times, have no choice but to find itself going backwards. There may be particular economic or political circumstances that mean that the current state of human rights cannot be maintained. Drastic cases would include countries under invasion or following a major natural disaster, but countries may also find themselves in straitened economic circumstances. In these circumstances, it is not a breach of human rights to go backwards – provided that the government is taking all possible means to restore and progress human rights. The country remains under an obligation to provide the core minimum rights and to devise strategies for improving the enjoyment of human rights.

In the context of a country whose economy is struggling, a position that the UK was in when the Conservative-led Coalition Government came into power in 2010, the central importance of human rights means that any spending cuts that are likely to hamper human rights must be minimised by firstly making full use of all available resources, and secondly by making cuts fall more heavily on the better-off. Any reductions in public spending must only occur after the government has made full use of its ability to increase its spending power. The UN says that,

> "any deliberately retrogressive measures in that regard would require the most careful consideration and would need to be fully justified by reference to the totality of the rights provided for in the Covenant and in the context of the full use of the maximum available resources..."[19]

'Balancing the books' therefore isn't just about cutting outgoings; it is about increasing spending power as well. We will discuss in Chapter 8 how an accurate understanding of fiat money releases governments from the ostensible need to collect tax or borrow in order to spend (fiat money is money that is backed by the government, rather than by a commodity such as gold). But even countries that are not the sovereign supplier of their own currency, such as users of the euro, have a number of options for increasing what is available to them to spend before they have to start thinking about reducing what they spend. Thinking only about taxation, revenue can be increased by collecting more of the tax that is owed, closing loopholes that allow tax avoidance, pursuing tax evaders, and reducing tax breaks to rich companies and individuals. All of these measures can be done without increasing the nominal tax rates; actually increasing tax rates or overhauling the tax system are further tools the government has available to it for increasing its revenue relative to spending. The UK Government could also have borrowed money; with interest rates at historic lows for several years after 2010, the UK could have borrowed substantial sums at little cost. This would have met the publics' demand for bonds as a secure investment whilst making available to the government money that it could spend on necessary goods and services. Money used in such a way easily generates enough economic growth to cover the debt incurred.[20]

The UK therefore had a number of options available to it for improving the balance between spending power and need. The UK could, and should, have maximised the resources available to it for spending, but it did not. Instead, the government has implemented a number of tax cuts for the richest in society, including by increasing the threshold for the 40% higher rate tax and by cutting the additional rate tax from 50% to 45%. This is the reverse of maximising resources.

1. A BREACH OF HUMAN RIGHTS?

Proportionate response

As well as being counter to the principle of maximising a country's available resources, tax cuts for the better off are contrary to the principle of proportionality.

The UN says that,

> "even in times of severe resource constraints whether caused by a process of adjustment, of economic recession, or by other factors the vulnerable members of society can and indeed must be protected by the adoption of relatively low-cost targeted programmes."[21]

The first step for a government suffering resource constraints is to maximise the resources available to it, such as through direct money creation balanced by appropriate taxation. If this is still insufficient, then governments can consider spending cuts. Such cuts must fall in areas where they least directly impact people's human rights. In order to protect vulnerable members of society, cuts must therefore fall upon the better-off: there is a vast difference between taking £20,000 from a family with £100,000 compared to taking £2,000 from a family with £10,000, even though proportionately they are the same. Examples of such cuts might be reductions in business subsidies and corporate welfare, an ending of public sector golden handshakes and a removal of charitable status from fee-paying schools such as Eton.

Only when no more cuts can be taken from the better-off does it become acceptable to enact cuts that reduce anyone's enjoyment of human rights.

It is therefore incumbent upon the government to identify which groups in society currently have most enjoyment of their human rights and which groups have least. Governments have a duty to continue to come up with plans for improving access to human rights, even during times of spending constraints, but this can only be done if the government knows where human rights currently are and are not being enjoyed. When determining on areas for cuts, the government should bear in mind its duty to increase human rights access for the most deprived in society and take actions to fulfil this even as it enacts spending cuts in other areas.

It would be sensible to order cuts from those which have least impact on human rights to those which have most. Whilst allowing for other objectives, such as preventative actions and long-term outcomes, cuts to government spending should still broadly fall in this order. This means that a reduction in the implementation of or access to human rights for people in poverty, deprivation or disadvantage should only occur after government has both raised all the revenue it can and has run out of cuts that it can reasonably make on people with greater incomes, influence and advantage.

The UN's findings from the CRPD

The UN initiated its inquiry into the UK's treatment of disabled people because it had received a number of reports alleging that social security and wider welfare cuts were having a negative effect on disabled people.[22] In April 2013, the CRPD received a formal request that they investigate the matter. The CRPD registered the request and, pursuant to procedure, asked the UK Government to reply. In the following April, having received two reports from the government, the CRPD concluded that it had reliable information that there may have been serious and systematic violations of disabled people's rights, and that therefore it would investigate.

During its investigation, the CRPD spent 11 days in the UK, interviewing over 200 people and receiving over 3,000 pages of evidence. The reports from the UK Government included statements that were at variance with the information received from the complainants. The CRPD therefore went to considerable effort to establish the truth by cross-referencing data from a variety of sources, including official government statistics. In some cases, the government's statements were either unsupported by the evidence or there was no data available to check the accuracy of the government's position. The CRPD, upon completing its investigation, concluded that there was reliable evidence of grave or systematic violations of the rights of disabled people in the UK. Not only were there numerous examples of regression, but many disabled people had been left unable to manage the bare essentials of life.

The CRPD stressed the importance that disabled people be able to choose where they live from the same range of options as non-disabled people, in particular to prevent disabled people being separated from their families. The government is therefore required to ensure that enough resources have been allocated to the care arrangements for disabled people to allow disabled people to live in the community, and not be constrained by the quality, availability or location of provision of care.

1. A BREACH OF HUMAN RIGHTS?

The benefits or social protection system should ensure that disabled people have an adequate income for a sufficient duration of time to enable an adequate standard of living. Instead, the CRPD found that people are left in significant financial, material and psychological hardship during assessment processes and benefit sanctions, even when people are assessed as unfit for work. Sick and disabled people who were assessed as fit for work generally still had substantial health-related barriers to work, and there was no evidence that these people were being adequately protected and cared for in the Jobseeker's Allowance system. Sick and disabled people, whatever benefit they received or none, were not getting any meaningful help to get and sustain work, whilst others who were previously supported in work lost their jobs after their support programmes were closed. This was despite the government saying that getting disabled people into work was both the reason and mitigation for benefit cuts.

Assessments for disability-related benefits "failed to take in account the support persons with disabilities need to perform a job or the complex nature of some impairments and conditions, or reflect the human rights-based approach to disability". Despite some measures to improve assessments, disabled people still "felt that they were merely processed rather than being listened to or understood" and that "the needs, views and personal history of persons with disabilities, and particularly those requiring high levels of support such as persons with intellectual or psychosocial disabilities, were not properly taken into account or given appropriate weight in the decisions affecting them." Evidence suggested that the assessors had "a persisting lack of awareness and limited knowledge of disability rights and the specific needs of persons with disabilities", despite the training given to them. Supporting information for helping disabled people with their benefit applications was limited and not always accessible; and the appeals process had been made more difficult by the addition of an extra bureaucratic step requiring benefit claimants to ask the original decision-making body, the Department for Work and Pensions (DWP), to reconsider before being allowed to proceed to an independent judgment.

The consequence of multiple cuts across social security, housing, social care and other welfare spending is that "core elements of the rights to independent living and being included in the community, an adequate standard of living and social protection and their right to employment have been affected: persons with disabilities affected by policy changes have had their freedom of choice and control over their daily activities restricted, the extra cost of disability has been set aside and income protection has been curtailed as a result of benefit cuts, while the expected policy goal of achieving decent and stable employment is far from being attained". Disabled people have been made more dependent upon others and many no longer have their essential needs met. The post-2010 austerity policies "have caused financial hardship to persons with disabilities resulting in, *inter alia*, arrears, debts, evictions and cuts to essentials such as housing and food". Although theoretically available, various hardship payments to help those most affected by social security cuts have not been promoted and are inadequate in scope or duration for the amount of need created.

The UN's findings from the CESCR

Although the government has not looked at how all of the cuts and changes cumulatively impact people, other groups have. The CRPD reported that the social security cuts are having a disproportionately adverse impact on disadvantaged and marginalised citizens, and the more disadvantaged a person is the more they have lost not just in proportional but in absolute terms. Several organisations have calculated a 'cumulative impact assessment' which show how the overall impact of government changes to tax and spending has disproportionately impacted the poor, for example Figure 1. By focusing cuts on the poorest people in society, the government has ignored the basic rule of ensuring that any cuts do not harm those in need, whilst falling proportionately across the rest.

In most cases the government was aware that its new policies were retrogressive but justified them on the grounds of resource constraints and 'being fair to the taxpayer'. But resource constraints are not a justification unless all other measures to mitigate such constraints, such as raising taxes, putting more effort into fully collecting tax, or targeting cuts at highly paid individuals, have been tried and found to be insufficient. The UK has not tried such measures; indeed, it was the combination of further cuts to a disability benefit alongside tax reductions for the better-off that led the MP Iain Duncan Smith, in charge of the social security cuts instigated between 2010 and 2016, to resign his position as head of the DWP.[23]

Because of this failure to fully utilise all resources available to it, a previous report by the UN Committee on Economic, Social and Cultural Rights (CESCR) had recommended that the government undertake a

1. A BREACH OF HUMAN RIGHTS?

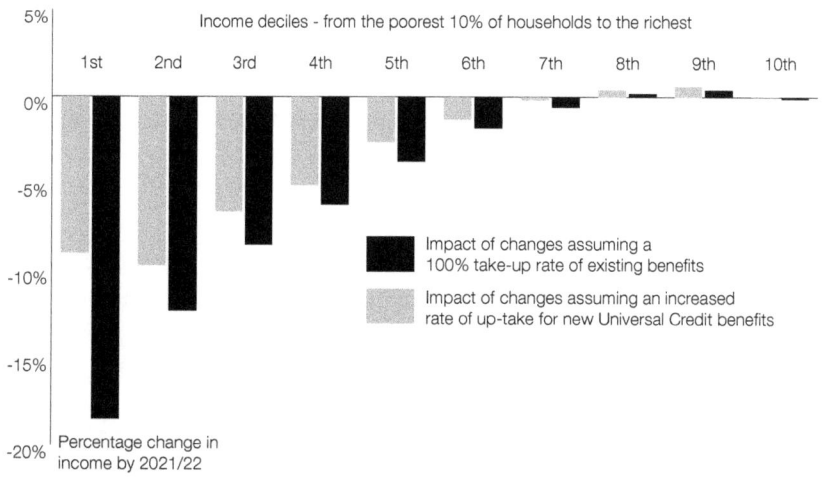

Figure 1. Cumulative impact of austerity policies

Analysis by the Equality and Human Rights Commission (EHRC) shows that poorer people have suffered more cuts in both absolute and proportionate terms than have better-off people. It is important to note that this analysis makes optimistic assumptions and the real world effect is likely to be even worse than this.

human rights impact assessment; increase measures to tackle tax abuse "in particular by corporations and high-net-worth individuals"; and create an "adequate, progressive and socially equitable" tax policy that "increases the resources available for spending on economic, social and cultural rights."[24] Essentially, the UN told the government that it should reverse and then progress away from its tax and spending decisions since 2010. The government should have increased tax receipts and increased spending, but instead it had cut spending and to some extent used this to subsidise tax cuts for the better off. This is unacceptable.

The UN did not consider that the UK could justify these cuts as necessary given the economic circumstances, because the UK Government had not done its best to use all of its available resources, increase its resources or spread the cuts in a way such that those with the most money and advantage experienced the largest cuts. The CESCR concluded that recent tax policies – such as reductions in inheritance and corporation tax, financial secrecy legislation and permissive rules on corporate tax – are making it harder for the government "to address persistent social inequality and to collect sufficient resources to achieve the full realisation of economic, social and cultural rights". The government cannot, therefore, use reduced resources as a valid justification for cutting support to sick and disabled people, because it has not done everything it can to increase the resources it has and to spread the burden of cuts proportionately according to people's ability to pay.

The CESCR therefore wrote to remind the government of "its obligations under the Covenant to use the maximum of its available resources, with a view to progressively achieving the full realisation of economic, social and cultural rights." It also wrote to remind the government that any cuts that do take place under austerity measures should be temporary, as well as necessary and proportionate. They should therefore be reversed as soon as possible and as a matter of priority. Instead, the decision to keep most benefits at their 2016 nominal rates until 2020 remains in place, and changes have been made that further cut the value and scope of disability benefits since the CRPD's report was published in October 2016.

Next steps

The UN and the UK Government have come to very different conclusions regarding the UK's provision for disabled people. The UK Government remains confident that it is a world leader in disability rights, and that in recent years it has improved its provision through better targeting of resources and more support to help disabled people get and stay in work. The UN, in complete contrast, has concluded that the UK Government is gravely breaching disabled people's rights. It considers that the government has cut too much support from disabled people, with the result that these people are unable to access all their basic rights, and are less able to do so than they were before 2010.

This book aims to present the evidence on the policy changes that have affected disabled people, and the impact that the changes have had, so that we can see whether the UN or the UK Government is more accurate in its depiction of disabled people's lives. But to do this, we need to start with answering what seems like a simple question: who are these disabled people? If we aren't sure who is included, then we can't be sure whose rights are potentially being breached, and we can't hold politicians to account.

1. A BREACH OF HUMAN RIGHTS?

NOTES FOR CHAPTER 1

1. **Committee on Economic Social and Cultural Rights (CESCR)** (2016) Concluding observations on the sixth periodic report of the United Kingdom of Great Britain and Northern Ireland: advance unedited version. UNITED NATIONS E/C.12/GBR/CO/6.
Committee on the Rights of Persons with Disabilities (CRPD) (2016) Inquiry concerning the United Kingdom of Great Britain and Northern Ireland carried out by the Committee under article 6 of the Optional Protocol to the Convention: Report of the Committee. UNITED NATIONS CRPD/C/15/R.2/REV.1

2. **Joint Committee on Human Rights** (2012) Implementation of the right of disabled people to independent living. 23rd report of session 2010-12. LONDON: HOUSE OF LORDS AND HOUSE OF COMMONS.

3. **Just Fair** (2014) Dignity and opportunity for all: securing the rights of disabled people in the austerity era. London: Just Fair UK Independent Mechanism (2014) MONITORING THE IMPLEMENTATION OF THE UN CRPD LONDON

4. **CESCR** (n 1)

5. **CRPD** (n 1)

6. **United Nations, Office of the High Commissioner.** Human Rights Bodies > Special Procedures > Communications. Available at www.ohchr.org/EN/HRBodies/SP/Pages/Communications.aspx

7. **Chapman J and Doughty S** (11/09/2013) Outrage as 'loopy' UN inspector lectures Britain: She's from violent, slum-ridden Brazil, yet still attacks us on housing and human rights. LONDON: DAILY MAIL

8. **Alston P** (16/11/2018) Statement on Visit to the United Kingdom, by Professor Philip Alston, United Nations Special Rapporteur on extreme poverty and human rights. United Nations, Office of the High Commissioner

9. **Kiai M** (2016) Closing space for civil society in the United Kingdom. UNITED NATIONS, OFFICE OF THE HIGH COMMISSIONER

10. **Achiume E** (2018) UN rights expert hails UK for anti-racism action but raises serious concerns over Immigration Policy, Prevent programme and Brexit. UNITED NATIONS, OFFICE OF THE HIGH COMMISSIONER

11. **Cannataci J** (2018) UK jointly leads Europe and world on privacy after big improvements, says UN rights expert. UNITED NATIONS, OFFICE OF THE HIGH COMMISSIONER

12. **The United Kingdom Government Response to the Report by the United Nations' CRPD under article 6 of the Optional Protocol to the Convention (2017).** Weald, O as referred to in Mortimer, C. (08/02/2017) Government refuses to accept austerity measures are breach of human rights. LONDON: THE INDEPENDENT.
Lidington D (12/01/2017) Business of the House, HOUSE OF COMMONS, HANSARD v619 c480

13. **United Kingdom Government Response** (n. 12)

14. **United Nations** (1948) Universal Declaration of Human Rights

15. **CESCR, Committee on Economic, Social and Cultural Rights, General Comment 3, The nature of States parties'**

16. **obligations** (Fifth session, 1990), U.N. Doc. E/1991/23, annex III at 86 (1991)
16. **BBC News** (21/06/2017) Otodo-Gbame: Nigeria court rules eviction unconstitutional.
17. **Jones A** (13/04/2017) Every flat in a new south London development had been sold to foreign investors. VICE CHANNELS.
18. **Batty D** (20/09/2017) Why are housing association flats lying empty when Grenfell survivors need them? THE GUARDIAN.
19. **CESCR** (n 15)
20. **Zenghelis D** (2016) Building 21st century sustainable infrastructure (part 1): time to invest. CENTRE FOR CLIMATE CHANGE ECONOMICS AND POLICY, AND GRANTHAM RESEARCH INSTITUTE ON CLIMATE CHANGE AND THE ENVIRONMENT. **Organisation for Economic and Cultural Development** (2014) Recommendation of the Council on effective public investment across levels of government.
21. **Committee on Economic, Social and Cultural Rights, General Comment 3, The nature of States parties' obligations** (n15)
22. **CRPD** (n 1)
23. **Duncan Smith I** (18/03/2016) In full: Iain Duncan Smith resignation letter. BBC NEWS
24. **CESCR** (n 1)

2

Who are the disabled?

In the last chapter, we saw how the United Nations had come to a conclusion that the UK governments since 2010 have breached disabled people's rights through their austerity policies and in particular the restrictions to benefits, housing and social care. The purpose of this book is to lay out in more detail the evidence underpinning the conclusion reached by the UN as well as why the UK Government so strongly disagrees. However, before we can do that we need to have a common understanding of the term 'disabled' and of who therefore is affected by disability-related policy. We will also, in the next few chapters, consider the history of UK support for disabled people, because as we have seen it is not only the actual position but also the possibility of retrogression that is of concern. History will also help us to understand how and why we have got to where we are and what could or should be done about it.

Traditional understandings of disability

For many of us, the first thing we think of when someone raises the topic of disability is a wheelchair user or maybe a guide dog. We see Blue Badge signs, ramps, lifts and priority seating all around us when we are out and about, all of which serve to remind us of limited mobility and in particular wheelchair users. 'Guide dog only' signs and, sometimes, Braille writing point to the presence of blind people whilst hearing loops highlight the needs of people with hearing loss. There are reminders all around us of these types of disability.

These are people like Fiona, who was born with the hereditary condition retinoblastoma bilateral, and had to have both her eyes removed before she was 2 years old.[1] Fiona uses a white cane to help her get around, and at school she had a dedicated teaching assistant to help her by converting the set work into something suitable for a child with no vision. She did well enough at school to go on to university to study maths.

They are also people like Gemma, who is deaf. When Gemma was a child, she went to a school that was specialised for teaching deaf children, but the focus was on teaching English – to children who could barely hear – and British Sign Language was banned. Gemma essentially grew up without a language. Although she didn't receive the help she needed as a child, as an adult she is now able to use assistive devices and is attending evening classes to improve her skills and abilities.

These more traditionally-recognised physical disabilities are often associated in our minds with persons of good physical, mental and cognitive health; people who are no different from anyone else, bar of course the loss of use of their eyes, ears or legs. It is easy to think that a few aids or adjustments can make up for that loss, raising the disabled person to the same level – or close enough – as every other healthy adult. So long as the right technology is in place – and why wouldn't it be? – disabled people are no longer disadvantaged, just different.

This view is supported by the increasing attention given to the Paralympics, the Invictus Games and the Commonwealth Games. The athletes competing in these para-sports show that disabled people can still be fit, active and healthy – often far more so than the average non-disabled person! The Commonwealth Games has gone so far as to integrate the para- and non-para- sports, so that both compete at the same Games and medals from both para- and non-para- athletes count towards a country's medals total. Para-athletes are widely touted as inspirational and positive proof of a 'can do', 'there's no such word as can't' attitude.

Another traditional disability is learning disabilities. These people are increasingly visible in society, as more young learning disabled people live into adulthood and the old hospitals, asylums or institutions are closed down. Learning disabled people are now more commonly supported to live as self-governing and independent adults in the community of their choice, where they are our neighbours and friends, and sometimes our work colleagues or the staff members who come to our aid.

In terms of numbers, approximately 360,000 people in the UK are registered as blind, although up to two million have reversible sight loss, moderate sight loss or have not registered as blind. At least 24,000 people are known to use British Sign Language as their main language, and 900,000 people are severely or profoundly deaf. There are around 40,000 people with spinal injury (paralysed), and 350,000 people with severe learning disabilities. Many of those who are blind or deaf are pensioners who have lost their sight or vision with age, whilst many of those who have learning disabilities are children or younger adults, because historically the life expectancy of people with learning disabilities has been very low.

At the same time, 12 million people are defined as disabled in the UK. It is clear therefore that many disabled people do not have one of these traditional disabilities, as their numbers are measured in hundreds of thousands, not millions (Box 1).[2] The typical disabled person, therefore, cannot be someone who is essentially in good health other than for a specific impairment of vision, hearing, limb use or cognition. There must be something else.

> **Box 1. Disability data**
>
> **360,000** people are registered blind.
> **24,000** people use British Sign Language as their first language.
> **40,000** people use wheelchairs because of spinal injury.
> **350,000** people have a severe learning disability.
> There are around **12 million** disabled people in the UK. This is almost **20%** of the population.
> Around **6 million** working-age people are disabled, or approximately **16%**.
> **6%** of children and **45%** of pensioners are disabled.

The definition of disability

Under UK law (Equality Act 2010), disability is any physical or mental impairment that has a substantial and long-term (longer than 12-months) impact on a person's ability to perform normal day-to-day activities. Whilst many people may experience symptoms common to various disabilities, if these are short-term then they are not included under the definition of disabled. However ill we feel when afflicted with the flu, or however restricted by a broken thigh, these experiences aren't counted as disabilities.

Many disabled people are elderly, as the ageing process results in the gradual breakdown of our bodies and our capabilities. Most people will end up disabled eventually. But around half of disabled people, or six million, are of working-age. Working-age disabled people have borne most of the changes in policy since 2010, as pensioners, whether disabled or not, have been explicitly excluded from most benefit changes, and benefits for disabled children have largely not changed. Disabled children and pensioners are, however, as impacted as working-age adults by the ability of local councils to pay for necessary services such as social care and education.

Because disability is any impairment that has a substantial and long-term impact, it is not just about the static, traditional impairments. It also includes chronic physical illness, severe and enduring mental illness, and personality and autism spectrum disorders. Danni, for example, was a normal, healthy child until she was nine years old, when she started to experience complications as a consequence of her congenital spina bifida. Her spinal cord twisted and left her with nerve damage to her bladder, bowel and left leg. She had to have repeated surgery, at one point leaving her wheelchair bound due to an unrecognised impinged nerve. For a long time she was told that there was nothing wrong and that her inability to use her left leg was merely psychological. Operations, kidney infections, pain and septicaemia became her life. Her local school failed to keep her up-to-date with educational material, and eventually Danni's father resigned his job in order to take the task of educating his daughter upon himself. The drop in income experienced by the family was harsh.

Moving into adulthood, Danni has tried to work, but repeated attempts land her in hospital battling septicaemia every time, even though she has only ever worked part-time. Over a period of more than ten years, Danni has persisted in trying to complete an Open University degree, despite the cost to her health. Danni can stay (relatively) healthy by not being active – not working or studying – but whether she is inactive as a necessary precaution or inactive because she's bed-bound, the effect remains that her illness disables her.

However, whilst useful as a base on which to agree, the legal definition is not the UK's only definition of disability. The phrasing used influences who does and doesn't report as disabled. For example, the Labour Force Survey referred to 'disabilities or long-term health problems' up until 2013, and after that used the phrase 'physical or mental health conditions or illnesses.' This shift resulted in a reduction in the numbers reporting a long-

2. WHO ARE THE DISABLED?

term health problem of nearly 400,000 (exact numbers are impossible to prove), largely due to people in work who have cardiovascular problems or diabetes no longer reporting themselves as in the disabled category.[3] The General Household Survey, which reports different levels and even different trends in disability to the Labour Force Survey, uses 'long-standing illness, disability or infirmity.'

The context can also influence self-reported disability rates. The Labour Force Survey used to ask people if they were disabled at work, disabled in day-to-day living, or neither. Whilst around 20% reported being disabled at work and/or in day-to-day life, around 5% were disabled at work without experiencing disability in day-to-day life and 3% were disabled in day-to-day life without being limited in work.[4] Some people may be limited in the type of work they do but able to work full-time, whilst others may be able to work in any one of a wide range of jobs so long as they work only a limited number of hours. Other surveys assess disability by asking about performance on a list of functional activities, such as climbing stairs or reading, and then noting the cumulative total; these are then dependent upon which questions they ask as to which people are defined as more or less disabled.

Definitions of disability have been likened to an archery target, with progressively smaller concentric rings representing tighter and tighter definitions of disability. On the outer ring may be people with a long-term health condition that is well-managed, such as some people with diabetes or cardiovascular conditions; whilst these people have a long-term condition, they are not disabled. The next ring in might represent people with minor functional impairments, such as people who need larger print or other small modifications that tend to adequately alleviate their condition. Progressively smaller rings end with the inner-most ring containing the people with the severest of impairments, who may need expensive mobility aids and 24/7 care, or are completely bed-bound.

Who counts as disabled therefore depends upon what exactly is being looked at. Critically, as will be seen throughout this book, the government is able to implement regressive policies by periodically tightening or adjusting whom it counts as truly 'disabled'. So when the government says that it is protecting disabled people despite cutting access to out-of-work sickness benefit, it does so by ignoring those disabled people who are assessed as able or nearly able to work. Yet in previous years, these disabled people would still have been recognised as needing help and support – as the governments' own figures show that they do.[5] This sleight of hand and moving of the goalposts allows successive governments to reduce support to some disabled people by hiding it under the cloak of help still provided to other disabled people.

Many disabled people use the social model of disability to define and describe the source of their disability. The social model posits that it is not the person's impairment (such as being deaf or paralysed) that is the problem, but the set-up of society which has more steps than ramps, and very few British Sign Language (BSL) users. The social model of disability is contrasted with the medical model, which locates the disability in the person's impairment. The different models tend to lead towards different solutions: the social model would see more ramps, wider passageways and BSL taught to everyone; the medical model would focus on healthcare to increase people's ability to walk or hear, or would teach people how to lip-read and how best to propel a manual wheelchair. By placing the main responsibility for adjustment with government and society, the social model shows that people who have an impairment do not have to be excluded from parts of society, nor bear the cost of access wholly by themselves.

Chronic physical illness

Chronic physical illness can be a whole host of different things: infectious diseases; blood conditions; bowel disorders; skin complaints; joint problems. These broad-brush categories sound innocuous and are reminiscent of childhood gymnastics and shin-pad rash. But in the context of disability, they refer to the more severe conditions such as Ehlers-Danlos Syndrome, where joints can dislocate so often that they can't be kept in place, or epidermolysis bullosa, where the skin separates from the tissues below and causes widespread debilitating blisters. When it comes to disability, it is not the name or type of condition that matters, but its severity and impact on normal life.

Some of the key features of chronic physical illness are chronic and severe pain or fatigue, variation in (dis)ability over a range of timescales, difficulties thinking or concentrating (often because of pain or fatigue) and generalised difficulty with any activity. Many illnesses come under this umbrella, often as auto-immune attacks on various different parts of the body or as one of a variety of ways in which the autonomic system can fail. Then, of course, there are the 'old age' diseases which don't always wait for a person to turn 65. Cancer, Parkinson's disease and dementia can all cripple someone long before they are ready to stop working.

Other conditions such as spina bifida, cerebral palsy and cystic fibrosis can sometimes seem to straddle the static disability/chronic illness divide. They tend to be present from birth or from a young age, and can cause problems with mobility whether due to spinal cord damage, brain damage or breathing difficulties. Their presence from birth tends to make people think of them alongside the static impairments, whilst their symptoms of pain or fatigue are more similar to the experiences of people with chronic illness. Again, a diverse range of causes can result in similar functional problems.

To make things even more complicated, not everyone with a long-term illness thinks of themselves as disabled. Danni, for example, does not think of herself as disabled. And the lived experience of chronic illness can be as different from a healthy person with a static impairment as it is from being fully healthy and able-bodied. Some people therefore prefer to use the phrase 'chronically ill' as a better reflection of their reality. Largely because of this difference, there is conflict within and between the more traditionally disabled communities compared to those disabled by chronic illness as to the extent to which the social model applies to people with long-term incapacitating illness. People with severe pain and fatigue tend to experience an overall limit on activity levels, with little that society can do or change to mitigate it. The lack of scope for amelioration, plus the origin as an illness or disease, leads some people to question whether chronic illness counts as a disability at all. This book uses the Equality Act definition of disability, which includes physical chronic illness.

Long-term mental illness

The other big group of disabled people is people with mental illness. Many countries have seen a large increase in severe and enduring mental illness over the last few decades. The reasons are not always clear and can vary from country to country, but in the UK it has been associated with an increase in low-skilled, high pressure jobs.[6] These are jobs that place a premium on speed and long hours over technical expertise and a decent working environment for employees. These jobs tend to come with high pressure and little autonomy, creating a toxic high strain environment that produces high levels of unremitting stress. Long-term stress results ultimately in the physical and mental breakdown of the body, including through common public health conditions such as cardiovascular disease, back pain, depression and anxiety. Researchers have found that this increase in low skill, high strain jobs is likely to be a significant contributor to the rise in incapacitating mental illness in the UK in recent decades.

Whilst depression and anxiety are the leading mental health problems, the other conditions are not insignificant. At any one time, around 220,000 people are being treated for schizophrenia, and over 700,000 have Obsessive-Compulsive Disorder (OCD), most of whom are severely affected. It is estimated that 1 in 50 people may have bipolar disorder, including people not yet diagnosed or receiving treatment. Diagnosis of a mental health condition requires that it has a substantial impact on a person's life, so it should not be surprising to find that many people with a mental illness would struggle to work, or that over one million people on sickness benefit are classed as being unable to work primarily for mental health reasons.

> ### Box 2. Mental illness data
>
> **1 in 100** people experience an episode of schizophrenia at some point in their life.
>
> At any one time, around **220,000 people** are being treated for schizophrenia.
>
> Approximately **13% of people** on sickness benefit have a psychotic disorder.
>
> Over **700,000 people** have Obsessive Compulsive Disorder (OCD). Most people with OCD are severely affected by it.
>
> Around **1 in 50 people** may have bipolar disorder, including people not yet diagnosed or receiving treatment. 1 in 8 people on sickness benefit screen positively for bipolar.
>
> Around **700,000 people**, or 1% of the population, have autism.
>
> **One third of people** on sickness benefit may have ADHD.
>
> Around **50%** of the 2.5 million people in receipt of sickness benefit have primarily a mental health condition.

Nor is every condition listed as 'mental illness' for benefit purposes actually a mental illness. The group includes people with learning disabilities and developmental disorders, as well as personality disorders and autism spectrum disorders. These conditions aren't the same as mental illnesses but they tend to be grouped with such, largely because they don't mesh easily with physical illness either.

2. WHO ARE THE DISABLED?

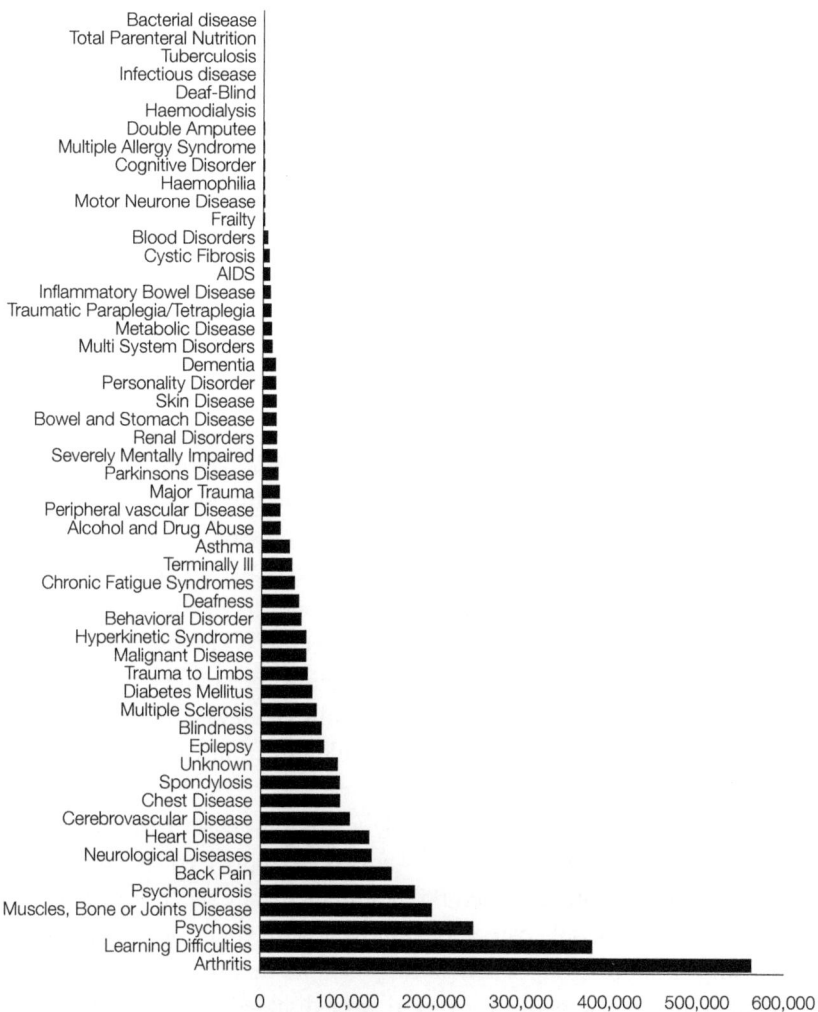

Figure 2. Complexity of disability

Taking data from DWP benefit tables (2011) it is clear that disability is a far more complex and wide-ranging reality than many people realise.

Natalie has Borderline Personality Disorder, also known as Emotional Instability Disorder. For her, it means emotions that rocket from 0-60 in the blink of an eye, and remain at that intensity for far longer than they would for anyone else. These emotions are often either hugely excessive relative to the situation, or even completely inappropriate – such as rage over a minor incident, or laughing at sad news. The sheer intensity is so emotionally painful that physical outlets, such as self-harm, are often sought as the only way to cope. Just living through those emotions and learning to remain safe in them is exhausting in a way that emotionally stable people cannot understand. Natalie has spent several years hospitalised and in community hostels whilst she received intensive support to learn to manage her condition.

People with these various disorders are particularly unlikely to view themselves as disabled and, along with others, may use phrases such as 'differently normal' to describe how their abilities and talents are different from neuro-typical people but not lesser. However, other people with the same conditions do feel that they experience some level of impairment and disability. In these situations, it is often best to use the individual's self-definition, as only they know whether or not they feel impaired or disabled.

The key point here is the sheer diversity of disability. From the traditional static-but-healthy disabilities to life-long chronic illness, and from debilitating mental illness to personality or autism spectrum disorders, there is no one image that reflects the experiences, needs and abilities of disabled people. For the purposes of this book, we will refer to all these people using terms like disabled, chronically ill and long-term sick, because listing all the caveats and conflicts of opinions would be clumsy and cumbersome. But this is not to suggest that disabled people can validly be viewed as a homogenous group. Different disabilities are as much different from each other as they are from a healthy, non-disabled person.

Support needs are therefore also widely varying, as we will see more of in this book. Some people can, and want to be, supported to work, whilst others need to be protected from the requirement or expectation that they try to work. Some people can, and want to, live in their own home, whilst others want a more group-based setting. Simple mantras of work or independent living as the goal for every sick or disabled person overlook the differing needs and abilities of the people concerned. It tends to result in giving everyone the same form of support, which whilst helpful for some will be at best neutral and at worst actively harmful for others.

Much of our stereotypical understandings of disability are rooted in historical views, passed down the generations with little scrutiny. These stereotypes are both inaccurate (when they consider the traditional disabilities) and too narrow (in excluding others). In the next chapter, we look at historical understandings of disability and treatment of disabled people. This sets the scene for the origins of the welfare state so that we can make an informed critique of the post-2010 changes that are the subject of this book.

2. WHO ARE THE DISABLED?

NOTES FOR CHAPTER 2

1. Unless otherwise specified, the people in this book are all people who have shared their stories with me for the purposes of this or other writing, and names have been changed.
2. **Papworth Trust** (2018) Disability in the United Kingdom: facts and figures. RNIB (2018) Eye health and sight loss stats and facts. NHS UK WWW.NHS.UK/CONDITIONS/LEARNING-DISABILITIES/
3. **Hankings M and Chandler M** (2016) Measuring disability in the Labour Force Survey. LONDON: OFFICE FOR NATIONAL STATISTICS
4. **Labour Force Survey,** April 2010 to April 2013 data
5. **DWP** (2013) Evidence based review of the Work Capability Assessment: a study of assessments for Employment and Support Allowance
6. **Marmot M, Goldblatt P, Allen J et al** (2010) Fair society, healthy lives. Strategic review of health inequalities in England post-2010. LONDON: STRATEGIC REVIEW OF HEALTH INEQUALITIES IN ENGLAND POST-2010. Marmot's report points to what he calls 'toxic' jobs. Toxic jobs combine pressure to work at high speed with little control over the tasks that are to be performed, low wages, long hours and high job instability. Toxic, high strain jobs are associated with increases in mental illness, cardiovascular disease and metabolic problems.
László KD, Pikhart H, Kopp MS, Bobak M, Pajak A, Malyutina S, Salavecz G and Marmot M (2010) Job insecurity is associated with an increased likelihood of ill-health, regardless of age, sex, marital status or education. JOB INSECURITY AND HEALTH: A STUDY OF 16 EUROPEAN COUNTRIES. SOCIAL SCIENCE AND MEDICINE VOL. 70 ISS: 6, PP. 867-874. People with little job control are more likely to claim sickness benefits in the following year. If the UK had not seen a decrease in job control in recent decades, fewer people would have become unable to work due to illness.
Baumberg B (2014) Fit-for-work – or work fit for disabled people? The role of changing job demands and control in incapacity claims. JOURNAL OF SOCIAL POLICY VOL 43 ISS. 2, PP. 289-310 DOI: 10.1017/S0047279413000810

3

Disabled people in history

In the last chapter, we saw that the traditional disabilities, such as sensory impairment and loss of use of limbs, make up only a small proportion of all disabled people. Most disabled people are people who have a long-term physical or mental illness that limits their ability to take part in activity.

In the next few chapters, the history of how disabled people have been viewed and treated sets the scene for the post-2010 changes to disabled people's rights.

Medieval and early modern history

Disabled people in medieval times were treated much the same as anyone else, as they lived and worked in the family and community groups. In these agrarian, subsistence-based economies, almost everyone could do something, although in fact quite often it was not necessary. Contrary to popular belief, the lives of peasant farmers weren't constant hard physical graft, but were marked by short hours and regular days or even whole weeks off.[1] It simply didn't take very long to produce the goods needed to provide for one's self and family and cover the rent owed to the local landowner. There was therefore no need for disabled people to live elsewhere to be specially catered for, and nor were they burdens dependent upon the goodwill and sacrifice of hard-striving others, whether family, friends, church or State. They were simply a normal part of community in which working the land took up only 150 days per household each year.

People held a variety of attitudes towards those with disabilities. There was a widespread belief in purgatory, a place of suffering that purified a person between death and entering heaven. Some people thought that disabled people were undergoing an earthly purgatory and purification; therefore disabled people must, as an outcome of their ongoing purification, be more holy than most. Others saw disability as a natural part of living in a world broken by sin, and that therefore disability neither brought nor indicated any particular status; it was simply the way that the world is. Still others held the negative view that those who were disabled were being punished for some past sin; disabled people were therefore in some way inferior or less holy. Both the 'saint' and 'sinner' explanations saw disabled people as 'other' and different to the main non-disabled population.

Regardless of the believed spiritual cause, people still considered themselves to have a Christian responsibility to care for the sick and disabled, and this they did; some simply by caring for their own family members, and others through donations to the local churches who would then distribute support to those in need. Monks and nuns would care for the 'passing poor' – people who would need somewhere to stay overnight as they roamed the country looking for work or selling goods that they had made. Such people were permitted to stay only one night in any one place before moving on.

Over time, it came to be common practice that those who were sick would be allowed to stay in monasteries until they had recovered, rather than moving on to the next place after only one night's stay. As many of these people had conditions from which they would not recover, this practice eventually resulted in the first hospitals, some of which specialised in particular conditions such as leprosy or blindness. These hospitals and almshouses provided a decent home, with the opportunity to work in the fields and gardens and to enjoy the natural world. Demand for places was high, and the work was funded by donations from well-off people, some of whom saw it as a way to smooth their own passage to heaven. However, there were always some cases of corruption around, where the siphoning off of funds to directors and managers left the people living in the hospitals vulnerable to neglect and abuse.

Tudor period

When King Henry VIII decided to become the head of his own church in England in 1531, distinct from the Roman Catholic church, he insisted that all the Roman Catholic monasteries be closed. Those sick and disabled people who had been supported in these monasteries were left without a home or means of support. However, as England was still primarily an agrarian society, most sick and disabled people were still living in community with their families; they were often married with children, and like everyone else would work at whatever they could do. Families who were unable or struggling to support a disabled family member could receive assistance from their local church. Because hospitals and almshouses were expensive to build, assistance after the closure of the monasteries was predominantly through 'outdoor relief', such as money, food or clothing, rather than through the 'indoor relief' of monasteries, almshouses and hospitals.

Over time, it became the prevailing view that the proper place for disabled people was in institutions. New poor laws condemned the workless poor who were deemed able to work, but did provide for the sick and disabled. So it was necessary that the sick and disabled be distinguished from the able-bodied poor. By living in institutions, sick and disabled people could receive protection from the typical requirement that people work to support themselves, and they could be safely (and cheaply) provided for. This took the work of care away from families, who could then focus on engaging in paid work, but it also meant that families were separated and disabled people were less able to live with their loved ones. This increased the tendency to view disabled people as in some way different and distinct from other members of society.

New hospitals and almshouses were gradually built to replace the monasteries, often as public rather than religious buildings, and paid for by wealthy tradesmen who were more interested in boosting their reputations than in considerations of purgatory. Some hospitals were built on a grand scale with public money; others came from charitable groups in a reaction against ostentatious building programmes. But whatever the origins, the quality of the institution itself still depended upon the people who ran it. As before, some people ran institutions for their own gain, taking large sums of money, whilst others focused on providing humanitarian care through kindness, reason and a family atmosphere.

The Bethlem, or Bedlam, hospital was one of those that had been caught up in Henry VIII's dissolution of the monasteries. In the following decades it passed through various hands before coming under the control of Helkiah Crooke in 1619. Sadly he, like many others, falsified accounts in order to steal money; to steal the money, he also had to deprive his patients of food and basic care and neglect the maintenance of the building itself. In 1676 a new, larger hospital was built to replace the ramshackle, uncared for building but, despite its added room and landscaped gardens, it didn't bring better conditions to its residents. Medicine still relied upon the idea of four 'humours' which were believed, when out of alignment, to cause illness. The treatment was to reduce one of the 'humours', such as by extensive blood-letting or causing people to vomit. Staff continued to use manacles, straitjackets and other physically controlling methods to contain what they saw as disruptive, out of control or dangerous people – people who often were merely reacting against the loss of freedom and basic rights in their lives. Life in Bedlam Hospital was so poor that its name has entered the English language as a word meaning uproar, disorder and confusion.

Around the same time, deaf and blind people established the first specialist schools for people with sensory impairment, where they could be taught useful trades that would enable them to support themselves economically. The church schools that provided education for the children of poor families typically did not cater for disabled children. Specialist schools were therefore the only option for many disabled children of poorer families. Although beneficial, in providing the opportunity for a useful education, it showed that society still thought of disabled people as different from non-disabled.

Industrial revolution

The industrial revolution brought a substantial change to the lives of disabled people. There was a mass urbanisation as individuals and families left the country to work in factories and mills. But the pressure and emphasis on speed in the new workplaces, and the technical and physical abilities required to operate the machines, were too high for people whose capabilities were reduced in one way or another. Disabled people could not participate in this new, industrial economy.

The machines and mills could produce very quickly what used to be produced slowly by hand. This had several impacts: fewer workers were needed; the price of goods fell; and hand-made items became unprofitable. It was also preferable to employers that they have fewer employees working longer hours, rather than spread the work over more people; training costs were reduced, for example, if there were fewer employees.[2] Consequently, unemployment rose, at the same time as hand-to-mouth work stopped being a viable alternative. People simply wouldn't buy hand-made wares anymore. Thus disabled people, alongside many able-bodied people, ended up being displaced from work without any alternative.

The population was also growing rapidly, which only increased the gap between the available jobs and the number of people looking for work. Because so many people needed support, it was becoming prohibitively expensive to provide outdoor relief. There was also a rising belief that outdoor relief was being abused by people who didn't really need it, rather than there genuinely not being enough work for everyone. So new laws were brought in, to stop the provision of outside support (at least to the able-bodied) and to increase the use of workhouses.

Workhouses were deliberately designed to be miserable places, to make any form of work preferable to being in a workhouse. The assumption was that able-bodied people who were not in work were workless by choice, rather than because of a lack of jobs or the loss of viability of working by hand. The workhouses were designed to incentivise these undeserving people to change their behaviours and attitudes and engage in paid work. Financial relief was thought to encourage laziness, whereas workhouses encouraged work.

As intended, able bodied people did their best to avoid workhouses – even if it meant dying destitute and homeless, as Charles Dicken's elderly character Betty Higden did in his novel *Our Mutual Friend*. So increasingly it was only the sick, disabled, orphans and elderly who lived in workhouses, where they received the same workhouse uniform, monotonous food and communal dormitories, but did not have to engage in hard labour. However, they were allowed very few visitors, so whilst not required to engage in demanding work they were not permitted to do much else either.

In the same era, improvements in medicine gave people hope that the mentally ill or handicapped could be cured of their condition and so returned to society as able-bodied workers. Thus it was better for these people to be in institutions, where they might be healed, than in communities where their disability would persist. Before the industrial revolution, only a few hundred mentally disabled people lived in charitable asylums at any one time. By 1900, over 100,000 such people lived in asylums and an additional 10,000 lived in workhouses. The early asylums were pleasant places, with gardens and orchards, farms and bowling greens, all with the intention of curing their patients and returning them to the outside world.

But it soon became clear that mental illnesses and impairments were not as amenable to treatment as had been hoped. As more and more people came, and very few left, the asylums became overcrowded and the hope of a cure was lost. The goal changed from cure to containment of disabled people in often unpleasant conditions, against which some not unsurprisingly rebelled. This provided managers with an excuse for physical or pharmaceutical restraint of residents, but it did nothing to help the residents themselves or ensure a decent quality of life.

The combination of the loss of suitable work and the lack of hope for a cure led to a change in the way that disabled people were perceived. No longer the deserving poor, who deserved help because they were not at fault, disabled people instead became merely a costly burden. They couldn't, and wouldn't be able to, work; so instead of their disability meaning that they were worthy of support it meant simply that there was no point in supporting them. These attitudes were supported by shifts in thinking associated with the decline of religious faith and development of social Darwinism. The Social Darwinist, Herbert Spencer, coined the phrase 'survival of the fittest' after reading Darwin's *On the Origin of Species by Natural Selection*. Social Darwinists took Darwin's theory of evolution as scientific proof that those who are most successful are naturally superior; conversely, the less successful – including non-whites and the disabled – were inferior and not fit to reproduce. The answer was eugenics: the disabled or deficient were a threat to society, and therefore should be removed.

The 20th Century

Eugenics was a major force in the Edwardian period. Many well-respected and powerful people advocated the compulsory sterilisation of disabled people, to prevent the passing-on of disability to future children. Winston Churchill wrote in a memo that, "the multiplication of the feeble-minded… is a very terrible danger to the race".[3] In 1909, William Beveridge – widely perceived as the author of the UK Welfare State – wrote that whilst the disabled should be supported by the state, it should be with "complete and permanent loss of all citizen rights – including not only the franchise but civil freedom and fatherhood".[4] It was believed that if the disabled were allowed to have children, then the whole of society would be undermined by the many people who were unable to work and support themselves. In contrast, if only the healthiest and most intelligent were to have children, then we could produce a superior human race.

The idea of eugenics fitted well with the existence of workhouses, as disabled people were already segregated from society and even from themselves – there was strict segregation by age, sex and ability within the institutions. There was therefore little chance of 'contamination' or of disabled people having children.

Over time, conditions in the workhouses gradually improved, with inmates given more variety in what they ate and access to reading material as well as occasional trips out. But from such a poor start, there was still a very long way to go to achieve the basic rights of disabled people. When workhouses were officially abolished in the 1930s, many of the old workhouse buildings simply transitioned into long-stay institutions for the people who had lived there when they were called workhouses. The change in name did nothing to change the underlying reality.

The First World War prompted a slight change in attitudes. Many returning servicemen were disabled in some way or another, and far from being a burden on society, these disabled veterans were people who had served heroically; they were people worthy of support. Rehabilitation, sheltered employment and housing were all set up to provide for ex-servicemen, although in practice only a small proportion received help. The level of need that WWI caused simply wasn't anticipated by the authorities. However, it did lead to new rehabilitation services for men injured whilst engaged in manual industry, as attention was brought to the existence of this deserving, hard-working or 'heroic disabled' category.

Things didn't really change for the civilian disabled. Many had taken on work during WWI, filling the gaps left by men who had gone to fight. But when these men returned, they also took back their jobs, displacing the disabled. Many mentally disabled people were sent to new colonies of 900-1500 people, separated into villas of up to 60. Here they lived in large sex-segregated dormitories, away from the rest of society. The colonies were self-contained with farms, kitchen gardens, kitchens, laundries, workshops, recreational facilities and even a mortuary in each one. There was no need for disabled people to go out into the rest of society.

The 1918 Education Act had made it compulsory for all children, including disabled children, to be educated. But in keeping with the eugenics ideology, it was thought best to keep disabled children away from their (non-disabled) families. So children also lived in colonies, separately from the adults, where they had their own residential schools. Innovative measures were put in place, such as 'open air' schools where teaching was done outdoors. Children were, as far as possible, given access to countryside and fresh air over the unhealthy air of cities and overcrowded buildings. They were taught trades and life skills rather than a more standard curriculum, in the belief that this was what they most needed if they were to be able to work and live independently as adults; deaf children were also taught to lip-read rather than to sign. But as with most schools at the time, discipline was harsh, and children were not always happy. Families were encouraged to forget about their disabled children, separating them even further from normal life and any semblance of a childhood, and leaving the children to grow up believing that they had been rejected by their parents.

The impact of history

Disabled people have been subject to a range of views throughout history, from saints to sinners and from the deserving to the burdensome. The economic structure of society has impacted society's view of disabled people, which in turn has affected how they have lived and worked. In pre-industrial times, disabled people typically lived and worked with their families as a normal and accepted part of society. Some were supported by churches, including in monasteries and church-based hospitals. With the closure of Roman Catholic monasteries came the need for a state-based system of support, leading eventually to new hospitals and workhouses.

In the industrial era, disabled people began to be pushed out of work, unable to keep up with the rate of production by machines. Instead of being a functional part of society, disabled people began to be seen as a burden. Increasingly, they were encouraged and expected to live in institutions where they could be protected from poverty and the deliberately stigmatising poor laws that were applied to able-bodied people. But as these institutions became overcrowded, conditions deteriorated. An initial hope that many disabled people could be cured was proved false.

Society began to take the view that disabled people were a burden and threat to humanity, despite a brief period when disabled people engaged in paid work during WWI. Though there were some positive initiatives, such as the attempts by specialist schools to fit disabled children for participation in society, the overwhelming assumption was that disabled people were best kept away from society. Many people agreed with and supported the new eugenics movement, and many disabled people who were not already living in institutions were taken to new colonies or placed under strict supervision. Consequently, disabled people did not have the right to determine where they lived, receive a full education or gain access to work. Often, because of the conditions in which they lived as well as their lack of choice and control, they did not have an adequate standard of life.

NOTES FOR CHAPTER 3

1. **Schor J** (1992) The overworked American: the unexpected decline of leisure. NEW YORK: BASIC BOOKS
2. **Kutner R** (02/02/1992) No time to smell the roses anymore. NEW YORK: NEW YORK TIMES.
3. **Churchill W** (1910) Letter to Herbert Asquith, then Prime Minister of the UK.
4. **Beveridge WH** (1906) The problem of the unemployed. SOCIOLOGICAL PAPERS VOL 3 PP 323-41

4

The dawn of welfare

We saw in the last chapter that perceptions of disabled people have varied throughout history. There has never been one view of disabled people; even before the Industrial Revolution, there were a range of ideas regarding the nature of disabled people, from sinners to saints. Disabled people have not always been expected to live in institutions apart from the rest of society; they have often participated in communities as full members, and some have excelled. Families have always been the main source of support, but the cultural assumptions about where responsibility should lie shifted from families to local communities to, more recently, central government. New ideas and ways of living resulted in large hospitals being built to house and, in theory, cure disabled people. But the need was overwhelming, and disability proved generally resistant to cure. Provision for disabled people began to fail.

Disabled people at the start of the 20th century did not have access to their full human rights. They were deliberately put out of sight, to be out of mind, and many prominent members of society supported the idea of eugenics through selective breeding. Then came a second world war, and with the uncovering of the horrors of the Holocaust the eugenicist movement fell dramatically out of favour. The Liberals had already been replaced by Labour as the Conservative's main opposition party, and the vote had been given to all adults and not just men with property. The ruling class became less powerful, and collectively the turbulent period of the first half of the 20th century led to a growing desire for change.

In this chapter, we look at the changes that came in during and after the Second World War, and the progress that they brought in the realisation of basic human rights. In particular, the new welfare state sought to address the rights of all citizens to an adequate standard of living, healthcare, education and work.

The need for a welfare state

Harry Smith grew up during the Great Depression.[1] His family moved from Barnsley to Bradford in 1929, joining what was essentially a slum occupied by the destitute and jobless. The poor relief that was available could cover rent or food – but not both. He describes being kept awake at night by ex-soldiers screaming as they dreamed of their memories of war, and disturbed during the day by the cries of dying cancer sufferers unable to afford morphine. In winter and at night time, his own gnawing hunger was compounded by cold. This was daily life before the welfare state.

The Second World War triggered a change in all of that. The evacuation programme saw poor urban children mixing with rural families. Class and country divides were brought down as rich met poor, and it became clear to the rich that charity had never ended poverty, and never could. London lost over one million homes and much of its docklands, whilst the entire centre of Coventry was destroyed in one night. It was clear, months before the end of WWII, that a rebuilding of society was needed, both socially and physically. There was hope that a new country could be built in such a way as to lock out the evils of past societies, and lock in a new peace and prosperity.

WWII also broke down the antipathy to large government with extensive control. The government had of necessity taken over a wide variety of industries and practices – from the control of factories to the rationing of fuel, and from control over who worked where to encouragement to 'dig for victory' and grow one's own food. It had done so with substantial success. Big government was therefore no longer anathema, but something that could be desired for the success it brings.

The place where Harry grew up has now been replaced by Bradford University. For Harry, this was a keen reminder of the difference that government can make. After WWII, a new government was elected on a manifesto promising a free National Health Service, education, housing and jobs. The post-war years saw strong economic growth over a prolonged period. Living standards for the poor improved substantially, and inequality fell. Children no longer lived in slums.

4. THE DAWN OF WELFARE

Building the welfare state

Rebuilding Britain to care for all its citizens was a bipartisan goal, and its importance and urgency was nationally recognised. As well as the need for physical and social rebuilding, politicians from more capitalist countries were very aware of the rising support for more communist economic systems. They were keen for capitalism to prove itself as a viable economic system, and in particular that it should not afford the working classes any reason to revolt against it. A new welfare state, in which government made provision for the wellbeing of its citizens, was seen as a way to maintain the stability of the country and stave off the threat of communism.

To advise it on how to rebuild the UK, the Coalition government that led Britain during WWII set up a Ministry for Reconstruction. It also commissioned a report on the matter, which once published had a revolutionary impact on people's thinking. Entitled *Social Insurance and Allied Services*, it became known as the Beveridge report after its author, Sir William Beveridge. It was comprehensive in scope, both in its analysis of the problems and in its proposed solutions. The report both reflected and set the tone for politics for the next 30 years.

The Beveridge report was greeted ecstatically, and not just by the poor. 76% of people in the upper income groups supported the implementation of the report, and 92% of professionals.[2] The concern amongst many was not the cost – an issue on which public and political opinion was divided – but that the proposals would be watered down. Amongst the Conservatives, more than 40 MPs signed a motion for the immediate creation of a Ministry of Social Security. Quintin Hogg, a Conservative MP and later Lord Hailsham, considered the report to be a "relatively Conservative document", and favoured the idea of "publicly organised social services, privately owned industry."[3]

Britain was tired of war-time austerity, and keen to avoid the inter-war Great Depression. The 'boys back from the front', and the men and women who had laboured at home, deserved a country worth fighting for. People wanted relief and hope: relief from the privations and restrictions of economic depression and world war; and hope for a peaceful, prosperous and happy country. It was clear that the previous economic consensus had broken down, and that a new approach was needed. Beveridge's report showed that it was possible.

In his research for the report, Beveridge found that there were five major factors contributing to individual poverty and economic retardation.

Famously referred to as the five "Giant Evils", these were, in his words, Want (poverty), Idleness (lack of jobs), Squalor (bad living conditions), Disease (ill-health) and Ignorance (lack of education). Three of these are covered in the core rights that the UN set out as the minimum starting point on which States must build: basic shelter and housing; essential primary healthcare; and a basic education. The remaining basic right, to essential food, is met through decent employment and adequate social protection.

The Beveridge Report made concrete suggestions on how to remedy these five evils. In doing so, the government and citizens of the UK would together rebuild the country on a fairer, more moral and ultimately more productive footing. Beveridge considered that it was entirely possible to build and fund such an economy, and that it was right to do so both pragmatically on economic grounds and morally on the grounds of human rights. The implementation of the welfare state coincided with, and arguably contributed to, years of strong economic growth and a rapid drop in debt as a percentage of GDP.

> **Box 3.** How the welfare state combats the five giants
>
> **SOCIAL SECURITY** - benefits including income replacements and child benefit - combating **WANT** (poverty)
>
> **JOBS** - creation and maintenance by the government of full employment - combating **IDLENESS** (worklessness)
>
> **HOUSING** - a government house-building programme to ensure enough houses for everyone - combating **SQUALOR**
>
> **NHS** - a national health service, free at the point of use - combating **DISEASE**
>
> **EDUCATION** - the state provided education free at the point of use - combating **IGNORANCE**

To combat poverty, the Beveridge Report recommended that the government provide income-replacement benefits for people who were in poverty because they were not in work, whether that was because of old age, illness, widowhood or insufficient jobs. This would ensure that people were protected from destitution due to factors outside of their own control. All such direct provision of money was called social security, whilst in-kind benefits – the provision of (free) goods or services as opposed to cash –

4. THE DAWN OF WELFARE

were part of the wider welfare state. Poverty would also be addressed by the government's efforts to secure and maintain full employment. By making sure that there were enough jobs, the government ensured that no-one need be poor out of idleness, where idleness means lack of something to do and specifically in this context the lack of a job to go to.

All those who could work would thus have the opportunity to do so, and so be able to provide for themselves. This brings a double benefit: personal responsibility is rewarded, and the government is not paying out unemployment benefit to large numbers of people. This fulfils the basic right as expressed in the UN's Article 23, that everyone has the right to work and to work that provides just and favourable conditions and just and favourable pay. As originally conceived, ensuring that society functions in a way that maintains full employment was a major part of the welfare state and the social contract that exists between private citizens and the government.

When jobs pay an adequate wage, they relieve the requirement on the government of providing directly for citizens through income-replacement benefits. This requires the basic wage to pay enough to keep someone out of material deprivation and to cover the costs of participating in the labour market. Thus by maintaining full employment and a national minimum wage (although this was not part of the original welfare state), the government protects its citizens from poverty through a method that is more socially desirable than the safety net of the benefits system. At the same time, the size of the out-of-work benefits bill would act as an indicator to the government of the success or otherwise of its policies to create and maintain enough jobs, and specifically jobs that paid a suitable wage.

Beveridge also planned a large house-building programme by councils and rent control in the private sector. Without such measures, people at the poorer end of society were unlikely to be able to afford housing. Building enough houses not only meant that citizens had somewhere to live; it also meant that they were not left in poverty after housing costs. So it helped to mitigate poverty (Want) at the same time as reducing the numbers of people living in bad living conditions (Squalor).

This was not just about building houses, but also about town and city planning, to ensure that urban environments were healthy and pleasing to live in. As with all of the social services, adequate housing serves a dual purpose: promoting the health, wellbeing and availability for work of citizens; and fulfilling the moral imperative on the government to ensure citizens' access to basic rights. And, as with full employment, house building and rent control helped to keep the cost of social security down by keeping the cost of housing low.

The Beveridge Report also recommended the provision of a National Health Service, to maintain citizens' health. The provision of comprehensive and free healthcare was considered to be a necessity as much on moral grounds as on economic ones: the "restoration of a sick person to health is a duty of the sick person and the State, prior to any other consideration", wrote Beveridge. Too many people were unable to afford healthcare, and consequently suffering from illnesses that it was possible to relieve and that reduced their capacity for work and participation in society. Universal healthcare meant that poor people could access treatment, recover quicker and return to work sooner – a positive for both the State and the citizen. In fact, when the NHS was introduced the sheer size of the backlog showed just how much unmet need there had been.

Following his investigation, Beveridge reported that the available mix of public, occupational and private insurance schemes of the time were failing to reach everyone, and that even those who were covered often did not get the level of support that they needed for the financial costs of unemployment, sickness or bereavement. Consequently, the inability to work or the loss of a husband or father resulted in many people being tipped into poverty or even destitution.

Where a person lost a job, this was tenable if jobs were plentiful and he suffered only short-term unemployment, such that savings – or even temporary loans – could adequately bridge the gap to the next pay day. But if jobs were not plentiful, then long-term unemployment ensued. Such people could not afford decent housing or adequate food; stress, cold, hunger and other attendant problems led to illness; illness and poverty prevented a person from returning to work. Thus, without an adequate income, whilst out of work for whatever reason, a person could end up losing the opportunity to work if and when a job became available, through no fault of their own.

This was not acceptable. The country, or its government, has a duty towards all its citizens both to care for them and to provide opportunity for them. By leaving people without jobs, housing, healthcare, training or money, a country failed on both counts. Citizens could not be held responsible for their poverty or worklessness when the opportunity to engage in secure work was limited or non-existent, whatever the reason: whether it was due to insufficient jobs, not enough housing near jobs, illness or lack of necessary skills. In contrast, providing the five pillars of welfare fulfilled the duty of care, ensured that opportunities to work were both available and viable, and ultimately led to a more productive economy and lower spending on healthcare and income replacements.

National Insurance

The Beveridge Report suggested some clear principles for how a welfare state should be run (Box 4). It was to be a holistic system, providing substantially more than just an insurance against income loss. The government would act to prevent income loss in the first place, through four schemes: national healthcare, to reduce the time spent out-of-work due to curable illness; state education, to ensure that people had the skills required by the existing labour market and were not locked out for being unable to afford to invest in themselves; the provision of full employment, to make sure that no-one was out of work due to a lack of a decent job to go to; and the provision of housing, so that citizens were able to rest well, live close to jobs and not be made ill through exposure to the elements. Together, these four schemes gave people the opportunity they needed to succeed, without which they could not be blamed for being unable to work, unskilled for work or unable to find work.

All of these benefits plus social security were to be available to all citizens as of right, without means-test or favour. People did not get more out of the system for being richer (such as with earnings-related benefits) or for being poorer (through means-tested benefits and some aspects of healthcare). People paid in according to their ability – an initial intention that everyone pay in the same monetary amount proved unaffordable – and received the same treatment as anyone else according to need.

The Beveridge Report recommended that the ad-hoc private, public and charitable schemes be replaced with one universal and comprehensive public scheme, National Insurance (NI). By pooling risk and taking insurance under government control, NI would ensure that all people were covered in the most cost-efficient and effective manner possible. It locked-out the problem besetting many non-public schemes, which is that the people who most need it tend to be excluded or face higher premiums and excesses, which only reinforces their need. And it made sure that everyone was covered at affordable rates.

> **Box 4. Principles of the welfare state**
>
> **HOLISTIC** - the adequate provision of jobs, housing, education and healthcare are all the responsibility of the government under its side of the social contract.
>
> **CONTRIBUTION-BASED** - workers pay National Insurance to the government, to get income-replacement benefits back during loss of earnings.
>
> **EQUAL CONTRIBUTIONS & EQUAL BENEFITS** - there are no earnings, age or cause related components.
>
> **UNIVERSAL** - there are no means tests: everyone can receive financial support, regardless of savings, during periods of income loss; and everyone regardless of income or savings enjoys the same access to in-kind support such as education and healthcare.
>
> **SUBSISTENCE PLUS** - benefits are adequate to live on, providing slightly more than what is needed for basic physical survival.
>
> **RECIPROCITY** - people claiming for an income caused by unemployment must be looking for work.
>
> **EQUALITY OF OPPORTUNITY FOR CHILDREN** - child benefit is provided to all families (except for the first child) regardless of work status, so that children are not penalised for their parents' circumstances.

Beveridge proposed a number of core principles for this system, some of which remain today. Firstly, there was to be a flat rate of contribution and a flat rate of pay-out, so that everyone was treated equally. The flat rate of contribution, however, proved unaffordable; people at the bottom of the income scale could not afford to pay in enough contributions to make the scheme viable without asking people on higher earnings to pay more. Instead, NI contributions are paid in proportion to one's ability, following the principle of taxation according to ability and support according to need. But this progressive principle has been reduced by not taking NI contributions on a person's pension either when they pay in to it or when they withdraw it, and by sharply reducing NI contributions on income above £50,000 per year.

Secondly, pay-outs were not means-tested, because of the adverse impact of such policies on families who tried to save money for future needs. It also meant that a sense of commonality was retained; everyone in the same situation of income loss, regardless of assets or savings, got the same subsistence support back. Richer people, who had paid in more, didn't lose out relative to people who had paid in less. There were no earnings-related components, because this would mean the State paying to sustain people in a higher lifestyle than they needed. Furthermore, these people could, and arguably should be encouraged to, take out any top-up insurance they wanted to or act prudently in laying by savings for future need – the latter of which only makes sense if the government does not reduce income replacements for people with savings.

People who were unemployed but able to work were expected to look for work in return for their income-replacement benefit. The provision of the State in ensuring the opportunity and capacity to work was to be met in return by citizens assuming the responsibility to provide for themselves and their family as far as they were able. Because there was full employment, secure jobs and long careers, it was reasonable to ask citizens to play their part by taking work when it was available.

Income-replacement benefits were to be slightly more than was necessary to live, which both protected against destitution and ensured that people continued to have the financial resources to make a job search meaningful and successful. It also ensured that one-off or random costs, such as household repairs, did not have to go undone or, if done, leave a household in deprivation. That extra bit of money can be crucial in providing the slack to manage the vicissitudes of life and still allow people to maintain an adequate standard of (subsistence) living as well as good health.

Benefits were not to be related to the specific cause of a person's loss of earnings. For example, a person whose disability was acquired whilst working in coal mines should not receive more assistance than someone whose disability was congenital, or whose injury or illness was acquired in a line of work that did not have its own compensation scheme. This principle was met in part by rolling most of the previous private, charitable and occupation-based schemes into one national scheme.

Beveridge also recommended that there be a child benefit or family allowance, so that children did not grow up in poverty. This was to be universal regardless of employment status, because whilst a family clearly needed higher unemployment benefits than did a childless couple, to make child benefits contingent upon unemployment risked making low-wage work worth less than unemployment for families. Beveridge also recognised that, as the future workers, children were important to the country, and it was worth investing in them. To protect against destitution, ensure that all children had a decent upbringing and remove any adverse financial consequences, Beveridge concluded that child benefit should be universal.

However, to protect against abuse of the system and to encourage a balance of responsibility between the individual and the state – as well as reduce the costs of the system – families would not receive benefit for their first child.

Unfinished business

Beveridge had a lot of ground to cover in his report, with less access to data and much less research available then than we have now. One area that was under-estimated by Beveridge was the cost of living. Beveridge had attempted to calculate the subsistence needs, plus a little extra, for the typical person, but he had underestimated them. The benefits suggested in his report were then not introduced until two years later, and were kept at the same amount for five years, meaning that right from the start they were insufficient for subsistence living and failed to keep up with price increases. They thus failed to meet people's most basic physical and material needs, let alone their social and cultural rights as recently defined and protected under the United Nation's Declaration of Human Rights.

For the non-typical person who had additional needs, there was a supplementary benefit awarded at the discretion of a governmental case officer to cover those needs. But because the basic level of need had been underestimated, far more people than expected ended up needing to have the top-up benefit in order to reach just a subsistence level income. It was estimated that the unemployment benefit was only 19% of the average industrial wage (itself not high – this was a long time before the National Minimum Wage) and well below subsistence needs. Similarly, the Family Allowance (child benefit) had been reduced from what was estimated as subsistence – nine shillings a week – to only five shillings a week.

Initially, this was seen as a strength of the system: it successfully targeted the necessary amount of money at those who most needed it. However, to critics, "it looked increasingly like an intrusive and inconsistent form of state charity."[4] It took a lot of work for case officers to determine the differing needs of individuals and decide what merited extra assistance and what didn't. Awards could vary from one case officer to another, leaving people unsure of what they could receive and why. The system recreated the gaps and inefficiencies of previous charitable systems, and required a high level of state intrusion into people's private lives.

In the 1950s, the Conservative Government's Minister for National Insurance, Osbert Peake, was in favour of subsistence-level benefits, but

4. THE DAWN OF WELFARE

the Treasury opposed him. The Treasury refused to raise benefit levels to a subsistence income or to increase them in line with prices, meaning that with each year people on benefits were placed in deeper and deeper poverty. Family Allowance was raised by three shillings a week when the post-war food subsidy was abolished, but by then inflation had eroded its value. It wasn't the last time that the Treasury intervened to block expenditure that other government ministers saw to be necessary for the sake of the poor.

The new welfare state also failed to remove all of its precursor benefits and provisions. The *Beveridge Report* stressed that extraneous circumstances, such as age, sex or the industry someone had worked in should not affect how much support a person received when in need. But with the retention of work-related benefits, such as industrial injuries benefit, people with the same functional impairment could receive substantially different amounts of benefit, simply because one was injured whilst working in industry and the other became injured by different means.

The make-up of the population was also changing in the years after the end of the war. It was not just that there were more pensioners; there were also more single parents, and more 'civilian disabled' – disabled children who survived into adulthood but were not eligible for benefits received by those who became disabled whilst at work in an industry or during war. Unemployment still remained low and typically a transitory experience, but it was beginning to rise, and with it long-term unemployment was also rising. Beveridge's contribution-based system may have worked sufficiently well for single or married men, but it did not work well for women, lone parents or the disabled who struggled to pay in the necessary National Insurance contributions but still needed support. It failed to consider the different ways in which people contribute, particularly through family but also through voluntary and community work.

Pensions were always going to be expensive. Beveridge suggested a gradual introduction of the basic state pension, taking 20 years before a newly-retired adult would receive a full pension. The new flat-rate state pension was to be contribution based, with the typical adult paying enough contributions over their lifetime to pay for their state pension; naturally, people who retired shortly after the introduction of the state pension and national insurance would not have had time to pay enough contributions to cover the cost of their pension. However, the government chose to introduce full pensions immediately. Combined with the growth of the pensioner population, and in particular the ex-army pensioners, it meant that the National

Insurance fund was about to become woefully inadequate. Consequently, reforms were introduced in the late 1950s to increase the contributions paid in and to slightly increase the state pensions of people who did not have occupational pensions.

Occupational pensions, almost unknown before WWII, had spread rapidly afterwards. With their rise, a new principle was introduced: better off workers were encouraged to pay in to a private scheme to top up their out-of-work incomes, rather than to expect a large public benefit that exceeded subsistence needs. However, as the government did not always make the public aware of when they would need to consider a private top-up to the benefits system, people could end up without having saved enough money to cover job loss or retirement to fund the lifestyle that they were used to.

One of Beveridge's biggest oversights was the needs of disabled citizens. Although people could claim sickness benefit, similar to the unemployment benefit but without having to look for work, this was insufficient for people's needs. A benefit that didn't cover subsistence needs was never going to be adequate for people who experience additional costs because of their disability, and nor was it enough to cover the costs of participating in society. Disabled people also lacked the opportunity that full employment offered to the able-bodied, of escaping poverty through paid work, because they were not able to work. This oversight rendered disabled people second class citizens in both thought and deed.

During all this time, between the end of WWII and the mid-1970s, social security policies remained largely bipartisan issues. Although one party or the other, depending on which was in government, claimed responsibility for particular benefits, in fact it was largely a case of continuing the work of the previous administration. Thus the redundancy payments introduced by Labour were also in the Conservative manifesto, and the disability benefits later introduced by the Conservatives had first been discussed during the preceding Labour Government. There continued to be a perception that the problems of poverty and the other four evils were soluble. In one welfare expert's summary, it was firmly believed that "the poor, the deprived and the distressed did not always have to be with us."[5]

Progress in human rights

The welfare state made a big impact to Harry Smith's life. After WWII, Harry lived in Halifax with his German wife, Friede. He had a job as a

4. THE DAWN OF WELFARE

labourer and lived only a short walk away from his work. Having grown up destitute and often hungry, his new bedsit with his wife and meals of beans on toast were sources of gratitude. And when Harry was treated, for free, for bronchitis, he knew his life and country had dramatically changed for the better. It was a huge contrast from the fate of his sister, who died of tuberculosis in a workhouse infirmary.

But what really made a difference to Harry was the way the NHS saved his wife and his marriage.[6] Friede had experienced harassment and stigma in Germany, for being the illegitimate daughter of a trade unionist who disagreed with Hitler. At 15, she had lived through the bombing of her native city, Hamburg, when many thousands of other residents were killed.

After moving to England, Friede began to become ill. She would tremble violently at night and experienced sudden mood changes. She became quiet, subdued and unhappy. Harry had no idea what to do, but a friend did. The friend insisted that Friede visit a doctor, and because of the NHS, Friede was able to do so. The doctor encouraged Friede to meet up with other immigrants to England who could help one another adjust to a new country and way of life. She also supported Friede to go and speak at the local Woman's Institute, where she could share her experiences in Nazi Germany and help diffuse the inherent suspicion that every German was a Nazi.

Friede recovered and was able to learn to love her new life in England with Harry. Harry doesn't know what would have happened without the NHS. But he does know the dramatic difference between a country with a welfare state and one without.

NOTES FOR CHAPTER 4

1. **Smith HL** (17/05/2017) Corbyn's inspiring manifesto takes me back to Labour's 1945 blueprint for hope. LONDON: THE GUARDIAN Harry Smith died in November 2018.
2. **Addison P** (1994) The road to 1945: British politics and the Second World War. LONDON: PIMLICO
3. **Hogg Q (Lord Hailsham)** (1990) A sparrow's flight. GLASGOW: HARPERCOLLINS
4. **Timmins N** (1995) The Five Giants: a biography of the welfare state. GLASGOW: HARPERCOLLINS
5. **ibid**
6. **Smith HL** (26/01/2016) My sister died because we couldn't afford a doctor. Then the NHS changed everything. LONDON: THE GUARDIAN

5

The campaign for inclusion

We saw in the last chapter how the UK, through the influential Beveridge Report, attempted to set up a comprehensive welfare state that would ensure the access to basic rights of all citizens. However, one particular group had been largely left out: the long-term sick and disabled. At the time of the Beveridge Report, many disabled people lived in long-term care facilities, and thus were not a typical part of a community of working men and their families. Others lived with their families, cared for by women who would have been unlikely to be in work anyway; consequently neither they as carers nor the disabled people they cared for were visible to policy makers. Poverty was seen through the framework of a lack of work earnings, with long-term disability for breadwinners catered for through compensatory, industry-based benefits. Asides from that, disabled people were essentially forgotten.

But as medicine improved, the disabled community changed and became larger. More people survived with illnesses which previously would have killed them, but from which they did not always recover to full health. People were living longer, and becoming subject to the diseases and illnesses which predominantly affect older people. Long-term disabling illness was becoming a significant cause of poverty. And with the State now committed to protecting non-disabled citizens from poverty and supporting them in equality of opportunity, it was inconsistent for it to fail to provide the same basic rights for its disabled citizens.

5. THE CAMPAIGN FOR INCLUSION

The disabled community began to come together to campaign for their rights as equals. For them, the 1960-80s were decades of significant achievement. The social model of disability was developed, giving disabled people the impetus and inclusive narrative that they needed to strengthen and drive forward their campaign for inclusion. As a result of their work and campaigning, two new benefits were introduced: an out-of-work sickness benefit specifically for the long-term sick and disabled, and an extra-costs benefit to meet the additional costs of living with a long-term illness or disability. The institutions in which disabled people lived began to be closed down, and care in the community became the new ideal.

The start of campaigning

In the initial National Insurance scheme introduced in 1946, those out of work due to sickness received a flat-rate sickness benefit. No formal recognition was made of the additional problems caused by long-term illness or disability relative to short periods of illness or unemployment. It seems to have been largely assumed that sick people would recover – through the medical care now available in the NHS – and so return to work, whilst the long-term disabled would continue to be cared for in institutions or by non-working female relatives (if, indeed, they were thought about at all). Some disabled people, such as those injured in the line of work or in war, could claim compensatory benefits, but the majority could not. The flat-rate sickness benefit, inadequate for short-term physical needs, was even less adequate for supporting people who could not expect to return to work.

Disabled people at the time were aware of this. Many disability charities which still exist today started soon after the end of the Second World War, including MIND, Mencap, Scope and the Leonard Cheshire Foundation. Most of these were started by the parents and families of disabled people, rather than disabled people themselves, but disabled people soon began to campaign as well: in 1951, 800 members of the British Limbless Ex-Servicemen's Association marched to Downing Street as a "silent reproach" to the government.[1] The National Cripples Journal pointed out that the new welfare state, allegedly providing security from cradle to grave, did nothing for "the civilian cripple who is incapable of earning a living." They wanted the "bold new society", fit for all, to include disabled people.

But it was not until the 1970s that disability campaigning became a major force. The Union of the Physically Impaired Against Segregation and the

Mental Patients Union, followed in the 1980s by People First (a learning-disabled group), became prominent campaigning groups. A previous attitude of 'disabled people can't do things' was being challenged by a new theory that saw disabled people as having been placed in an oppressive relationship by the able-bodied, and particularly by those traditionally seen as their carers or helpers.[2] Vic Finkelstein argued that it was the machine-based production systems of the industrial revolution that had excluded or 'disabled' disabled people, compared to the previous agrarian communities.[3] Thus in this new conception of disability, people with impairments were disabled more by modern production methods and controlling carers than by their own bodies or minds.

The emerging disabled people's movement sought to reclaim the term 'disability' with a new social model of disability. In the social model, as we saw previously, it is not the impairment per se that causes disability, but the set-up of society which fails to include people with impairments. In many cases, society could be set up differently, such as through the provision of ramps instead of steps, or the dual use of auditory and visual information systems. Disability therefore ceased to be something that was a feature of an individual, which was unavoidable and therefore necessarily caused exclusion. Instead, disability was a feature of society, and was both unnecessary and entirely avoidable.

Because governments could do something about this exclusion of their disabled citizens, they therefore had a responsibility for actually doing something about it, just as they had a duty to ensure the access of non-disabled citizens to their basic, inalienable rights as far as the government is able. In fact, many would argue that part of the raison d'être of a government, and one of its most basic duties, is to ensure the access to rights of its citizens in general and its poor and disadvantaged citizens in particular.

The disability community successfully campaigned on this basis for new forms of support for disabled people, leading to the creation of new benefits specifically for the disabled, and new ways of supporting sick and disabled people in their homes.

The social model

Fiona and Gemma are two people for whom the social model can be transformative. In the medical model, Fiona is disabled because she can't see, and Gemma because she can barely hear. It is Fiona's responsibility to learn

5. THE CAMPAIGN FOR INCLUSION

to walk using a white cane and all the tips and tricks of managing blindness – how to locate and repair tears in clothes; how to determine whether clothes are clean or stained; how to identify which apples are bruised and which bacon is tinged green. It is Gemma's responsibility to learn to read a language she can't hear or speak; to set up visual alarm systems for her front door, alarm clock and mobile phone; and to work out how to communicate with hearing people.

In the social model, the problem as such is not with Fiona or Gemma, or with their sight or hearing, but with society. It is because society tries to sell substandard goods alongside high quality ones that Fiona is unable to make an informed choice. It is because society doesn't provide braille writing on accurately-stocked supermarket shelves that Fiona can't identify which box has the cereal she wants. It is because society doesn't teach British Sign Language as part of the curriculum that Gemma can't easily communicate with hearing people, and it is because society failed to give her a good education that she is having to catch up now, as an adult.

However, the social model doesn't work well for all disabled people. Olivia is a university student who has hemiplegia, a form of cerebral palsy caused by a stroke whilst in her mother's womb. It causes fatigue, pain and problems with her joints. There are things that can be done to help, such as living in catered accommodation and being close to where her lectures are held. Good quality splints can also make a big difference. But nothing can be done to counter the effects of pain and fatigue, beyond medication, and medication for pain often itself causes drowsiness or other fatigue. When it comes to pain and fatigue, disability is more accurately placed in the body than in the environment, and a person often has to accept that that does mean a reduction in the activity in which they can take part. Indeed, it is typically this fatigue and pain and the activity limitation it creates that is the essence of disability for people with chronic physical illness.

Sickness benefits

The distinction between short and long-term sickness was first formalised in 1971 by the introduction of Invalidity Benefit for sickness lasting longer than six months. The benefit was claimed on the basis of a medical note or certificate from a person's GP confirming their incapacity for work.

Age-related top-ups were quickly introduced. This breached the principle that extraneous factors should not influence the benefit that a person received. A separate benefit that topped-up the incomes of those able to work only part-time remained available as a further compensatory mechanism for people with reduced capacity for work; again going against the principle of one benefit to meet one type of need. However, it did mean that people who could do some work could receive some top-up benefit to help them achieve an adequate income, whereas Invalidity Benefit was for people who essentially could not work at all.

Invalidity Benefit failed to meet the principle of being universally available. It was not available to people without NI contributions, and thus excluded the majority of married women. Whilst this followed the principle of a (NI) contributions-based system, it ignored the impact on people who had not had the opportunity to pay enough NI contributions, whether because of age, sex or other reasons. It also ignored the human rights which the UN had set up: every person, regardless of ability or work status, should have access to a liveable income. The result was that two people with the same functional incapacity could receive very different amounts of benefit.

To provide for people who had not been able to make NI contributions before becoming ill or disabled, a Non-Contributory Invalidity Pension was established in 1975. Disabled people successfully argued that people who had not had the opportunity to work were still people with a right to a decent standard of living; and that the government had a particular role in providing access to a decent living standard for those people who for whatever reason, including reduced health, would struggle to provide it for themselves. However, it was worth only 60% of the contributory pension, leaving people far from achieving a basic standard of living that was adequate for their health and well-being.

The new benefit was primarily for those whose illness or disabilities started during childhood or adolescence. Married women were specifically excluded from this pension on the grounds that they would have been at home anyway, regardless of their capacity for work. Because the system was still predicated upon a family structure in which a father or husband provided for the whole household, it failed to properly meet the needs of women and young adults.

A non-contributory benefit was added in 1977 for married women who could not carry out housework themselves, in recognition that this work would then have to be done by someone else, at cost. However, the household duties test for the Housewives' Non-Contributory Invalidity Pension was deemed to be so harsh that it essentially discriminated against women.[4]

5. THE CAMPAIGN FOR INCLUSION

In effect, women had to pass a harsher test of invalidity than did men: they had to be assessed as both unable to work and unable to carry out most of their household tasks. Yet two in five of those who receive benefits because they are too sick or disabled to work do not receive benefits for being disabled at home.[5]

Significant disquiet with the pension, as voiced by disabled people and their organisations, led to the development of a new benefit, introduced in 1984, which replaced both of the non-contributory pensions. However, the changes made to the assessment criteria did not materially improve the eligibility of married women for sickness benefit. It was felt that the new benefit simply rendered the discrimination against married women less overt, whilst doing nothing to actually address it.

Overall, the "piecemeal and reactive" development of sickness benefits up to the end of the 1980s resulted in what the researchers Walker and Walker described as "an incoherent mixture of benefits which do not mesh together easily, overlapping considerably for some groups while missing out others altogether."[6] The ideal system that provided universal protection for income loss due to illness or disability had not, at this point, been fully realised. Benefits were still based on criteria other than need, such as sex or the reason for an illness or injury, when the Beveridge Report had specifically advised against this. The result was that instead of pay-outs being consistent across people with similar levels of functional (in)capacity, there were a variety of benefits being paid based upon extraneous factors such as the reason for illness or injury, or the age or sex of the person concerned. Not everyone who needed it could get support, and those who did get support did not receive enough to compensate for their disability and place them on an equal footing in society with the non-disabled.

The first extra-costs benefits

Extra-costs benefits are a relatively new phenomenon. Prior to the welfare state, many disability-related benefits were compensation-based. They were intended to compensate someone for an injury or impairment incurred in a line of work, and in many cases this required proving not just that harm had occurred but that the employer was at fault. The welfare state introduced the insurance principle, in which neither fault nor cause had to be identified. But both compensation- and insurance- based payments missed a key issue: that people with disabilities don't merely have lower incomes;

they also have higher expenditure. The new extra-costs benefits were therefore designed with the intention of improving disabled people's footing in relation to non-disabled people by covering some of the extra costs that disabled people face.

The first extra-costs benefit, Attendance Allowance, was introduced in 1971 following a survey which showed that disabled people experienced widespread extra costs as a consequence of their disability.[7] Attendance Allowance covered disabled people for the extra costs incurred in their home, and was paid at two rates depending upon the amount of assistance needed for specific home-based activities, such as washing and dressing.

As with sickness benefits, the development of extra-costs benefits was heavily influenced by the historical understanding of a household as a man, his wife and their children. A tribunal judge ruled that the ability to perform domestic tasks was not to be included in assessments for Attendance Allowance, because these were tasks that a wife or daughter carries out, as opposed to the disabled person himself.[8] Yet if that wife or daughter were sick and unable to carry out household tasks, she was at the time unable to receive either a sickness benefit (as a man would if he could not work) or the new extra-costs benefit. This somewhat discriminatory ruling has influenced extra-cost benefits ever since.

Four years later, in 1975, Mobility Allowance was introduced to cover some of the costs associated with the difficulty of getting around. However, it was not available to those aged less than five years old or over 65, on the grounds that people of these ages had mobility needs even if not disabled in any other way. Later, a new benefit was brought in, which made benefit available for children of three to five years with very severe mobility problems. Disabled pensioners, however, continue to be unable to get any support towards the cost of mobility problems, despite the fact that loss of mobility does not occur uniformly with age, and that lifting and moving an adult is very different from lifting and moving a baby. In this way, the social security system fails to meet the principle that when age is an extraneous factor, as it is in the case of pensioners, it should not impact the awarding of a benefit.

Further surveys in the late 1980s showed that the two Allowances were still not meeting disabled people's needs.[9] The extra-costs benefits failed to reach many people who experienced extra costs, and did not cover enough of the extra costs incurred by those whose disabilities were severe enough to merit at least some award. For the same income level, disabled people were still financially disadvantaged in relation to non-disabled people. Following further campaigning, the two benefits were scrapped for children and working-age people and replaced with a new benefit, Disability Living Allowance. Pensioners, however, continued to be restricted to Attendance Allowance only.

Social care

One of the earliest themes of the new disability campaign movement was the right to independent living. Independent living could mean a variety of different things, but at its core were always the concepts of individual choice, control, freedom and equality. It is "the right we all have to build a life of our own, with family, friends and neighbours; enjoying the same housing and other social rights that everyone else should be able to enjoy."[11] Disabled people should be able to choose where they live, and when and from whom they receive any assistance they need, with the same level of choice and control as non-disabled people; and they should have the same opportunity to take part in work, leisure and family life as easily and fully as anyone else.

But in the 1970s, the legacy of Victorian public asylums was still present in the form of large, dehumanising residential institutions. These were supposed to be places of refuge, moving the work of care from (unpaid) families and the church to paid staff. But a brief period of good ventilation and extensive gardens had collapsed under the sheer numbers of people in need, and saw a return to physical and drug-induced restraint of residents. Erving Goffman, one of the most influential sociologists of the 20th century, spoke of these institutions as "social arrangements that regulate according to one rational plan and under one roof, all spheres of individuals' lives; working, playing, eating and sleeping."[10] A standard routine included getting up at 6:30am and going back to bed by 7:15pm, with food available only at prescribed times.

Campaign work brought the existence of long-stay hospitals and institutions back into general awareness amongst the public and politicians. The idea behind institutionalised care, that people with long-term disabilities could be cured, had been proved wrong, making hospital-type institutions unnecessary. Tales of abuse were being uncovered and reported on the front pages of newspapers and in television documentaries, rendering such institutions unpopular. Several disability campaigners released books documenting the poor quality of care in certain institutions and campaigning for their closure and the provision of care within the community.

Prudhoe hospital was one of the better institutions, but strong-suits were still in use to restrain patients and low staffing levels meant that many patients were drugged to keep them quiet.[12] Family visits were confined to one day a month. Kay, a resident in Prudhoe, described a typical meal time:

> "the staff feeding them by holding their noses, that's not right. I was trying to speak up for the people in wheelchairs. They dragged me out, took me back and doped me. I was just speaking up for the people in wheelchairs, they shouldn't get fed by their noses, it's wrong."

Another resident, Metallica, reported that:

> "The staff were very strict when I was in Prudhoe hospital. Staff put them to sleep to control their temper. I remember an awful lot of people who got injections."

Virginia Moffat has spent her career working in social care. She started off at L'Arche, an organisation that supports people with learning disabilities to live in the community. Typically, this is in the form of a house-share including one non-learning disabled person who is there to support the other residents. This approach is referred to as 'intentional community', which means that the individuals in the house have chosen to live together and often have shared values. This contrasts with larger residential homes, where the location and housemates are not 'choose-able'.

In a submission to the Adult Social Care Inquiry in 2016, Virginia wrote:

> "At the time I had little understanding of the history of people with learning disabilities, having grown up in the 1970s when disabled people were not visible in our communities... I knew nothing of the long stay hospitals where so many people were incarcerated for years and had never stopped to think where all the disabled children were when I was growing up.

> "L'Arche changed all that for me. It was there that I first heard of the horrors of long stay institutions from two of my new housemates, Doris and John. They'd both been sent away at the age of ten to St Lawrence's

5. THE CAMPAIGN FOR INCLUSION

Hospital in Caterham, swapping loving families for an institutional life. They had no possessions, were often referred to by a number, slept in massive dormitories, whilst living in a system where the nurses were at best indifferent and at worst totally cruel. Family contact was not encouraged so Doris was never told when her parents died. John, who was interested in learning despite his disabilities, was mockingly called The Professor. No wonder when people from L'Arche asked them if they wanted to leave they were eager to do so."[13]

The governments of the 1980s responded to this campaigning with a renewed commitment to end institutional care and bring in care in the community. The main focus was to allow disabled people to live and receive care in homes. New residential and group homes, which were on a smaller scale and provided individual bedrooms rather than multi-bed wards, were created, and the provision of day-care expanded. However, the full shift to disabled people, particularly those with mental illnesses or learning disabilities, actually living in their own homes had not been made; essentially, all that happened was a down-scaling in institution size. Many others lived with their parents, rather than in their own home, with the attendant fears of what happens when their parents have passed away.

An audit in 1986 found a number of problems with the movement from institutional to community care.[14] The change in responsibility from hospitals and health systems to local government and social care systems had not included an adequate financial shift. Responsibility for the implementation of policy had been fragmented and consequently the shift of resources and personnel was slow. Without a comprehensive framework for planning the transition of disabled people between institutions and community care, the actual delivery on the ground was quite poor. In particular, the community care initiative had not properly listened to disabled people and what they had to say about their needs and abilities, and the forms of support they wanted. Altogether, the policy goal was desirable but under-funded and inadequately thought through.

Accessibility

At the end of the Second World War, there were 300,000 war-disabled people. At the same time, society was becoming more and more urbanised; consequently, it became increasingly important that architecture be designed in a way that was accessible to disabled people and in particular the war veterans. Pressure from campaigners, including leading disabled people, led the way for more inclusive design. Ken and Maggie Davis set up the first cooperative housing development, which allowed disabled and non-disabled people to live alongside one another in a shared community, whilst the Direct Action Network campaigned for improved accessibility on public transport.

Selwyn Goldsmith, himself disabled by polio, committed himself to overcoming architectural disability and institutional discrimination, i.e. the blocking of disabled people from participation because physical buildings and spaces are not accessible. He spoke with many disabled people about their needs, highlighting the need for public disabled toilets as well as access to the restaurants, local shops, churches and other buildings and public spaces that non-disabled people visited in normal life. Goldsmith also developed the first dropped kerbs, which made getting around outdoors easier and safer for wheelchair users. Other innovations, like tactile paving slabs which assist blind people with road crossings, also spread around the country.

Goldsmith championed the idea of universal design, which aimed to see all buildings built in ways that were accessible to everyone, thus protecting against institutional discrimination and preventing the need for expensive retrofitting as and when disability discrimination cases are brought or recognised. Public pressure for accessible buildings resulted eventually in the 1995 Disability Discrimination Act, which required all public buildings to be accessible. However, with the burden for ensuring access falling largely upon individual disabled people bringing access requests or legal challenges, inaccessibility remains far too common a problem.

Education

The original movement to educate disabled children had focused on teaching them basic work and life skills, rather than the formal curriculum. Although there was a desire at the time that at least the less severely disabled children should be educated in mainstream schools, in practice it was not happening. A combination of funding constraints and a lack of teachers meant that class sizes were simply too large to accommodate children with additional needs. In contrast, specialist schools were typically located in old town houses and country mansions, where there was adequate room at relatively low prices.

5. THE CAMPAIGN FOR INCLUSION

Specialist education therefore by necessity became synonymous with specialist schools, rather than as a feature within mainstream school. Disabled children throughout the 60s and 70s continued to be sent to specialist residential schools, usually segregated according to their disability. Children with Down's Syndrome, along with other children of low IQ, were considered ineducable and were sent to Junior Training Centres, which acted more like day centres and respite for parents than as education for the children. In the early 1970s, these were converted to schools for the Educationally Subnormal (Severe), but these schools largely continued with the same model of care as when they were Junior Training Centres.

Campaigns for inclusion led in the 1980s to the right for all disabled children to be educated in mainstream schools. Children with 'special educational needs' were to have an assessment of their educational needs, rather than just a medical assessment, and this would help to determine their school placement. The responsibility for education was devolved to Local Educational Authorities, not all of which had access to adequate funds, and so not all progressed very fast in their provision for disabled children. At the start of the 20th Century, the best authorities placed 67% of 5-6 year-olds and 58% or more of 10-11 year-olds with Down's Syndrome in mainstream education, but in the worst 25% of authorities the figures were 28% or less and 9% or less respectively.[15] Many children are still educated in specialist schools, sometimes by choice rather than necessity, but this may reflect more on the quality of provision within mainstream schools than on the benefit of specialist schools.

Not there yet

The new social model of disability created a means for sick and disabled people to successfully argue for the removal of many barriers in society. New benefits provided sick and disabled people with an improved income that enabled them to purchase more of the support that they needed as well as access more of the basic necessities of life. Simple structures such as ramps, dropped kerbs and tactile paving stones made the public environment more accessible to disabled people. New ideas in housing and education were leading the way for disabled people to live, learn and work in the same communities as everyone else.

But society wasn't there yet. Many barriers remained, including poverty and inaccessible structures, both physical and attitudinal. Benefits were not adequate to meet need and were something of a hotchpotch when determining who got support and why. They relied upon extraneous circumstances and particularly failed those who had not had the opportunity to build up enough National Insurance contributions. De-institutionalisation had resulted more in a shrinking of the size of institutions than in an actual shift in policy towards a more emancipatory understanding of disability. Whilst the public environment had improved, it was not universally accessible, and disabled children still struggled to access a standard education. Political will was not committed to the cost of ensuring full inclusion of disabled people, and improvements depended upon disabled people themselves raising the public and political awareness of their need. There was still a long way to go to make the UK fully inclusive of its sick and disabled citizens.

In response to an audit of community care, the British Council of Organisations of Disabled People summed up the state of disability policy up to the late 1980s: "Existing policies do conflict and often appear irrational to disabled people who have to live by them. In the opinion of BCODP, this confusion cannot but be so because existing policies and practices have been based in incomplete and inadequate information. This has come about because of the long, historical exclusion of disabled people from mainstream social life in general, and from policy development in particular. Public policy in this field has been dominated by non-disabled perception of our problems which can only yield a limited view of their solutions. The information which is derived from direct experience has been systematically limited or excluded from the decision-making process. Attempts to correct this have been desultory both on paper and in practice."[16]

5. THE CAMPAIGN FOR INCLUSION

NOTES FOR CHAPTER 5

1. **As quoted in Jarrett** (2012) Disability in time and place. ENGLISH HISTORY
2. **Oliver M** (1999) Capitalism, disability and ideology: A materialist critique of the Normalization principle. In Flynn RJ and Raymond AL (eds) A quarter-century of normalization and social role valorization: evolution and impact. OTTAWA: UNIVERSITY OF OTTAWA PRESS
3. **Finkelstein V** (1981) Disability and the helper/helped relationship: an historical view. In Brechin A, Liddiard P and Swain J (eds) Handicap in a social world. LONDON: HODDER AND STOUGHTON
4. **Walker A and Walker L** (1991) Disability and financial need – the failure of the social security system. In Dalley G (ed) Disability and social policy LONDON: POLICY STUDIES INSTITUTE
5. **Department for Work and Pensions** (nd) Benefits statistical summary LONDON
6. **Walker and Walker** (n 4)
7. **Harris A** (1971) Handicapped and impaired in Great Britain, part one. LONDON: OFFICE OF POPULATION CENSUSES AND SURVEYS
8. **R v National Insurance Commissioner ex p Secretary of State for Social Services** (1981) 1 WLR 1017
9. **Martin J and White A** (1988) The financial circumstances of disabled adults living in private households. LONDON: HMSO
10. **Goffman E** (1968) Asylums. LONDON: PENGUIN
11. **Duffy S in Foreword to Squire A and Richmond P** (2017) No place like home: The economics of independent living. SHEFFIELD: CENTRE FOR WELFARE REFORM
12. **Keilty T and Woodley K** (2013) No Going Back. SHEFFIELD: CENTRE FOR WELFARE REFORM
13. **Moffat V** (2016) Submission to Adult Social Care inquiry: A career in Adult Social Care. SHEFFIELD: CENTRE FOR WELFARE REFORM.
14. **Audit Commission** (1986) Making a reality of community care. LONDON: HMSO
15. **Buckley S and Bird G** (2000) Education for individuals with Down's Syndrome: an overview
16. **BCDOP** (1987) Comment on the report of the Audit Commission 'Making a reality of community care.'

6

Moving away from the welfare state

In Chapter 5 we saw how the rise of disability activism, alongside the new social model of disability, significantly improved the welfare state. New cash benefits were introduced, giving disabled people additional funds towards what they needed to live and to purchase their own care and assistance. The old institutions were closed down and more people were provided with care in their own communities. Education and the general environment were made more accessible. Full inclusion and enjoyment of all basic rights had not been achieved, but progress had been made.

The work of disability campaigners created the political space for additional spending on disabled people and raised awareness of the level of unmet need. However, at the same time the political arena itself was starting to move away from the idea of a comprehensive welfare state. This has had major implications for the welfare state and, consequently, not just how but whether citizens' human rights are achieved.

Moving away from the Beveridge Report

The Beveridge Report's underlying principles for the social security system had not yet been achieved at the end of the 1970s. The sickness benefits depended too much upon a person's age, sex and previous line of work. Because living costs had initially been under-estimated, and benefits had then been increased at below-inflation levels, benefits had yet to be raised

6. MOVING AWAY FROM THE WELFARE STATE

to a level that met subsistence needs plus a little more, as had originally been intended. Consequently, not all needs were being met, and this was compounded for disabled people by the lack of support for those who struggled to carry out household tasks.

In the original report, it was intended that there would be no means-test for the receipt of benefits. This would ensure that there was no us/them distinction between better-off people (who received no state aid) and the poor (who did). It also meant that the principle of the scheme as insurance was retained: insurance companies do not pay out based upon a person's wealth and income, but based upon what they have lost (up to a point). So in the National Insurance system, it was the intention that everyone who could paid in to the scheme to insure themselves against loss of earnings, and everyone who subsequently lost earnings – regardless of their other wealth or savings – could then receive back a subsistence income replacement.

But from the 1960s, means-testing as a concept began to become more popular. Crucially, at this time it was not about re-targeting a fixed amount of resources, but about which groups should be given more, on top of what was already being paid out. Both the Conservative and Labour parties were confident that economic growth would continue, and that therefore the question was not how to use the same pot of money differently, but where to spend an additional pot. The Conservative Party's Research Department, for example, concluded that, whilst the idea of means-testing would be used when considering "how to distribute the additional resources that will flow from renewed prosperity under the next Conservative government", they should still "state loudly and categorically" that they would not restrict any current social services, such as by charging for hospital treatment or reducing the monetary value of the basic pension.[1] Indeed, the intention was to direct extra resources towards disabled people and the elderly, as was achieved with the introduction in the early 1970s of the first disability and sickness benefits, rather than the redistribution of current resources. As the 1970 Conservative manifesto had said, "The only true solution is to increase what we can afford."

In the 1970s, however, the economy began to slow down, and the political mood changed. A key shift occurred, from the belief that the economy could grow enough to meet all needs, to a belief that economies grow more slowly and can't keep up with what people want. Labour MP Richard Crossman argued that the belief that a growing economy could afford the costs of social services was a "complete delusion". It was thought that demographics, technology and rising expectations would always "be sufficient to make the standard of social services regarded as essential to a civilised community far more expensive than that community can afford... there is no foreseeable limit on the social services which the nation can reasonably require except the limit that the Government imposes."[2] Therefore, because the public would always place growing and unreasonable demands upon the State, the State must deliberately impose artificial limits on what it made available.

What this meant in practice was more nebulous. Citizens still had their human rights, and it wasn't clear that the State at any point was providing more than this, or that the State itself, as opposed to individual endeavour, was expected to. What people wanted was the fulfilment of their right to a warm, weather-proof house; a fulfilling job with decent pay; the alleviation of pain, sickness and injury; and an education that allowed one to participate in society and the labour market on an equal footing with everyone else. A previous inability on the part of the State to ensure these rights didn't mean that peoples' expectations had risen insatiably, but merely that a pre-existing right had subsequently become satiable.

Arguably, the same technology blamed for making growing expectations unaffordable – people demand first landline, then mobile, then smartphones, for example – could in fact be what makes it affordable, as the same goods and services can be produced at lower cost. No longer does a string of horses race from one side of the country to another to deliver an urgent message, nor are clothes made laboriously by hand; and consequently the costs of messaging and clothes have come down. In healthcare, robotic surgeons carried out around 1000 operations at the start of the 21st century, at an additional cost of $11,500 compared to normal.[3] By 2009, over 200,000 operations were carried out by robots each year. Robots were so good at reducing complications, hospital stays and recovery times that hospitals saved money by using this expensive technology.

Still, the political arena was becoming more concerned with the idea that the welfare state in its current form could not meet what the public wanted from it. The first oil crisis only reinforced this view. A significant restriction in the sale of oil by the Organisation of Petroleum Exporting Countries to some western countries created an immediate economic shock. In the UK, it was experienced as a period of rapid inflation and a recession at the same time, a combination that the reigning economic paradigm indicated could not occur. Politicians in the 1970s found themselves wrestling with trying

6. MOVING AWAY FROM THE WELFARE STATE

to reconcile the idea of insatiable demand and rising costs with an economy that wasn't growing as fast as they wanted.

Economists such as Milton Friedman had already been developing a different view of how economies should be run. They suggested that inequality was a positive: rich people bought the latest expensive technologies, which then provided the profit for companies to develop new technologies or cheaper versions of existing ones; eventually the poor could afford these technologies too. Seeing the wealth of hard-working people at the top would also act as an incentive to those at the bottom, to encourage them that hard work is worth it. Thus there was a rising tide that lifted all boats, and wealth trickled down from top to bottom. Unfortunately for the decades that followed, this understanding of how economies work is increasingly being shown to be wrong.

These events and developments in political and economic theory coalesced into a new approach to government. British Prime Minister Margaret Thatcher and US President Ronald Reagan both took their economic advice from Milton Friedman, who was advising a much smaller role for government. Friedman and other economists recommended that, where previously the government had sought to maintain full employment as part of its side of the welfare state, in fact governments should focus instead on restraining inflation. Given the (oil crisis-induced) high inflation at the time, this was an attractive proposal. The idea was that by curbing inflation, the economy would recover and the short-term increase in unemployment would soon disappear as the economy returned to a healthy state. The UK has not experienced full employment since.

Ironically, Margaret Thatcher later argued that "industry and trade are the basic social service because they provide a large number of jobs and without a job there is no way of looking after one's family."[4] Yet with the rejection of government's previous function of maintaining full employment, the governments of the 1970s and especially the 1980s cut this most basic of social services. As well as ending the general commitment to full employment, Thatcher's subsequent governments oversaw the loss of many manual industries and skilled trades which had previously been the life support of entire communities. The government claimed that it wanted industry and trade to thrive, but its actions led to the opposite.

Benefit scroungers

The 1980s also saw a resurgence in the popular belief of an undeserving workless poor, created through an overly generous welfare state. This narrative of 'shirkers and scroungers' made an appearance in the Conservative manifesto that saw it take up power in 1970. In comparison to three million unemployed in the early 1980s, unemployment in the 1970s was very low (less than one million), but at the time it was perceived as high because it was higher than the most recent preceding years. However, once in power in the early 1970s, the Conservative Party soon realised that the scrounger narrative was unfounded. Jonathan Bradshaw recorded of the 1970s Conservatives that they "appear to have been more convinced [now] than in opposition of how small a problem abuse really is, and how difficult it is to introduce further controls without making the process of claiming so unpleasant as to deter bona fide claims."[5]

Still, tales of benefit scroungers began to abound, building upon the Conservative's message in its 1970 manifesto, even though diligent searching failed to verify the stories. It was convenient to blame the unemployed rather than the government's response to the oil crisis and decision to stop committing to full employment. One historian summarised how "high tax rates [83%] and even higher unemployment brought out the worst in people… Company executives had their suits bought for them, or took payment in crates of wine, to avoid top rate tax. Lesser mortals negotiated fictitious allowances, to be paid as expenses to avoid lower rates of tax. The jobless at the bottom took small jobs on the side to make ends meet."[6] The result, as the welfare rights expert Timmins said, was "envy and suspicion" which was "exploited remorselessly" to undermine the benefits system as a producer of welfare cheats and dependents. Tellingly, tax dodgers at the top were not demonised, even though their tax avoidance was on a much bigger scale, and actually harmful to the country, than poor people taking on a few hours of work without telling the benefits system.

The Conservatives were already talking about social dependency. "The only really lasting help we can give to the poor," it was argued, "is helping them to help themselves."[7] Blame was placed on the "permissive society" for 'divesting' parents of "their duty to provide for their family economically, of their responsibility for education, health, upbringing, morality, advice and guidance, of saving for old age, for housing". Thus the government was able to put political distance between its duty to provide full employment, and its failure to do so as seen in the rise in unemployment, and in long-term unemployment in particular.

The counter-argument, that up until a global economic recession there had been no reason to believe that there was any welfare dependency, received little attention. Britain had had full employment for three decades; it seems unlikely that there had been a sudden, substantial and intra-national change in individuals' behaviours and beliefs just at the time that a recession came and government abdicated its role in ensuring full employment. Welfare dependency was a myth, but it was one with a political purpose, and that drove it to prominence.

The 1980s cut-backs

Margaret Thatcher's government came in with the belief that it needed to reduce government spending in order to restart the economy and make way for private enterprise. It was hoped that government cut-backs would restart the economy, struggling as it was after the first oil crisis and worldwide recession, and that a restarted economy would negate the need for the government to directly provide for poor and disabled people. The overall government policy was to reduce spending on sickness and disability benefits, not to improve coverage or ensure that benefit levels met the needs of their recipients. This policy was supported by the increasingly popular narrative of welfare dependency.

Spending cuts in the 1980s were achieved by changing the eligibility criteria so that fewer people were eligible for and received benefits, and by reducing the amount of benefit received by those who still counted as eligible. Short-term sickness benefits (26 weeks or fewer) became flat-rate rather than wage-related; Industrial Injuries Benefit was reduced; and Reduced Earnings Allowance; (compensation for reduction in earnings following industrial injury or disease) was abolished. These changes helped to bring the social security system more in line with the principles of universal, flat-rate income replacement over compensatory, industry-specific or wage-related benefits. But as part of a parcel of social security cutbacks, it risked causing more harm than good. The cuts were enacted to make savings to the exchequer, rather than to release the money for spending in a more equitable way, and nor did they come with an intention of topping up all disabled people's incomes to an adequate amount.

The Labour MP Mr Flynn commented at the time that the abolition of the Reduced Earnings Allowance:

> "represents an obvious cut in benefit. To introduce some of the Government's promised reforms – the disablement employment credit and the disablement allowances – the Government must first cut. They are robbing Peter to pay Peter. This follows the Treasury's edict, which has dominated the 11 years of Thatcher's misrule in social security – that any apparent improvement must be self-financing. To reward the disabled with long overdue benefits, they must first be robbed of existing benefits."[8]

This approach is still used today.

Statutory Sick Pay was introduced at this time as a means of transferring administration from the government to the employer, but it also resulted in a cut in sick pay for many workers, particularly couples and low-paid workers. When the government consulted on this change, it received overwhelming opposition from both employers and workers. It was felt that "injury-prone industries would bear the brunt of the cost; workers with poor health records would be discriminated against by employers; and bad employers might risk avoiding sick pay altogether, preferring to sack any worker who complained and pay compensation if any were due."[9] And this is what has happened.

These step-changes in the level of benefits were then exacerbated by reductions in the year-on-year increase; previously, benefits increased each year in line with wages, but now they increased in line with prices. Prices were rising slower than wages at the time, which meant that each year the incomes of those on benefits fell further behind that of the rest of society.

As Walker and Walker describe:

> "The theme running through the [spending] reviews was the overriding importance placed upon the reduction of public expenditure. The ethos underpinning the subsequent legislation was of 'targeting' resources on 'those most in need' – generally accepted as implying more means-testing – reducing the 'dependency culture' by limiting eligibility, and simplification of the system...

6. MOVING AWAY FROM THE WELFARE STATE

> *"The preoccupation of the reviews with simplicity, arguably not the paramount goal of social security, combined with the failure to consider the adequacy of benefit levels, resulted in a system which takes little account of individual need, and therefore causes particular problems for people with disabilities."*[10]

Thus the previous discussion of means-testing switched from a positive – giving additional money to certain groups – to a negative – taking money from (or giving less to) certain other groups. Instead of being about the wisest spending of additional resources, targeting came to mean the reduction of current resources. Its previous positive connotation was manipulated to hide a negative fact.

As well as ending the commitment to full employment and reducing the value of social security pay-outs, Thatcher's government made significant changes to the provision of housing. In the post-War years, the governments of the time took on board the recommendation that they undertake a national building programme. If the supply of housing met demand, then the cost of housing would remain low, and any contributions to rent required by people in poverty would also remain low. Thus, house building met both the moral need to provide access to housing for citizens, and the economic goal of providing goods and services at low cost.

Thatcher's government changed this. Whilst the right to buy council homes was not a new concept, what was new was the scale of the discount offered, ranging from 33% to 50% depending upon how long a person had lived in their council property (in reality, most lived in flats, whilst the majority of purchasers lived in houses). The Conservative manifesto that promised these changes, including 100% mortgages, did not discuss whether the country could afford to lose the rent from these homes, or whether there would be enough properties left in council ownership, or how to meet future demand for housing if the population grew. At the time, there was not a significant housing shortage, and the public and private sectors between them were keeping up with demand for new houses.

In the initial plans, Thatcher's housing minister, MP Michael Heseltine, successfully argued that councils should keep at least three-quarters of the money raised from selling off the council housing, and councils still managed to build around 50,000 houses per year between 1980 and 1985 (down from 100,000-200,000; Figure 3).[11] But Heseltine was moved to the Ministry of Defence, and the amount of money given back to councils fell year on year.

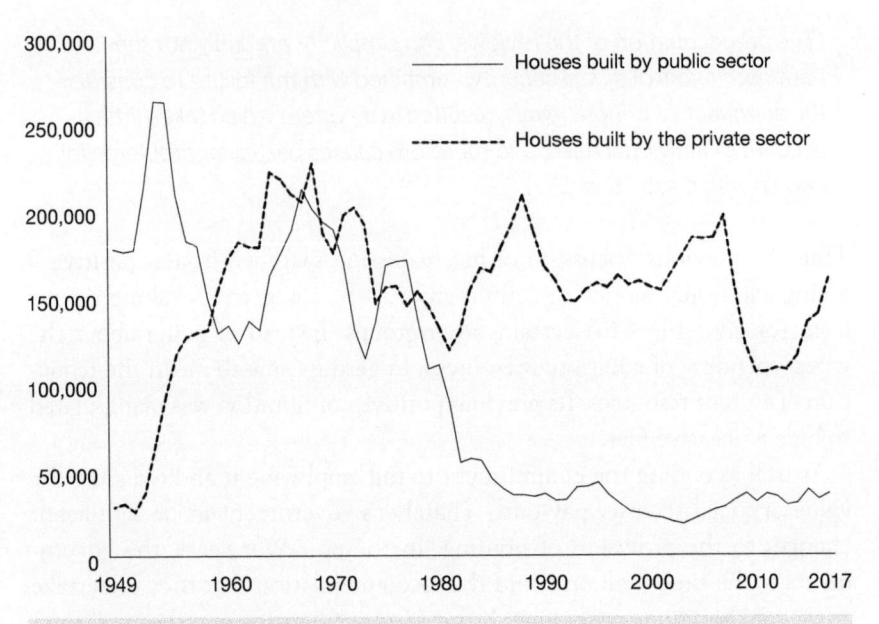

Figure 3. Housebuilding over time

There has been a dramatic fall in the number of houses built by the public sector since the mid 1970s; however there has been no balancing increase in the number of houses built by the private sector.

Because so much stock had been and was being lost, and in particular the higher value, higher rent stock, councils were forced to raise rents on the remaining stock. Jones and Murie concluded that, "if it were not for the right to buy, the council housing sector as a whole would have generated huge surpluses [from rental income] and the rise in real rents... would not have been necessary."[12] Thus the sale of council housing, predominantly the better-quality housing to better-off tenants, was effectively subsidised by the poorer tenants who were unable to buy.

The consequences of 1980s economic policy

The cuts to social security and the ending of commitment to full employment and a sufficient supply of housing did not end up saving the government any money. Unemployment reached three million in the early 1980s, from a previous 1970s high of one million under a Labour government. Many people who previously would have received universal and contribution-based benefits simply moved onto means-tested benefits, rather than

6. MOVING AWAY FROM THE WELFARE STATE

off the system altogether, because people were poorer than the government had realised or allowed for. The sale of council housing without adequate replacement by the public sector, and the failure of the private sector to take up the slack, resulted in a lack of houses relative to demand and therefore higher rent and higher social security costs. Consequently, whilst individuals personally received less support because of the social security cuts, many more people ended up needing support, and social security costs did not fall.

As social security spending continued to grow, a government committed to cutting spending on welfare had to find other cuts from somewhere. Unemployment benefit for people with savings – often the same people who had paid the most National Insurance contributions – was reduced from 12 to 6 months. Those who had mortgages lost their access to mortgage interest payments for the first 9 months of need, on the assumption that they would, could or should have taken out private insurance. Housing benefit was reduced, in particular by only paying rent to the value of a single room in a house share for those under 25.

Thus the social security part of the welfare state lost a key principle: that of universality. By reducing the duration of support to people who had paid in more (higher earners with savings or private insurance) or had had less opportunity yet (young adults), the system lost its sense of fairness. And at the same time as the principle of universality was lost and means-testing came into increasing use, income replacement benefits still failed to meet the basic core test of adequacy. Previous Conservative governments had agreed with Labour governments that no-one should fall below a subsistence level of income, but no government had actually ensured that this was the case. The result was that the 1980s cuts were taking money away from people who couldn't afford to lose any of what they had, rather than reducing excess to people who didn't need it.

Thus the welfare state shrank and became smaller than originally envisaged, as it now failed to provide not just the indirect benefits of employment and housing, but also the income protection that would in some part have mitigated government failure in the other areas. And ironically, because of these failures, it did not cost any less. Compounding this cost was the introduction of a new disability benefit, Disability Living Allowance, in 1992, in response to evidence that Attendance Allowance and Mobility Allowance were inadequate. But because this meant an increased spending on disabled people at a time when the government was still trying to decrease social security spending, more cuts had to be made elsewhere. Fuelled in part by a belief that many people being awarded Invalidity Benefit were well enough to work and in part by the desire to cut social security, Invalidity Benefit was scrapped and replaced with Incapacity Benefit.

Incapacity Benefit

In 1995, Incapacity Benefit (IB) was introduced to address fears that Invalidity Benefit (IVB) was overly accessible. The number of claimants on sickness benefits had more than trebled between IVB's introduction in 1971 and its replacement in 1995. Much of this increase represented increases in the number of disabled people with sufficient National Insurance contributions, and an increase in the proportion of claimants with long-term illness or disability. These people naturally take up an increasing proportion of claimants due to the length of time they remain on benefits compared to claimants with short-term conditions, who recover and leave the benefit system quickly.

Although there is some reason to believe that the eligibility threshold for incapacity had gradually lowered over the period up to 1995, preliminary evidence after the introduction of IB did not support a conclusion that many of those previously on IVB were fit for work.[13] Very few of those who were reassessed under IB and found fit for work actually returned to work. Instead, the increased labour supply relative to jobs, as more women entered the workforce, meant that it was becoming increasingly difficult for sick and disabled people to get work; at the same time as these "conventions about who should work have changed, it may now be more accepted that people need not take employment if their impairments make it extremely difficult for them to do so." But the difficulties that people with severe illness or disability faced in getting work did not stop the government from putting a new, harsher sickness benefit in place.

The new "all-work" test for IB was criticised for having an "exclusive focus on medical criteria, ignoring the interaction between impairments and other relevant circumstances such as age or previous experience." Whereas Invalidity Benefit could give consideration to how other barriers to work interacted with or exacerbated the impact of a claimant's health conditions, Incapacity Benefit looked only at a select group of activities (functional impairments) and whether or not the claimant could perform them. Thus Incapacity Benefit ignored a range of relevant factors that can interact with ill-health or disability, including the impact of commuting, personal care needs, household maintenance and any caring responsibilities.

No significant consideration appears to have been given to the possibility that work-related disability could have increased. Although the researcher Berthoud mentioned that employers may have become more selective, he did not discuss how work requirements might have changed. Instead, it has typically been assumed that increases in longevity mean that health has improved, and that a switch away from manual industry means that work has become easier. Unfortunately, neither assumption is borne out in the data. The number of people living with two or more long-term illnesses is increasing, and more of these people are of working-age than of pension age.[14] The stresses that work can put on people have not been ameliorated with a switch away from industrial work; they have simply changed.[15]

The UK in particular has a high proportion of high strain jobs that both cause and contribute to illness. Such bad jobs are not about the work itself, but about the conditions in which that work is carried out. Amazon warehouses, JD Sports, Sports Direct and meat and poultry factories have all been lambasted for imposing working conditions on low-waged staff that make their staff sick. These toxic jobs cause stress for employees by pressurising them to sustain high speeds of work whilst not permitting much, if any, autonomy, job control or decision latitude. Workers typically find themselves penalised for being ill or stopping to have a drink of water; going unpaid whilst queuing through security; being monitored to the second with public exposure for any failings; and having to ask permission to use the toilet. The mental strain and distress that is created leads in turn to mental illness and even physical illness, as long-term stress produces a cascade of physiological changes that promote general ill-health. In many ways, the UK workplace is not only no healthier now than 40 years ago, but worse. The diseases are just less overtly linked to work.

Erosion of the welfare state

The policies under Thatcher led to a gradual erosion of the welfare state. Benefits lost their value relative to the incomes of people in work. The ending of the commitment to full employment meant that more people were unable to find work, whilst the rise of the benefit scrounger narrative demonised the same people for what was a natural consequence of government policy. By the time Thatcher left the premiership in 1990, the poor were worse off after housing costs, and the number in relative poverty (earning less than 60% of the median income) had also increased.[16] Council housing had become more expensive and less available to poor people as a consequence of the right-to-buy policy. The government was moving away from universal and in-kind benefits, provided as of right, towards means-tested benefits provided only to those considered sufficiently deserving. Whilst the idea was to reduce costs, it turned out that holistic and universal welfare states were cheaper to provide and run whilst doing a better job of keeping the bottom income brackets out of poverty.

Although a new disability benefit, Disability Living Allowance, was introduced, it still didn't reach all who needed it, nor provide a top-up income adequate to meet their extra costs. It was paid for by pushing some people off sickness benefits, whilst reducing the award for others. Sick and disabled people therefore continued to struggle in poverty, perhaps now living in small institutions or even their own or, more likely, their parents' homes, but still unable to afford to participate in society and often struggling to meet their needs.

NOTES FOR CHAPTER 6

1. **As cited in Raison T** (1990) Tories and the welfare state: a history of Conservative social policy since the Second World War LONDON: PALGRAVE MACMILLAN
2. **Crossman R** (1969) Paying for the Social Services
3. **Mohr C** (20/07/2010) Is robotic surgery cheaper? FREAKONOMICS
4. **Thatcher M** (1976) Speech to Social Services conference dinner: The healthy society
5. **Bradshaw J** (1972) Social Security under the Tories in Jones K (ed) The Year Book of Social Policy in Britain 1971 LONDON: ROUTLEDGE AND KEGAN PAUL
6. **Timmins N** (1995) The five giants: a biography of the welfare state. HARPER COLLINS
7. **Joseph K** (1974) Speech by the Rt Hon Sir Keith Joseph BT MP (Leeds NE) Conservative spokesman on home affairs speaking at the Grand Hotel Birmingham
8. **Flynn P** (1990) Reduced Earnings Allowance and Retirement Allowance. HANSARD HC DEB 03 APRIL 1990 VOL170 CC1099-111
9. **Alcock P** (1980) Social Security under the Tories
10. **Walker A and Walker L** (1991) Disability and financial need – the failure of the social security system In Dalley G (ed) Disability and social policy LONDON: POLICY STUDIES INSTITUTE
11. Housing completions, Communities and Local Government, 1950 to 2010

12. **Jones C and Murie A** (2006) The right to buy: analysis and evaluation of a housing policy HOBOKEN: BLACKWELL
13. **Berthoud R** (1998) Disability benefits: A review of the issues and options for reform YORK: JOSEPH ROWNTREE FOUNDATION
14. **Royal College of General Practitioners** (2016) Responding to the needs of patients with multimorbidity: a vision for general practice LONDON.
    Barnett K, Mercer SW, Norbury M, Watt G, Wyke S and Guthrie B (2012) Epidemiology of multimorbidity and implications for health care research and medical education: a cross sectional study. LANCET VOL 380 ISS. 9836 PP. 37-43 DOI:10.1016/S0140-6736(12)60240-2.
15. **Theorell T** (2004) Democracy at work and its relationship to health In Perrewé PL and Ganster DC (eds) Emotional and physiological processes and positive intervention strategies. AMSTERDAM: ELSEVIER.
    Green F (2008) Work effort and worker well-being in the age of affluence In Cooper C and Burke R (eds) The long work hours culture: causes, consequences and choices. BRADFORD: EMERALD GROUP PUBLICATIONS
16. **Jones J** (10/04/2013) Margaret Thatcher in 6 graphs. London: The Spectator. Institute for Fiscal Studies (no date) Living standards poverty and inequality in the UK LONDON

7

The ongoing welfare dependency narrative

In the last chapter, we saw how concerns about public spending coupled with a belief in the dependency narrative were linked with a contraction of the welfare state. Welfare ceased to include the provision by the government of enough jobs and enough housing, and the provision of social security was cut back, leaving people more vulnerable to poverty when they could not work or find affordable housing. In this chapter, we see how this narrative continued through the 1990s and 2000s, leading to the creation of a new, tougher benefit for people who were unable to work due to chronic illness or disability. The same narrative has been used for the post-2010 changes, and its accuracy is key to whether or not cuts to support for sick and disabled people represent breaches in human rights.

The case for welfare dependency

The idea that providing support to workless people would only encourage them to remain workless is not new. As we saw in Chapter 3, there is a long history of belief in, and political fear of, welfare dependency. This subsided slightly in the post-war period, when the economy was growing and full employment meant that there was little opportunity to accuse people of a culture of worklessness. But with the start of a more turbulent economic period and a new political approach to the economy, the narrative of welfare dependency came to the fore again.

7. THE ONGOING WELFARE DEPENDENCY NARRATIVE

Governments since the 1980s have been particularly concerned by the possibility that the social security system undermines individuals' desire to work. A second major shift, building upon the 1970s and 80s discourse of scroungers, occurred during the 1990s. Positive references to welfare plummeted, and negative representations increased, as politicians began to speak about welfare – often used incorrectly, and narrowly, to refer only to social security – as ineffectual and wasteful. Scroungers were believed to be no longer a minor problem within an otherwise successful poverty alleviation programme, but were the moral fall-out of a benefit system that was itself a failure. It was not that the public became concerned about fraud, waste and moral failure with the politicians merely going where the votes were. Rather, politicians led the way in framing benefit recipients as scroungers and frauds and the benefit system as a costly mistake, and the public followed them.[1]

The argument is that the system provides workless individuals with a source of income which, by giving them enough to live on, makes work unnecessary. Individuals can end up with a sense of entitlement to state provision, simply because they are used to it being there. If living on benefits is comfortable and easy, then individuals may prefer and so choose this lifestyle compared to going out to work. Such behavioural choices may be contagious and spread amongst the poor to result in distinct communities where it is culturally normal and acceptable to live off benefits without bothering to consider paid work. The problem for social security, then, is how to provide for people in need without encouraging workless behaviour or rewarding poor choices amongst those who could work.

It is this problem which successive governments have referred to when they speak of an "over-generous benefit regime" resulting in a "dependency culture."[2] This was a theme which New Labour picked up on and continued, with references to a "social evil of dependency," "culture of dependency" and "culture of attitude and mind" amongst those who claimed out-of-work benefits.[3] Such language has enjoyed a high degree of consensus across political parties since the 1980s, when it became a mainstream prejudice.

The welfare dependency narrative is a central principle of post-1980s social security policy.[4] The idea is that the poor and unemployed deserve to live in poverty if they will not be flexible enough in terms of the pay, working conditions, occupation or distance to work that they will accept.[5] Not only that, but it would be immoral to alleviate that poverty, because these people need to experience the consequences of their inadequate work-ethic, in order that they may learn the right behaviours. The moral response to poverty therefore is largely to let poor people remain poor, so that they will be induced to work harder.

In order to properly serve those citizens who exhibit more lax work ethics, therefore, we must first stop subsidising their lifestyles. Work should be the only viable option for people capable of work. To do this, there are two main options: make work more attractive by increasing its pay and improving working conditions; or make benefits less attractive by reducing benefit levels and making the work search requirements more onerous. Rather than place requirements on employers, governments have largely chosen to reduce benefit levels and to increase the activity requirements placed upon benefit recipients, including those who are too sick or disabled to work.

Recipients of unemployment benefit have always been required to look for work in order to receive benefit. What has changed is the level of activity required and the degree to which the government monitors it. Since 2010, jobseekers have been required to spend 35 documentable hours each week looking for work, must apply for at least six jobs every week, and must also carry out any other activity that they are told to do. Such activities can include full-time (unpaid) work in entry level jobs, for which work the individual receives no additional money. Rather, the government supplies free labour to private companies whilst paying the individual less than minimum wage.

The imposition of sanctions for those who fail to complete a full job search every week reduces the benefit level even further, whilst placing substantial stress upon the jobseeker. A person who complies with every requirement except that they applied for only five jobs that week will lose their unemployment benefit for four weeks, during which time they must still fully comply with all requirements. If they fail again, further sanctions are added, up to a limit of three years; if they sign off benefits, they can't sign back on without finishing the rest of the sanction. Essentially, job-seeking is now a full-time job with illegally low pay and very large penalties.

The conclusion from this line of reasoning is that, in the end, the best help we can give poor people is to help them help themselves, by leaving them to experience poverty. This includes sick and disabled people. Changing the benefits system to make work more attractive relative to benefits therefore serves multiple purposes. It can help to form, or at least not malform, individuals' character; it results in people leaving poverty by encouraging the take-up of work; it shapes our country's culture; and it improves the economic functioning of society. In all these ways, it is alleged, getting people off benefits by cutting those benefits is a moral, as well as economic, goal that every society should endorse.

The case against welfare dependency

The dependency narrative of the last few decades has not been supported by any evidence, with MPs and others who hold this view relying instead on anecdote and their own assumptions regarding the behaviours, attitudes and incomes of others. Conservative MP Iain Duncan Smith, in charge of the post-2010 changes to social security, famously, when queried on this, could point only to his interpretation of worklessness on a Glasgow estate many years previously.

It is not that there is an absence of evidence. Rather, the evidence is that there are no such workless behaviours and beliefs amongst the long-term unemployed. The vast majority of long-term unemployed people do want to work, even when too ill to do so. There are no shared values of dependency within families or between peers, with no examples of entire families being out of work: workless adults have siblings, children and/or parents who are in work, as well as friends and peers in work. Working-age children are keen to avoid the poverty and worklessness experienced by their parents, and working-age parents are equally keen for their children to do better than themselves. Workless parents of working-age children have almost always been in work in the past, sometimes in insecure work and the low pay/no pay cycle; their children, even in job-poor areas, are also more likely to be in work than not, even when they have only recently left education.

Generations of worklessness, as claimed by Iain Duncan Smith, do not exist: extensive searching amongst deprived neighbourhoods found that even two generations of concurrent unemployment is rare, and usually results from the impact of long-term deprivation on the parental generation, including chronic disabling illness, and young age combined with limited job availability for the children (grandparents were retired or deceased, but had long work histories).[6] The researchers, who started by asking people 'in the know' – such as doctors, vicars, drug workers and Jobcentre staff – to point them to families with three generations of worklessness, were forced to gradually loosen their criteria as the people they asked, whilst confident of the existence of such families, either did not personally know any or used "generations of worklessness" to refer to cases where the parents were in and out of work, often with other social or health problems. From three generations of worklessness to two, and from worklessness in both generations to current long-term unemployment in the older generation, the researchers finally had to also include families where the younger generation had also previously had work. This was despite only looking for ten such families in each of two very deprived areas.

The researchers found that the younger generation, typically aged 16-25, had experienced multiple disadvantages during childhood yet "clung to conventional values and aspirations about jobs". The researchers concluded that, "the main explanation for their worklessness was that they were attempting to make their transitions into the labour market in a period of national economic downturn, and of high national and very high rates of local unemployment." In fact, the culture we have places such a strong emphasis on work as a sign of moral character that not being in work often leads to distress and depression, as unemployed people internalise the stigmatising messages that they receive from society.[7]

Despite ongoing claims of a dependency culture amongst sickness benefit recipients, research has found that there are no differences in attitudes towards work between people who return to work after a period of unemployment and those who do not.[8] This led DWP-commissioned authors to "question the policy assumption behind [replacing Incapacity Benefit] about the lack of work aspirations among recent Incapacity Benefit claimants". The fundamental difference amongst the mild to moderately ill is that one person simply happened to get a job when another person did not; for the moderately to severely ill, the crucial factor in a return to work is an improvement in health. This conclusion is a recurrent theme of DWP research reports, as well as academic papers.

Overall, what we actually see is that people actively desire to earn their own income rather than be dependent upon benefits, even when their only experience of work is of low-quality, dead-end jobs.[9] 'Hand-outs' from the government – or anyone else – are undesirable; people want to be able to support themselves and be independent of others. People who are too sick to work, who have been long-term unemployed, or who are trapped in the low pay/no pay cycle still retain a strong work ethic and a strong desire to work, despite the rhetoric. What astounds researchers in this area is not the existence of long-term unemployment, but the tenacity of the commitment to work amongst people who have never had the opportunity to enjoy a decent, secure job. Despite bad working conditions, illness and the misery of the low pay/no pay cycle, unemployed people – including the sick and disabled – remain strongly committed to and desirous of work.[10]

Stigma and malingering

Catherine has personally felt the impact of stigma and the assumption that she and people like her are malingering. When she was placed in the Work-Related Activity Group for people considered too sick to work but well enough to prepare for work, she was initially pleased and hopeful. She put her faith in the DWP having a plan for people like her, who have chronic illness, pain and debilitating exhaustion. Whilst stable, permanent work is beyond her, she has managed with a great deal of ingenuity to be a disabled mother. The list of things she can't do is too long to mention. But she outsources, compensates, cajoles, persuades and most of all gives 100% of her guts and passion to the job of being a mother. If she could do that, she thought, maybe she could manage 'work-related activity'.

She wasn't prepared for what happened. At her first back-to-work support meeting she was aggressively interrogated for fraud on the basis of allegations that the adviser made up as she went along. Catherine pleaded with the adviser to understand how much she wanted to work; how she'd tried every treatment possible to get better – including many not on the NHS – with no success. But all she got back was the command to try harder to get better, or her benefits would be stopped.

Catherine was referred to the Work Programme, the government's outsourced provision of employment support. It was totally inflexible and impersonal, and seemed geared mainly to instill punctuality and curtail any sense of control over one's own time. For someone who can only get through the parenting day with military-style planning, pacing and control that kind of regime, imposed from above and accompanied by the threat of losing her benefits, was stressful beyond words. When she was too sick to attend she was labelled a failure; when she was too exhausted to stand in a queue to sign in on time she was left in a breathless heap in the hallway, risking sanctions for being late.

Then she started to receive summons for workshops too far from public transport for her to be able to reach. Despite asking repeatedly for adjustments to help her to take part, the only answer she received was five referrals for sanctions. Then she had to do pretend job applications for jobs she couldn't possibly do, all because the government thinks that a person who has been ill for over 25 years is going to recover in the next five months. The harassment only stopped when Catherine instigated the process for taking the government to judicial review, although in the end she dropped the case because she would have had to sign a gagging order if she were to continue.

For Catherine, it is heart-breaking. Nothing has ever been offered to her to develop her skills, or to engage with employers who might be able to use her skills despite her disabilities. The question of who pays for the relatively poor productivity of a person who can only work a small amount, irregularly, and lying in bed, has not been answered. Catherine's children can't choose a healthier, fitter mum, but employers always have the choice of someone many times more reliable than her.

Are sick and disabled people malingering?

If unemployed people are assumed to lack the necessary commitment to work, it is not a big step to assume that sick people are playing-up a minor – or even non-existent – illness. It is assumed that the increase in sickness benefit receipt between 1971 and 1995 cannot be because of either an increase in work demands or an increase in illness or impairment, because it is assumed that the loss of heavy industry has reduced work demands whilst improvements in medical care have reduced illness and impairment. Therefore, the increase in sickness benefit receipt must be because people with mild to moderate illness are exaggerating their disability in order to avoid work. This is used as an excuse to cut support to sick and disabled people.[11]

The concern is that some, or even many, people on sickness benefit are not genuinely sick: they may be deliberately fraudulent; or, more likely, they have slipped into a 'sick role', in which they continue to perceive themselves to be sick and act accordingly, even though the original illness has long passed. This may be more a matter of habit than of deliberate intention to refrain from activity; they aren't deliberately fraudulent but merely misguided. In some cases, people may have a false perception that they are unable to work because the benefit system assessed them as such and did not offer the type of support they needed to make it possible for them to work. The award of a sickness benefit may therefore act as a negative label, unnecessarily putting people off from trying to work. In contrast, assessing someone as fit for work may help them to shake off the sick role and make a return to gainful activity.

7. THE ONGOING WELFARE DEPENDENCY NARRATIVE

But just as there is substantial evidence that sick and disabled people are not work-shy, there is also substantial evidence that people on long-term sickness benefits are not well.

A variety of measures of health and functional ability verify that most people on sickness benefits are severely and chronically sick or disabled. The increase in receipt has not been because of a growth in people with mild to moderate disability, but because of an increase in severe disability.[12] Government-recruited experts consider that those people who are assessed as fit for work typically have substantial health barriers which require several adjustments from employers – such as part-time work, work from home or unpredictable hours – before a person could be employed.[13] Even researchers who have previously referred to chronically sick and disabled people as hidden unemployment report that "health is central" to understanding sickness benefits.[14]

In weak labour markets, the poverty and stress of joblessness can themselves cause incapacitating illness. So even where someone leaves work in a relatively healthy state, they may not stay well, particularly if they are financially dependent on the benefits system.[15] This and other research has shown that the typical pattern for people entering sickness benefits is one of gradually deteriorating health and increasing spells of sick leave from work over as many as six years, before a person finally moves onto long-term sick leave.[16] Many soldier on for years, in many cases only making themselves more ill in the process.

Common stereotypes include the ideas that injured workers are irresponsible and that people with long-term illness or injury are lazy workers, looking for easy money or playing the system. However, research shows that such stereotypes are not only unfounded, but are themselves part of the cause of the problems for which they blame the victim:

> "Like most other members of society, injured workers want to work and to feel productive, proud and accomplished. These findings resonate with those of Stone whose research revealed that injured workers cherish their identity as worker and that this identity is central to their sense of self. Like the findings of this research, her work reports little evidence of a desire to move away from the work ethic. Claims to the contrary frustrate and anger injured workers, and lead to adversarial relationships with those who embrace and perpetuate these stereotypical notions."[17]

Sick and disabled people typically retain a strong desire to work, and do not want to take on the sick-role persona that the DWP believes is keeping unwell people from work. It is not that chronically sick or disabled people don't want to get well or return to work, but that they can't.

Replacing Incapacity Benefit

Concerns about over-accessibility of sickness benefits creating benefit dependency remained long after Incapacity Benefit was brought in, even though it was one of the harshest tests of capacity for work in the developed world.[18] Once the ongoing narrative of benefit dependency had been extended to sick and disabled people, it was easy to argue for an even tougher benefit that admitted fewer people to long-term benefit receipt.

But there was no evidence at the time that Incapacity Benefit was over-accessible. The number of people entering Incapacity Benefit each year had been falling, and after ten years was a third lower than when it was first introduced. The caseload had remained relatively stable, at around 2.5 million people, but this was because people with long-term illness or disability tend not to (be able to) leave sickness benefits. People did, of course, leave Incapacity Benefit, either because their health improved or because they were reassessed as fit for work, but it is the nature of long-term incapacitating illness and disability that people who have become unable to work remain so for long periods of time.

In fact, when government researchers tracked what happened to people after they left Incapacity Benefit, they found that the only group where a reasonable proportion of ex-claimants got and sustained work was those who had left the benefit of their own volition, usually because their health had improved.[19] These people were generally recent claimants who had a job contract to go back to; it was natural that as and when they recovered they returned to their contracted job. In contrast, when people were forced off the benefit because they were reassessed and told that they were capable of work, only a small proportion got, let alone sustained, paid work. Some ended up back on Incapacity Benefit, via an appeal or reassessment, but most ended up on no benefits at all. This included people who started claiming the basic unemployment benefit for jobseekers, Jobseeker's Allowance (JSA), but later stopped claiming and nor were they seeking work outside of the benefits system. These people simply left the system and were forgotten, still sick but now without financial support.

7. THE ONGOING WELFARE DEPENDENCY NARRATIVE

A reasonable inference is that Incapacity Benefit was already too harsh. People denied the benefit were not typically able to work; in fact, they often couldn't sustain job-search activity either. Despite this, and the fact that fewer people were entering the benefit each year, the 2007-10 Labour Government used the size of the caseload as a reason for introducing a new benefit, Employment and Support Allowance (ESA), under the allegation that Incapacity Benefit wrote too many sick and disabled people off to a lifetime of benefits.

The introduction of ESA had a significant impact on people like James, who has been on sickness benefits since 2005. In the post-1980s political language, James is the kind of person described by the government as abandoned to fester out of work. The political narrative implies that the issue is not whether there are enough jobs, or whether those jobs or suitable, or even whether the type of support that sick and disabled people need is available. It certainly isn't about whether people with chronic illness or disability are actually able to work. Instead, the narrative has increasingly been that unemployment is a choice made by individuals. People like James have chosen to be malingerers and scroungers, supported in this lifestyle choice by governments who are willing to give them financial support without conditions or employment support.

But the reality is not like that. James had been ill for some time before he finally admitted that he needed to stop working. It was not an easy decision. He had experienced JSA briefly after university, many years previously, and had been mistakenly sanctioned for not being offered a job by an employer at the end of a trial period. His JSA had been cut in half for six months, during which time he continued to seek work and comply with the conditions of JSA. But with so little money, he was struggling to survive. In poverty, living in a bedsit, choosing between food or electricity or heating, challenging the sanction and continuing to look for work, James became depressed and unhappy. It was the start of a series of mental illnesses that have continued to plague him, and which made James very chary of the benefits system.

James returned to education after successfully having his sanction overturned and all the money that he should have been receiving over the last 6 months was paid to him. From there, he continued in work for over 20 years, including running an off-license and holding various management positions. In government language, at this point James was doing the right thing as a hard-working taxpayer who deserved support (in the form of tax reductions) – right up until the point he had a breakdown, when he slipped back into the character of feckless scrounger who needed low benefits and tough conditions to teach him the right behaviours and attitudes to work.

Incentives to work

As part of the dependency narrative, the government believes that social security benefits are too well paid relative to work, and that in order to get people into work it is necessary to make work worth more relative to benefits. This is called making work pay, and is done not by making work pay more but by making benefits pay less. In Douglas McGregor's analysis of workforce motivation, this is Theory X: individuals as a whole lack motivation for work, and have to be in some way forced into work through rewards, penalties and strict supervision.[20] This is what the benefit system provides, albeit without the rewards. It is also the typical style of management for the dull, repetitive and high-pressure work at the bottom of the labour market that comes with little chance of promotion.

However, the evidence shows that it is actually Theory Y, job satisfaction, which motivates people. Jobs bring status, social contact, collective purpose, activity and a time structure.[21] Necessary as money is for living, people with enough money to live off, as well as people without and people dependent upon others, still want to work, because work is desirable in and of itself.

Neither JSA, ESA or their Universal Credit equivalents are lifestyle choices that individuals can routinely make in order to avoid work. JSA is only available to people who work at finding a job. It is not possible to refuse work and still claim JSA, or even to lose work either voluntarily or through misconduct and then receive JSA; all of these situations require 13 weeks of full conformity to JSA rules before any JSA will actually be paid. You can't even simply leave JSA for a time and reapply later as any uncompleted sanctions will be added to the start of a new claim. These sanctions can last for as long as three years.

To claim ESA, an individual has to have an illness or disability that demonstrably causes substantial limitation on their ability to work. Without an illness or disability, a person cannot claim ESA, however high their other barriers to work are. ESA uses the harshest test for work-related incapacity in the developed world, and even those assessed as fit for work typically have substantial health problems that prevent them from being able to work full-time. For claimants, ESA is not the easy option. Rather, claiming and retaining sickness benefits takes substantial effort and comes with stress, insecurity, poverty, stigma and high state surveillance.[22]

When additional finance is made available in order to incentivise work, such as by topping-up a person's earned income, it has no impact on the take-up of work.[23] Although this additional money can have a positive impact on a household's financial position, for example by clearing debts accrued during unemployment, it is not itself a significant contributor to the desire to work. The impact of a higher income in work on the desire to work is drowned by the size and strength of other motivators.

This is not to say that there is no relationship at all between benefit levels and unemployment. Higher benefits do result in benefit recipients, on average, spending a little longer out of work. But there is also an effect on people who are not receiving unemployment benefits: they get work faster when unemployment benefits are higher.[24] Higher benefits do not so much cause extra unemployment, as simply rearrange where the unemployment is. And the longer time spent searching for work means that benefit recipients are able to find a higher quality job; one that leads to a more complete use of their skills and is more stable.[25] Ironically, individuals may spend less time unemployed if they are given the time and support to find a permanent job than if they are forced to take a job at the bottom of the labour market, because these jobs usually don't last.

For people with illness that hinders work, a longer time on benefits promotes a fuller recovery and a more sustainable return to work.[26] In the UK, there is a strong sick-work culture, in which people attend work whilst too sick to work efficiently and productively. This might be acceptable if it still resulted in a higher quality and quantity of work being performed over the period in which a person is ill, compared to if the person had taken some time off. But it does not. People who attend work whilst sick prolong their illness and increase their likelihood of needing sick leave in the future.[27] The cost of this sickness presenteeism is difficult to estimate, because employees by definition are concealing their illness from their employer. But it is thought that the cost of sickness presenteeism is substantially more than the cost of sickness absence. It would potentially be better for the economy as well as the individual if a sick person were encouraged and supported to rest and recover rather than push on at work.

Conditionality and sanctions

As an extension of the government's use of Theory X, it is alleged that "conditionality is necessary to ensure that claimants take the steps required to move back in to employment."[28] Sanctions, it is claimed, are a positive force because they reduce the time spent on benefits and increase the movement into work. Without sanctions, claimants would cost society more (through longer periods on benefits) and jobs would either be left empty, or employers would have to pay a higher wage than the job merits in order to attract workers. But in reality, because people tend to want to work, it is rare that any negative inducement needs to be present to encourage people to apply for jobs.

As with inadequate benefit levels, conditionality and sanctions cause bad outcomes: people end up taking short-term, poorly paid jobs as part of a low pay/no pay cycle rather than being supported into a career, whilst others leave the benefit without anywhere else to turn for income. Recipients report that the system is degrading and harmful to their mental health and wellbeing, whilst the "arbitrary nature of requirements and the perfunctory, tokenistic nature of provided support" is frustrating.[29] And far from making work pay, harsh benefit systems with low benefit rates actually encourage the growth of the toxic, high strain, low pay work that dominates so much of the UK's labour market and which causes ill health.

For people with chronic illness or disability, sanctions create pressure to accept jobs or take part in work-related activities that are beyond their capabilities, resulting in a deterioration in health.[30] Sanctions "have no tangible positive effects" and "routinely trigger profoundly negative personal, financial and health impacts" that drive sick and disabled people further away from being able to work.[31] Those people who are not subject to sanctions and conditionality report that this gives them the freedom to engage in health management and work preparation that is actually beneficial and, whilst they may not become well enough to work, they are enabled to participate in and contribute to society in other ways.

Researcher Tania Rafass observed of enforced activity programmes that:

> "to make living off benefits unbearable is their direct if not always stated or publicised function. It is known that greater employment protection and generous income replacement rates during unemployment raise the general levels of life satisfaction. Yet both of these conditions (aka social rights) were deliberately undercut through neoliberal labour market and

7. THE ONGOING WELFARE DEPENDENCY NARRATIVE

welfare reforms on the grounds that they had purportedly exaggerated the sense of entitlement and etiolated the sense of social duty with regard to economic participation."[32]

We have now had several decades of responsibility-focused social security that is predicated on the assumption of welfare dependency. The emphasis has been on the citizen to prove that they are trying hard enough, and not on the government to provide enough jobs. Yet the positive impact of benefit systems with such high conditionality and sanctions as ours is very limited, and even non-existent, whilst the harm – in severe poverty, distress and demoralisation – is clear. These claimant-focused, demand-heavy benefit systems serve mainly to drive people into low paid, low skilled, insecure work, where they often need top-up benefits to get by and make repeated returns to unemployment.

The only real purpose of such programmes is to lower wages and working conditions, as they have done. To then impose such a system and labour market on poor, sick and disabled people is particularly pernicious. The high strain and low wage work that such a labour market provides risks making sick and disabled people more ill at the same time as blocking people from meaningful work and trapping them in poverty.

NOTES FOR CHAPTER 7

1. **O'Grady T** (2017) How politicians created rather than reacted to negative public opinion on benefits. LONDON SCHOOL OF ECONOMICS BLOG
2. **Dean H and Taylor-Gooby P** (1992) Dependency culture: the explosion of a myth. ROUTLEDGE: TAYLOR AND FRANCIS GROUP.
3. **Blair T** (1995) The rights we enjoy reflect the duties we owe. The Spectator. Blunkett D (2000) Enabling government: the welfare state in the 21st century: A speech by the Rt Hon David Blunkett MP Secretary of State for Education and Employment. POLICY STUDIES INSTITUTE
4. **Grover C and Stewart J** (2000) Modernising social security? Labour and its welfare-to-work strategy SOCIAL POLICY AND ADMINISTRATION VOL34 ISSUE3 PP 235-252
   Alcock (2003) The benefits system. In: Work to welfare: how men become detached from the labour market. CAMBRIDGE: CAMBRIDGE UNIVERSITY PRESS
5. **Byrne D** (2005) Social exclusion (issues in society). OPEN UNIVERSITY PRESS, 2ND EDITION
6. **Shildrick T, MacDonald R, Furlong A, Roden J and Crow R** (2012) Are 'cultures of worklessness' passed down the generations? JOSEPH ROWNTREE FOUNDATION

7. **Kirsh B, Slack T, and King CA** (2011) The nature and impact of stigma towards injured workers. JOURNAL OF OCCUPATIONAL REHABILITATION VOL22 PP143-145 DOI: 101007/s10926-011-9335-z.
   Dean H (2003) Re-conceptualising welfare-to-work for people with multiple problems JOURNAL OF SOCIAL POLICY VOL32 ISSUE3 PP441-459 DOI: 101017S0047279403007062.
8. **Kemp PA and Davidson J** (2010) Employability trajectories among new claimants of Incapacity Benefit. POLICY STUDIES VOL31 ISSUE2 PP203-221 DOI: 101080/01442870903429637
9. **Shildrick T, MacDonald R, Webster C, and Garthwaite K** (2012) Poverty and insecurity: life in low-pay no-pay Britain. Bristol: The Policy Press
10. **Garthwaite K** (2012) Incapacitated? Exploring the health and illness narratives of Incapacity Benefit recipients. PHD THESIS, DURHAM UNIVERSITY
11. **Hetzler A** (2009) Labor market activation policies for the long-term ill – a sick idea? EUROPEAN JOURNAL OF SOCIAL SECURITY VOL11 ISSUE4 PP369-401
12. **Berthoud R** (2011) Trends in the employment of disabled people in Britain. NATIONAL INSTITUTE FOR SOCIAL AND ECONOMIC RESEARCH, UNIVERSITY OF ESSEX
13. **DWP** (2013) Evidence based review of the Work Capability Assessment: a study of assessments for Employment and Support Allowance
14. **Beatty C and Fothergill S** (2009) Incapacity benefits in the UK: an issue of health or jobs? CENTRE FOR REGIONAL ECONOMIC AND SOCIAL RESEARCH
15. **Kemp and Davidson** (n 8)
16. **Bratsberg B, Fevang E and Røed K** (2010) Disability in the welfare state: an unemployment problem in disguise? IZA
17. **Kirsch et al** (n 7)
18. **OECD** (2003) Transforming disability into ability
19. **Ashworth K, Hartfree Y, and Stephenson A** (2001) Well enough to work? DWP RESEARCH REPORT 145
20. **MacGregor D** (1957) The human side of enterprise. First published in: Adventure in Thought and Action. Proceedings of the Fifth Anniversary Convocation of the School of Industrial Management. MASSACHUSETTS INSTITUTE OF TECHNOLOGY, CAMBRIDGE APRIL 9 1957 REPRINTED IN THE MANAGEMENT REVIEW (1957) VOL46 ISSUE11 PP22-28
21. **Jahoda M** (1981) Work, employment and unemployment: values, theories and approaches in social research. AMERICAN PSYCHOLOGIST VOL36 PP184-191
22. **De Wolfe** (2012) Reaping the benefits of sickness? Long-term illness and the experience of welfare claims. DISABILITY AND SOCIETY VOL27 ISSUE5 PP617-630
23. **Clayton S, Barr B, Nylen L, Burstrom B, Thielen K, Diderichsen F, Dahl E and Whitehead M** (2011) Effectiveness of return-to-work interventions for disabled people: A systematic review of government initiatives focused on changing the behaviour of employers. EUROPEAN JOURNAL OF PUBLIC HEALTH VOL22 ISSUE3 PP434-439 **Cordon A and Nice K** (2006) Pathways to work from incapacity benefits: a study of experience and use of Return to Work Credit. DWP

24. **Levine PB** (1993) Spillover effects between the insured and uninsured unemployed. INDUSTRIAL AND LABOR RELATIONS REVIEW VOL47 PP73-86
25. **Arni P, Lalive R, and van Ours J C** (2009) How effective are unemployment benefit sanctions? Looking beyond unemployment exit. BONN: THE INSTITUTE FOR THE STUDY OF LABOR (IZA)
Griggs J and Evans M (2010) Sanctions within conditional benefit systems: A review of evidence. YORK: JOSEPH ROWNTREE FOUNDATION.
Klepinger D, Johnson R and Joesch J (2002) Effects of unemployment insurance work-search requirements: the Maryland experiment. INDUSTRIAL AND LABOR RELATIONS REVIEW VOL56 ISSUE1 PP3-22
26. **Krueger AB and Meyer BD** 2002 Labor supply effects of social insurance. CAMBRIDGE MA: NATIONAL BUREAU OF ECONOMIC RESEARCH
27. **Post M, Krol B and Groothoff J** (2006) Self-rated health as a predictor of return to work among employees on long-term sickness absence. DISABILITY AND REHABILITATION VOL28 ISSUE5 PP289-297.
Bergström G, Bodin L, Haqberg J, Aronsson G and Josephson M (2009) Sickness presenteeism today, sickness absenteeism tomorrow? A prospective study on sickness presenteeism and future sickness absenteeism. JOURNAL OF OCCUPATIONAL AND ENVIRONMENTAL MEDICINE VOL51 ISSUE6 PP629-638.
Bergstrom G, Bodin L, Haqberg J, Lindh T, Aronsson G and Josephson M (2009) Does sickness presenteeism have an impact on future general health? INTERNATIONAL ARCHIVES OF OCCUPATIONAL AND ENVIRONMENTAL HEALTH VOL82 ISSUE10 PP1179-1190.
28. **Pickles C, Holmes E, Titley H and Dobson B** (2016) Working welfare: a radically new approach to sickness and disability benefits. REFORM
29. **Raffass T** (2017) Demanding activation. JOURNAL OF SOCIAL POLICY VOL46 ISSUE2 PP349-365 DOI:101017/S004727941600057X
30. **Nevile A and Lohmann R** (2011) "It is like they just don' trust us:" Balancing trust and control in the provision of disability employment services. CANBERRA: SOCIAL POLICY ACTION RESEARCH CENTRE. **Hale C** (2014) Fulfilling potential? ESA and the fate of the Work-Related Activity Group. MIND.
31. **Dwyer P, Jones K, McNeill J, Scullion L and Stewart ABR** (2018) Welfare conditionality final findings: disabled people. ECONOMIC AND SOCIAL RESEARCH COUNCIL.
32. **Raffass** (n 29)

8

The austerity programme

So far, we have looked at how sick and disabled people had been treated up to 2010 as a foundation against which we can compare the post-2010 policies. We have seen that there has never been a 'golden period' in which sick and disabled people enjoyed their rights to an adequate standard of living and full participation in society. Improvements to social security in the 1970s and early 1980s have been countered since the start of the 1980s by cutbacks to not just the social security system but to the welfare state as a whole. Poor people have been increasingly blamed for their poverty without any consideration of the government's role in shaping the quality and availability of education, healthcare, housing and jobs. Although there is less enforced institutional living now than there has been in the past, sick and disabled people have never received enough financial support, and access has never been uniformly applied or universally available.

In this chapter, we move forwards to 2010. Many of the arguments that have been used to justify the post-2010 social security cuts have had support from across the political spectrum, and have been building up since the 1970s. This includes the belief that welfare encourages unemployment and dependency, which we have already considered and shown to be flawed and even false, but also the post-2010 austerity narrative which massively extended the popular thinking that government spending needed to decrease. The outcomes of the post-2010 policies are addressed in Chapters 9 to 15, whilst in this chapter we will consider whether the government's spending cuts were justified economically. Whether they were justified or not is an important part of determining potential breaches in human rights. Short-term harm that leads to long-term good, or harm that was wholly unavoidable, is less likely to constitute a breach of human rights.

8. THE AUSTERITY PROGRAMME

Real Per Capita Expenditure on Social Security for Working Age Adults in the UK

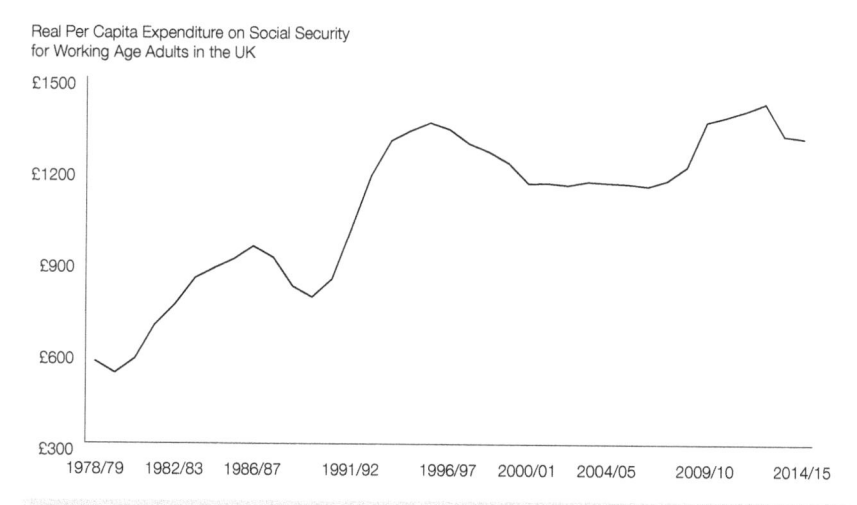

Figure 4. Trend in social security for working age adults

Real-term per capita expenditure on working-age people fell between 1995 and 2006, and even after the 2007/08 financial crisis it only peaked at around the same level as during the recession of the early 1990s.

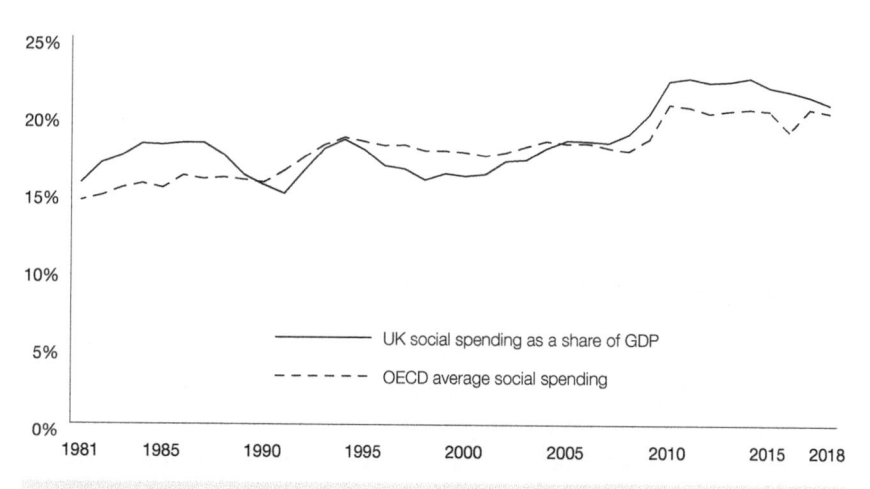

Figure 5. UK social spending compared to OECD average

Social spending as a percentage of GDP was below or very close to the average spending of other developed countries in the OECD, only going slightly above the average after the financial crisis of 2007/08.

Too much social security?

The cuts to social security, social care and the wider welfare system form part of general efforts to achieve a closer balance between government spending and tax receipts following the 2007/08 global financial crisis. The government elected in 2010 considered the social security budget to be particularly bloated and a large contributor to the deficit it inherited. Therefore, there was, it alleged, an economic need, as well as the moral need identified (and disproved) in Chapter 7, to reduce spending on social security.

The government wanted to prune down the social security system, to leave it available only to the most needy and remove less needy people from its remit. The expectation was that unemployed, including many sick and disabled, people can and therefore will choose to work when their benefits are made less valuable. Without such moves into work, cuts to social security and welfare will result in negative consequences for not just poverty rates but also "inclusion in society, independence, quality of life, well-being, housing, work, mobility and mental health."[1]

But the data does not support the contention that social security was excessive. Real-term per capita expenditure on working-age people fell between1995 and 2006, and even after the 2007/08 financial crisis per capita spending peaked at around the same level as during the recession of the early 1990s (Figure 4). Social spending as a percentage of GDP was below or very close to the average for developed countries from 1989 until 2007/08, and although the UK went slightly above average after the financial crisis this gap has now shrunk to half a percentage point (Figure 5).[2] So the pre-crisis benefit levels were neither excessive nor out of control; rather, they were average amongst developed countries and stable relative to the financial cycle.

The post-2010 Governments' claim of excessive social security spending ignores the importance of the government's role in maintaining demand and preventing unnecessary poverty during a recession. During a recession, the private sector stops providing an income for as many people as previously, as people are made redundant or otherwise have their pay reduced. This creates a downward spiral as people who have lost work have less money to spend, so demand for goods and services fall, so businesses have to let even more people go. Social security at this point provides both a moral and economic role by providing people who would otherwise have nothing with money that they can spend on basic living costs. Morally, social security protects people from becoming completely penniless; and economically, it maintains a minimum level of demand for goods and services in the economy. It is therefore both right and good that social security goes up during a recession.

8. THE AUSTERITY PROGRAMME

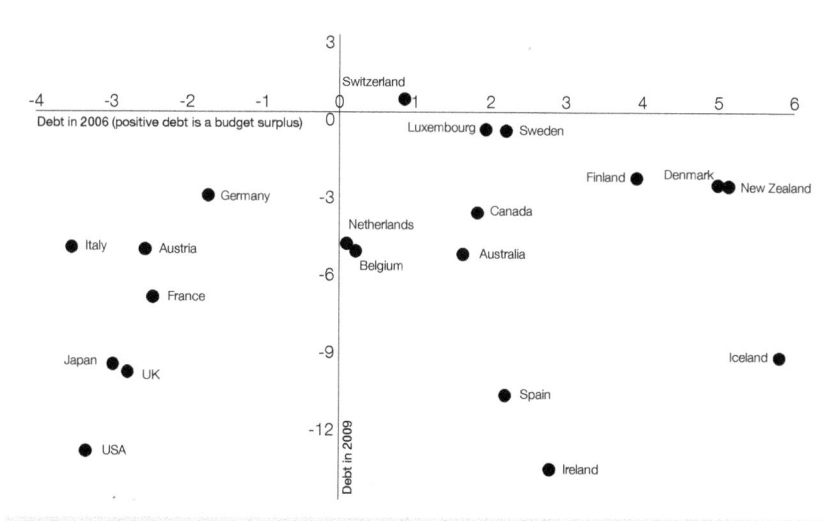

Figure 6. Debt as a percentage of GDP before and after 2007/08

If we compare government debt as a percentage of GDP before and after the 2007/08 financial crisis there is no positive link between the level of debt before the crisis and after the crisis. (Norway is excluded as an outlier with high budget surplus in both years.)

The government's argument, of cutting benefits to get more people into work, also ignores the necessity of jobs if employment is to be maintained. People can't stay in or obtain work if there aren't enough jobs, so making people more keen to work isn't the answer to insufficient jobs. During the recession, the number and (in terms of hours, pay and working conditions) the value of jobs fell. This wasn't because a whole group of people had suddenly decided that they didn't want to work, or that benefits offered a better lifestyle than paid work; it was because there were fewer hours of work available in the economy. Cutting income-replacement benefits for those without work could not drive these people into work, because the existence of income-replacement benefits was not the cause of job loss. There simply were fewer hours of work to go around – from a peak of 950,000 hours per week at the start of 2008, to 910,000 in mid-2009 (seasonally adjusted hours). It took until 2013 for the number of hours worked to recover to pre-crash levels, and 2015 to return to trend.

So both morally and economically, there was no justification for the UK Government cutting social security. In fact, cutting social security at a time of recession is morally and economically wrong.

Spending cuts

It was argued by the Conservative Party that Labour's failure to reduce government debt as much as it could have done before the 2007/08 financial crisis was a significant issue that caused serious harm to the economy. But the reality is that for countries with their own fiat currency, such as the UK, the amount of debt preceding a financial crisis has a remarkably small effect on what happens afterwards (Figure 6).[3] In the UK, the gap between spending and tax receipts soared after the financial crisis, and the large majority of this cost came from buying-out banks. Having a budget surplus (tax intake exceeding government spending) rather than deficit (spending exceeds tax intake) before the recession would have made very little difference to the size of the subsequent debt and deficit.

In fact the relationship between debt before and debt after the crisis is weak, with two countries that had surpluses before the crisis - Ireland and Spain - being amongst the most indebted nations afterwards. Running a budget surplus before a recession has little impact on debt afterwards.

But the 2010 Conservative-Liberal Democrat Government believed that the deficit was a major negative constraint on the economy. It was therefore considered important to reduce the deficit. There are two main approaches to this: growth-based policy, which uses government spending to boost the economy and thereby naturally bring down the deficit as tax revenue increases; and austerity, which works the other way around in that the government focusses directly on reducing the deficit through spending cuts and tax increases, in the expectation that this will boost private sector spending. The 2010 Government chose austerity over growth-based policy, and it also chose to implement 60% of austerity through spending cuts rather than tax increases.

Some government departments were protected from spending cuts. The NHS and non-investment education spending were protected, whilst the (admittedly small) Cabinet Office (No.s. 10 and 11) and the Department of Energy and Climate Change received increases. The remaining departments lost an average of 20% of funding for the government business that they manage. The DWP and the Ministry of Justice lost over a third of their financial resources, whilst local government – which in 2010 received 70% of its income from central government – lost over 50% of central government funding.

The cuts mean that departmental spending in 2019/20 will be the same, in real terms, as 2002/03 – but with a larger and older population. Civil servant numbers are now at their lowest level since at least 1971, both

8. THE AUSTERITY PROGRAMME

absolutely and as a proportion of the total workforce. Making these cuts particularly pernicious was the government's programme of welfare reform, which required the DWP to not only function on a substantially reduced budget and loss of civil service capacity and expertise, but to also introduce numerous cuts, entirely replace one disability benefit with another, manage a failing sickness benefit, and bring in a novel, untested mechanism for benefit payments (Universal Credit). All at the same time that local councils were finding it increasingly difficult to provide social care, child protection services and other valuable in-kind support such as parks, libraries and sure-start centres, which previously would have reduced the need for direct financial support.

But it doesn't make economic sense to base austerity on spending cuts and policies measures that increase deprivation and poverty rather than on raising taxes on the better-off.[4] It is well-established that poorer people are more likely to spend any additional money they receive than are richer people. This is called the marginal propensity to consume. Poorer people tend to spend all of their income, because that's what subsistence living and a limited amount of social participation cost, whilst richer people usually have money left over even after spending on luxuries. Richer people can therefore absorb a reduction in income by putting less money towards savings, and may not have to reduce spending at all, whilst poor people are forced to reduce spending by the same amount as the reduction in income. Therefore, a change in the income of poor people has a bigger impact on the overall economy than does a change in the incomes of rich people; and cutting social security has a more harmful impact on the economy than would increasing taxes by the same amount.

The consequence is that poorer people have been hit harder by austerity then have richer people: the government has focused more on spending cuts, which affect poor people, than on tax increases, which would affect richer people. And the departments that have been worst hit include the DWP – responsible for managing cash benefits – and local government – responsible for valuable in-kind support and social care. So the balance of austerity has disproportionately impacted the poor.

If austerity is to be imposed at all, raising taxes on the rich is better than cutting spending on or to the poor. It is much better for the economy to redistribute some money away from the rich, where the money is left idle, to the poor or the public sector, where it is spent and contributes to economic growth. And if spending cuts are to occur, they could fall on other areas, such as the salaries and pensions of the top public sector staff, and the removal of tax relief from fee-paying schools. But the UK Government did not do this: whilst it did raise some taxes, it lowered others, and the bulk of the measures adopted were not just based on spending cuts, but on cuts that disproportionately impacted the poor.

Tax and borrowing

Economics tells us that austerity, if implemented, should target the better-off. But should austerity be implemented at all?

Those who argue for austerity do so because they believe that any damage will be short-term or will simply not occur. They believe that governments that cut spending now can (and most likely will) cut tax in the future, and that low government spending and low taxation will result in substantially improved business spending and investment. The theory assumes that government spending has to be funded by either tax or borrowing (or one-off sales of assets), and that both of these reduce private spending. Tax reduces people's ability to spend by both directly reducing income and indirectly reducing the incentive to earn (because the return on work or investment is lower when some of it goes to the government). Government borrowing results in increased interest rates, which makes borrowing to invest more costly for businesses and so reduces their level of investment (this is called 'crowding out'). So a country that uses high tax and high public spending is expected to suffer reduced private investment and thus lower economic growth than one with a smaller tax and spending system.

It follows from this argument that a government can grow its economy by cutting government spending. The reduced government borrowing means interest rates are lower. The reduced government spending means that in the future, once the deficit has been turned into a surplus, the government can afford to cut taxes. Businesses will be attracted to such austerity-based economies because the cost of investment is low (low interest rates) and returns on investment will be high (less tax). They will also have confidence in the economy because they deem its government to be economically prudent. Government spending cuts that are "credible, decisive and of the right kind" should therefore result in increased private spending, which proponents of austerity claim will outweigh any direct negative impacts of reduced public spending.[5] This expectation of quick recovery underpins the EU's *Stability and Growth Pact*.

8. THE AUSTERITY PROGRAMME

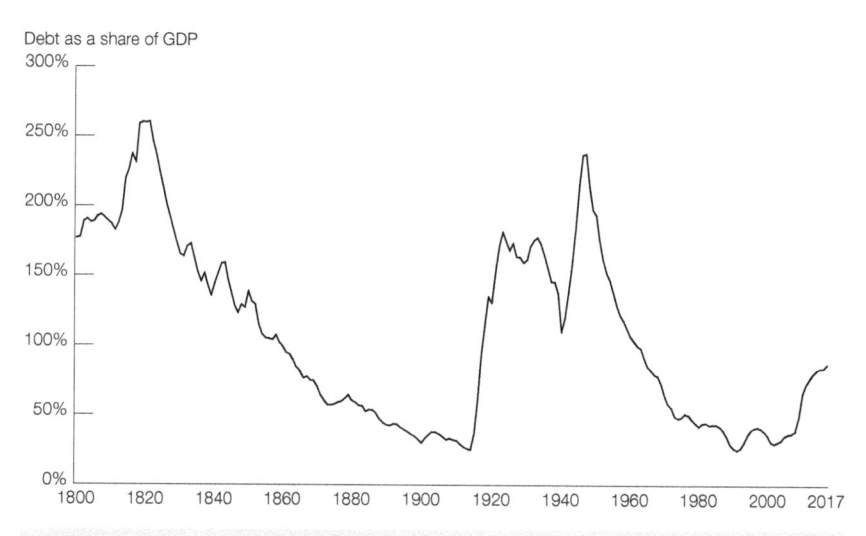

Figure 7. History of UK debt and GDP

The ratio of government debt to GDP fell twice as fast after WWII, the Golden Age of the Welfare State, as it did after the austerity that followed the Napoleonic Wars of 1803-1815. Furthermore, austerity since 2010 has so shrunken the state and the economy that debt to GDP has not started dropping, even ten years after the 2007/08 global financial crisis.

But the evidence does not support the hypothesis that austerity leads to improved economic growth. The direct negative impacts of public spending cuts are simply too high, especially during recessions.[6] When the problem is insufficient (private) spending, the remedy isn't to add to this by deliberately reducing government spending. This will only depress the economy further, and heighten the risk of bankruptcy for private businesses. Far from encouraging private business, austerity weakens the economy and makes investment more risky. Economist Anis Chowdhury observes that, "inaction by the government for the fear of crowding out will not help private investors."[7] Instead, government spending into a depressed economy is necessary to create the demand for private businesses, by putting money into people's pockets so that they in turn can spend.

Government cutbacks demonstrably have not resulted in private investment and economic growth, whether nationally, internationally or historically. Even the few examples where austerity co-occurred with economic growth were not due to the austerity measures, but rather to other growth-enabling factors that were able to offset the negative impact of austerity.[8] After WWII, at a time of high national debt, the UK Govern-

GDP relative to the start of the recession

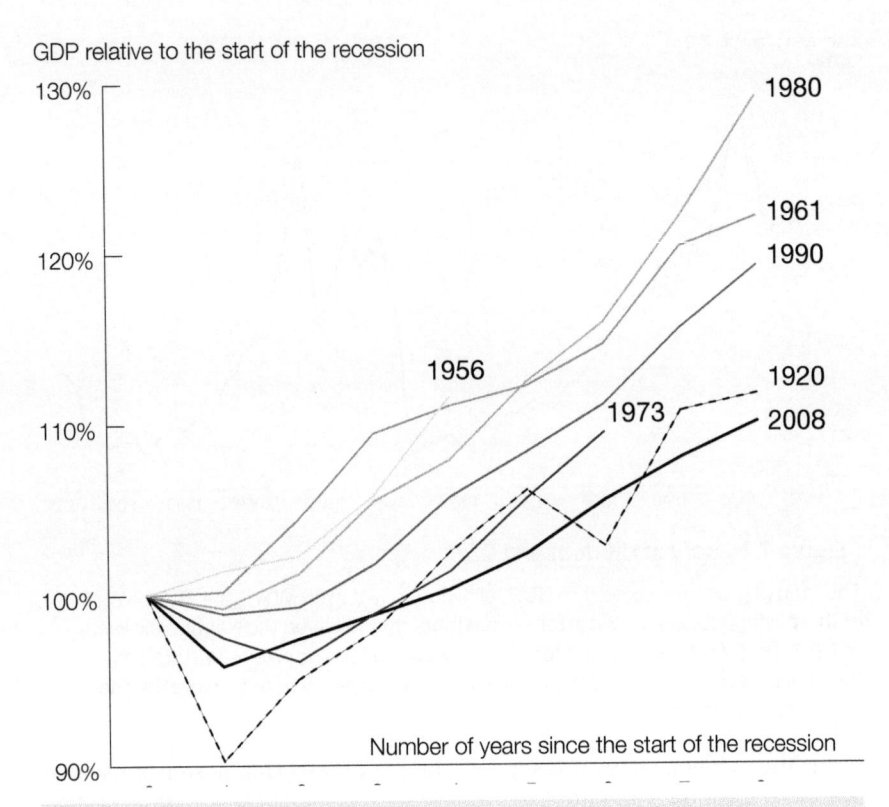

Figure 8. UK recovery from recessions

The UK's recovery from the 2007-08 crash has been the least successful in the last hundred years, even worse than the recovery from the Great Depression of the 1920s. Although the 1920s Depression was deeper, the recovery rate was faster.

ment protected and invested in its people, and the economy grew. As a result, government debt dropped rapidly relative to the economy – twice as fast as after the Napoleonic wars, when the government chose the path of austerity (Figure 7).

It turns out that businesses take confidence not from the hope of a strong economy in the future, but in the fact (or not) of a strong economy now. Austerity can only result in a strong economy if private businesses create that strength themselves. It therefore relies upon circular behaviour: businesses investing on the basis that the economy *will be* strong, so long as enough of them invest – but the cost if no-one else invests is high. So businesses much prefer to invest into economies that are already strong. The data shows that private business spending follows boom and bust cycles

8. THE AUSTERITY PROGRAMME

and perpetuates, rather than corrects, them. It is therefore not austerity but steady economic growth created by government spending that supports private investment and business.

This is not to say that governments can spend willy-nilly with no consideration for what the economy needs or the rate of inflation, but that austerity is not the same as economic prudence. Austerity neither gives businesses confidence in the economy, nor enables increased private investment. But if the private sector is not spending, and reductions in government spending don't result in increased private sector spending, then a different approach is needed. What actually works is growth-based policy: economic growth created by government investment. This then creates the strong economy that private businesses like to invest in. Government spending in key areas, such as education, social housing or counter-cyclical spending (spending that naturally increases in bad times, e.g. social security) therefore has a positive effect on the economy.

The next section shows why it is not a good idea for a government try to reduce its deficit during a recession. But even if it were the right aim, the post-2010 governments have on their own terms made the wrong decision. The right way to reduce a government deficit is to stimulate economic growth through government spending, thus increasing tax receipts; it is not to engage in wishful thinking that reduced government spending will somehow give businesses confidence in a (even more) sluggish economy.

The result of austerity was that the UK experienced the worst recovery from a recession on modern record (Figure 8). An initial expansion during the last year of the Labour government was lost when austerity policies were introduced after the 2010 general election. Although initial fears of a double-dip recession were revised away by the time of the final data release of quarter-on-quarter change, the subsequent years have seen stymied and uneven growth, unusually low interest rates and inflation, and a lack of growth in productivity. Whilst politicians hail increasing numbers of people in work, the actual hours worked have not been so positive, taking until 2015 to recover fully, and the government's employment claim is bolstered by including people working as little as one hour a week or working unpaid on government programmes as 'employed'.

The UK did not need to implement spending cuts. The economy is still struggling and is nowhere near full capacity, which means that the UK has ample fiscal space for public spending. Fiscal space is only restricted when a country is at or nearing the full utilisation of all its resources, which would include genuine full employment. At such a point, more government spending would serve no useful purpose. But we are not near that point. So the UK Government can safely increase its spending, protect the poor and stimulate the economy. Instead it chose to focus on artificially cutting the deficit rather than promoting full employment; austerity instead of spending for growth; spending cuts over tax increases; and to target cuts on areas that disproportionately impact the poor. The government should have used expansionary fiscal policy – tax cuts (best directed at the poor) and increased government spending – instead of trying to reduce the deficit and thereby harming the economy and especially harming the lives of the poor.

What is money, and does it matter?

The government has justified its desire to reduce the deficit by using the 'household' analogy. The argument is that an individual, household or business cannot continually spend more than it earns. If it borrows money, then it will need to pay that back at a cost in the future. The wise action is to keep spending below one's income, whilst putting aside savings for future income or expenditure shocks, such as worklessness due to major illness. It is argued that the government must do the same: it must seek to have no debt, and to perpetually spend less than it receives in money coming in.

But a currency-issuing government like the UK is not in the same group as individuals, households and private businesses, or even the euro-using countries. It is fundamentally different, because unlike the others who are recipients of currency, the government is the issuer of currency. The government doesn't receive an income and then spend it; rather, the government must spend before it can ever collect anything in tax. The pound sterling would not exist if the UK Government did not create it. For anyone to ever be able to pay tax to the UK Government in pound sterling, the government must have first created that pound by spending it into existence. Phil Armstrong explains:

> "Governments use their position of authority to place members of the community in their debt; they impose a tax liability upon them. The government has the power to decide upon the unit of account in which the tax must be paid (pound, dollar etc.) and the 'money things', denominated in the unit of account, that must be used to satisfy the tax liability. The state is able to provision itself by first imposing a tax liability, creating

8. THE AUSTERITY PROGRAMME

> willing private sector sellers of goods and services who require the state money to satisfy their tax bill. State money can thus be conceptualised as state debt which acts as a tax credit; the government spends money into existence and taxes it out when it accepts the return of its own debt in settlement of a tax liability."[9]

These insights are provided by Modern Monetary Theory (MMT); once grasped, it is reasonably intuitive, but explaining it in the first place can be somewhat harder! To help explain how money works, MMT economist Alan Hutchison developed the following riddle:

> I am made of paper and have interesting designs printed on my surface. I am usually associated with a nation and if that nation is a monarchy it is commonplace for me to have a representation of the monarch included in my design.
>
> I am created and issued on demand by the state (although the state may contract my creation to the private sector). It is illegal to create counterfeits of me.
>
> I have monetary value and I am denominated in varying amounts of the national unit of account. In comparison to my denominated value, it costs the state virtually nothing to create me.
>
> I can be used to pay for goods and services supplied by the private sector or by the state.
>
> I can also be used to pay taxes to the state. When I am used to pay tax, or to pay for services from the state, I am cancelled.
>
> Until I am cancelled I represent debt owed by the state.
>
> Quite a few people desire to hoard large quantities of me and forego using me for payment. In certain circumstances the state will pay interest to the people who have collected me.
>
> Some foreign entities like to hoard me and are happy to accept me in return for real resources.
>
> The fact that some people like to hoard me means that the state issues more of me than gets cancelled.
>
> Finally, my greatest fear is hyperinflation.
>
> What am I?[10]

There are two answers to this question: One is currency in the form of cash – a coin or note. This is the obvious answer. But what many of us have probably never realised or thought about is that this is also true of postage stamps.

Like money, postage stamps are created with patterns that are difficult to counterfeit. In the UK, they usually include a picture of our monarch. The state produces the stamps at negligible cost, but despite their negligible 'real' value they are carefully guarded and audited to prevent theft, and it is illegal to counterfeit them. Although postage stamps are not legal tender, people can use them to purchase goods or services, and used to do so regularly when adding stamps to fixed-value postal orders in order to make up an intermediate value. Some people may remember using stamps to buy small items over mail order as children.

Before postage stamps existed, people used small labels called 'revenue stamps' to record the payment of tax. This morphed into the first postage stamp, the penny black, which recorded that a tax had been paid to the government for the delivery of post. The state is obliged to provide postal services in return for a stamp, so people who have unused stamps have a 'postal credit' from the government: the government has promised to accept the stamp back at some point, and in return deliver some post for the individual. Similarly, money is a tax credit. The government has promised to accept the money back at some point, and in return cancel the tax that the individual owes them.

After use, the stamp is marked to show that it has been used and cannot be reused. In effect, it is cancelled. If used stamps were not cancelled, then every time the government printed new stamps the circulation of stamps in the economy would increase, causing inflation as the stamps drop in value relative to goods and services. Similarly, the government cancels any currency it has issued into the economy by receiving that money back in lieu of tax.

Crucially, at each printing round the government has to print more stamps than have been cancelled by going through the delivery system. The reason is that some people collect stamps, which means that they fall out of the system without being used. If 5% of stamps are collected, then only 95% of the stamps that the government issued in the first round are cancelled. If, at the next printing round, the government can only issue as many stamps as have been cancelled, then the government can only print 95% of the stamps actually needed. As this goes on, more stamps end up in collectors' books and fewer are in use. People end up unable to send letters or parcels,

8. THE AUSTERITY PROGRAMME

not because there is a lack of desire to send and receive, but because there aren't enough stamps.

The same happens with money. If the government matches its spending in each period to its tax receipts, then the amount of money that is usefully flowing around the economy gradually reduces. More and more of it is sat in banks or people's homes, doing nothing, like the stamps in the stamp collectors' books. The government needs to issue more money than it receives back in taxes, to account for the money kept in savings. The negative gap between what the government spends and what it gets back in taxes, called the deficit, is simply the sum total of all the privately held savings. Conversely, if tax receipts are higher than government spending – a budget surplus – then this has only happened because the government has withdrawn money from people's or businesses' private savings. This is like forcing stamp collectors to hand over some of their stamps unused.

Alan Hutchison explains:

> "Tax destroys money which was previously created out of nothing by the state. The state doesn't need the tax money in order to continue spending. Tax money is not re-spent. Anyone who thinks that it is should ask themselves why the government is not obliged to soak stamps off envelopes in order to keep the postal service running."

Anyone can create a currency: you could create a currency denominated in Units by writing 'I owe you 5 Units' and offering it to someone as payment. You might hope that they would later buy something from you that was worth 5 Units, and then your IOU is neatly cancelled without anything of real value (it was a bit of paper, after all) being exchanged. But you probably won't find many people willing to accept your IOU, which will make it difficult for you to buy things. Your ability to spend money into existence is limited by the public's reluctance to accept your IOUs.

Similarly, you could lend money into existence – give the person the IOU without requiring anything in return now, whilst agreeing that the person owes that amount of IOU plus interest in the future, and that you will accept the repayment of that loan and interest in the form of more of your IOUs. But again, you won't find many people who want a loan of your IOUs, because they know that not many other people want them either, so the loaned IOUs would be of little use to them.

People do, however, want the government's currency, because it is the only way they can pay the tax and any other charges that they owe to the government. The government promises to accept its IOUs back as payment of tax owed, and will only accept tax in its own IOU currency. Consequently, everyone needs to acquire at least some government IOUs in order to pay tax, and government IOUs have a reliable value. So when the government writes IOUs to the people or businesses from which it is buying, those people or businesses are happy to accept the IOUs. They know that they can use the IOUs to pay the tax they owe and, because others also want government IOUs for the same reason, to buy goods and services from others.

The government doesn't have to lend money into existence, because it can spend money into existence. The government may lend money into existence in order to satisfy the demand for government bonds, which are desirable for investors who don't need much return on their money but do want to be sure of getting something, but it isn't itself constrained by how many bonds it can sell. The government does not at any point need to borrow, tax or sell in order to raise money to spend. It simply creates the IOUs by spending them into existence. Private banks can also create money, but only by making loans to people (denominated in the government's currency), which those people have to repay in the future with interest (thus making profit for the bank).

The problem with money therefore is not that it is sometimes created out of 'thin air', for it is always created out of thin air. The problem with money is how much is being created and who or what for. Government spending to meet public needs is good, but not if the government tries to spend money beyond the capacity of the resources of the country. Prudent lending by private banks is good, but banks can make too many loans, and they can lend to people or businesses who are not credit-worthy. This leads to market bubbles that subsequently crash, as in the 2007/08 financial crisis and ensuing recession.

Money is the oil that keeps the machine of the economy moving, enabling resources to move to where they are needed, but it is not the resources themselves. By targeting creation of money where the private sector is running dry, and taking it out where there is too much, the government keeps the economy moving smoothly and efficiently. Taxation is important, but its role is not to generate government revenue, but to enable the state to provision itself and allow the government to control the level of demand in the economy, to prevent both deflation and excessive inflation. It is a tool for managing the economy. Constraints on government spending do exist, but for a country with its own government-backed currency these constraints are real, not monetary.

The outcome of MMT is that governments faced with falling tax revenue do not have to cut their spending or raise taxes. Indeed, if demand is falling and unemployment rising, to do so is foolish, because this removes money from circulation and thus hinders people from engaging in the market activity which they wish to pursue. The desire for spending remains, but is hampered by the lack of money. The government can enable the economy by giving poorer people benefits, such that they can afford to meet their needs; and by spending on public services such as housing, education and healthcare, where poorer people cannot afford to buy what they need and consequently the private sector cannot afford to provide. This government spending can reverse any deflationary pressure, whilst a return of inflationary pressure can be met by increased taxation to prevent the economy from overheating. Appropriate taxation and targeting of spending will ensure that the economy neither shrinks nor overheats, but instead grows at a sustainable rate over the long-term.

Big government isn't bad

We saw in Chapter 4 that the welfare state was made possible by the realisation that big government isn't automatically bad. Big government had proved itself not merely necessary but effective and successful during WWII. But the debate over the 'right' size of government was still going on. When the oil crises hit in the 1970s, it was easy for those in favour of smaller government to argue that a key contributor to the economic problems of the times was that the government was too big. Politicians, particularly on the right-wing, were listening more to economists like Milton Friedman, who was arguing that big government is bad and that it gets in the way of private business.

Two of Friedman's keenest disciples were Margaret Thatcher and Ronald Reagan. Although the 1970s governments had already been moving 'rightwards' economically, it was Thatcher in the UK and Reagan in the USA who really consolidated the position of neoliberal economics in politics and government. Neoliberalism generally is used to mean a form of economics that advocates the removal of regulations in order to open up the market, and a reduction in the size of the government by cutting public spending and contracting private companies to deliver public goals. The idea is that the wealth that is thus permitted at the top will trickle down to the people at the bottom, giving them more money and improved quality of life than if the state had intervened to ensure minimum wages, decent working conditions and full employment.

But this is not what happens. When the income share of the top 20% increases, economic growth slows over the next five years, suggesting that wealth does not trickle down (if the converse happens – the income of the bottom 20% increases – then economic growth increases).[11] The two key planks of neoliberalism – reduced regulations and a small state – are both associated with increased income inequality, which in its turn is associated not only with reduced economic growth but also with more frequent recessions. Neoliberalism tends to result in rapid growth for a short period of time, followed by a crash. These crashes occur with such frequency and severity that, in the long-term, unequal countries grow slower than if they had been more equal.[12] This is exacerbated if governments, believing that the problem is too much government spending, respond to reduced growth by cutting spending further.

Between 1945 and the early 1970s, financial crises and recessions were rare events. There might be economic downturns, but they lasted only one quarter. Since the shift to neoliberal politics, which broadly occurred in most countries during the 1980s, financial crises have occurred in at least one country almost every year, and recessions have become the norm. Ironically, neo-classical economics on which post-1980s politics is based relies on models of the economy that are incapable of predicting these recessions. Yet recessions happen more often in neoliberal type countries and in countries with higher inequality than they do in more equal countries.

In contrast to neoliberalism's focus on small government, economists Gill and Raiser report that, "big government is systematically correlated with better quality of government" and "more equality".[13] This equality is not just associated with better and more durable economic growth, but a wide range of other wellbeing factors including physical health, mental health, obesity, child wellbeing, teenage pregnancies, drug abuse, violence, imprisonment, education, social mobility, and trust and community life.[14] In contrast to the neoliberal belief that wealth from the rich will trickle down to the poor, it is the wealth of the poor that lifts the rich: quality of life for the rich is higher in more equal countries, largely because of factors such as improved health and community cohesion along with reduced violence, crime and distrust.

8. THE AUSTERITY PROGRAMME

Gill and Raiser go on to say that:

> "Big government is associated with better enforcement of property rights, better regulation, and more independent judiciaries in both the world sample and Europe... Big government is related to effective government, better control of corruption, and small informal economies in both the world as a whole and in Europe. Low informality means, for example, a larger tax base, which in turn makes it easier to fund big government without imposing high taxes...
>
> "Big government goes with stronger institutionalised democracy, more voice and accountability, and greater political stability... Big government does well with public goods. It is correlated with higher years of schooling, lower infant mortality, longer healthy life expectancy, and more equality in both the world and Europe."

The government does not need to reduce its size on economic grounds, nor on ideological ones. A bigger government in the UK would be likely to result in improved democracy, justice, public provision and equality of opportunity compared to our current size, which is simply too small to function properly. It would also create and sustain a healthy economy that can grow without being as susceptible to market bubbles.

The importance of government

Governments have a key role in recessions, as they determine the total level of demand in the economy (aggregate demand). Without sufficient demand, the economy slows down and starts to break, like a machine run without oil. Crucial industries, like healthcare, social care and education, fall apart. But if the government continues to spend then it maintains public sector jobs and stimulates economic growth, thus protecting citizens against poverty whilst strengthening the economy. A strong economy attracts private business investment, creating a positive spiral of growth and investment. Judicious taxation stops the economy from overheating and so prevents the excessive booms that inevitably end in an economic collapse.

There was therefore no need for the UK Government since 2010 to make spending cuts, particularly those to local government and social security which disproportionately harm the poor, disabled and disadvantaged. The government not only didn't need to reduce spending levels to match tax receipts, but economically should not have done so. Government deficit and debt is necessary for a successful private sector.

Claims that the size of the welfare state is damaging are unfounded. Big government does better on a wide range of measures, including political stability, quality of life and a broad tax base. Government spending can continue to increase until there is full employment of the nation's resources, being used to make up any deficiencies in the private sector. This does not crowd out the private sector, as private businesses take their confidence from government investment and economic growth, and in any case are unable to provide necessities for people too poor to pay at least cost price. The government therefore has a crucial role both in ensuring provision for the poor and in maintaining a strong economy that attracts private investment. Governments that step back from this don't create space for private business but instead weaken the economy and make private business more reluctant to invest.

The result is that the UK's response to the Great Recession has not been proportionate. Firstly, the government chose austerity over investment and social protection, when it didn't have to; consequently the poor have suffered from a stymied economy that needn't have been stymied. Secondly, the government made its austerity occur more through spending cuts than through tax rises, thereby making austerity fall more heavily on the poor than the better-off. And thirdly, the predominant proportion of spending cuts was taken from social security and local government, again hitting the poor hardest, who most need these services.

The government should have invested in the UK using its power as a sovereign supplier of government-backed money to spend on what the country and in particular the poor, disabled and disadvantaged needed. This would have protected the poor from the harmful effects of both recession and austerity. Instead, the ideological commitment to a small state has resulted in a reduction of poor and disabled people's access to basic rights, without any moral or economic justification or necessity.

The financial crisis occurred because the private sector got into unsustainable debt. But the harm that has occurred since 2010 is the fault of the government, for pursuing economically illiterate policies that directly and indirectly make the poor worse off in both financial and material terms.

8. THE AUSTERITY PROGRAMME

NOTES FOR CHAPTER 8

For a further exploration of the issues described in this chapter, interested readers may wish to consult: **Mitchell WF, Wray LR and Watts M** (2016) Modern Monetary Theory and Practice: an introductory text. CREATESPACE INDEPENDENT PUBLISHING PLATFORM
Wray RL (2015) Modern Monetary Theory: a primer on macroeconomics for sovereign monetary systems. 2ND ED LONDON: PALGRAVE
Armstrong P (2015) Heterodox views of Money and Modern Monetary Theory (MMT) pp.10-13 YORK

1. **CRPD** (2016) Inquiry concerning the United Kingdom of Great Britain and Northern Ireland carried out by the Committee under article 6 of the Optional Protocol to the Convention: Report of the Committee. UNITED NATIONS CRPD/C/15/R.2/REV.1
2. Social spending is defined by the OECD as expenditure old age, survivors, incapacity-related benefits, health, family, active labor market programmes, unemployment, housing, and other social policy areas (ie. it is broader than, but included out of work benefits). The OECD calculated that UK social spending in 2012 was 22.23% of GDP versus 20.34% for the average of other countries in the OECD.OECD (2019) Social spending (indicator). DOI: 10.1787/7497563B-EN
3. **Ostry J, Loungani P and Furceri D** (2016) Neo-liberalism: oversold? FINANCE AND DEVELOPMENT. ISSUE: JUNE
4. **Romer C** (02/07/2011) The rock and the hard place on the deficit. NEW YORK: NEW YORK TIMES.
5. **Chowdhury A and Islam I** (19/07/2010) The fallacy of austerity-based fiscal consolidation. VOX CEPR POLICY PORTAL
6. **Islam I and Chowdhury A** (2014) Fiscal consolidation, growth and employment: What do we know? G24 Policy Brief No.57 NEW YORK: UN
7. **Chowdhury and Islam** (n 5)
8. **Islam and Chowdhury** (n 6)
9. **Personal communication** (2019)
10. **Hutchison A** (27/09/2018) Lovers of exemption from tax. Blog: Matches in the dark. Available at WWW.MATCHESINTHEDARK.UK/LOVERS-OF-EXEMPTION-FROM-TAX/
11. **Dabla-Norris E, Kochhar K, Suphaphiphat N, Ricka F and Tsounta E** (2015) Causes and consequences of income inequality: a global perspective WASHINGTON: INTERNATIONAL MONETARY FUND
12. **Berg AG and Ostry JD** (2011) Inequality and unsustainable growth: two sides of the same coin? Staff Discussion Note SDN/11/08 Washington: International Monetary Fund. Ostry JD, Berg AG and Tsangarides C (2014) Income distribution, inequality and growth. STAFF DISCUSSION NOTE SDN/14/02 WASHINGTON: INTERNATIONAL MONETARY FUND
13. **Gill IS and Raiser M** (2012) Golden Growth: restoring the lustre of the European economic model. WASHINGTON: THE WORLD BANK.
14. **Wilkinson R and Pickett K** (2009) The Spirit Level: Why more equality is better for everyone. LONDON: PENGUIN

9

Employment and Support Allowance

Now that we have seen the background to the post-2010 cuts, we can turn to those cuts themselves. So far in this book we have followed a broadly chronological pattern, from the medieval period to the 21st century. We have seen how disabled people's lives have varied over the centuries, with the industrial revolution disrupting the agrarian communities in which disabled people were able to live as ordinary people, through a time of eugenics and segregation, to the creation of the welfare state. We have seen that disabled people, perhaps due in part to the earlier eugenics and segregation thinking, were largely left out of the welfare state. And even once they were included, it was not long after that that politicians began to cut the welfare state back.

Moving into the 21st century, we have seen that the post-2010 cuts weren't economically necessary. Big government beats small government easily on a range of measures of health, wellbeing and prosperity; it improves economic equality which reduces the frequency, depth and duration of recessions; and it results in improved opportunity and quality of life for all. Government spending is not dependent upon tax, nor does it crowd out the private sector; instead, government spending is the source of money and gives the private sector the confidence to invest as well.

Nor were the social security cuts morally necessary. Far from there being a dependency culture, what the UK really has is a sick-work culture: people attend work when, for their own health and their employer's productivity, they should rest and recover; and jobs at the lower end of the job market

9. EMPLOYMENT AND SUPPORT ALLOWANCE

actually make people ill. The UK has a particularly high proportion of such bad or toxic jobs.

In this and the following chapters, we move from a chronological to a parallel view of history. The preceding chapters were largely by way of background and setting the scene for the question that the government has to answer: has it breached disabled people's rights? In these coming chapters, we will look in turn at some key post-2010 policies and consider whether the government's specific rationales for each one are sound, as well as whether they achieved what the government claimed to want or whether they had a negative impact on sick and disabled people.

We will start by looking at a policy inherited by the 2010-2015 Government from Labour: Employment and Support Allowance (ESA), the sickness benefit that was introduced in 2008 as a replacement for Incapacity Benefit. The 2010 Government expressed concern that ESA abandons sick and disabled people to benefit dependency without a chance to try to find work. To rectify this, the government reduced the financial value of ESA (to make work more attractive relative to benefits) and increased both the number of people who are forced to engage in work-related activities and how much activity is required. The government hoped by this to get more sick and disabled people into work through their increased participation in work-related activity and greater financial incentives to work.

Whether the government achieves its aim is central to whether or not the cut in benefit levels represents a breach of human rights. If sick and disabled people are now in decent, adequately paid work when otherwise they would have remained on poverty level benefits, then this is an improvement. But if what has happened is that sick and disabled people have to engage in activities that are harmful to them, whilst now living in deeper poverty and not moving any closer to work, then the government's cuts to ESA are a breach of human rights.

Experiencing ESA

Colin used to be a nurse, progressing from a generalist nurse to become a psychiatric nurse with a psychology degree. His wife worked as a GP, and they had two small children. Colin was also on the Parish Church Council at his local church and took part in other church and community activities. They were the epitome of the Conservative Party's "hard-working family", who deserved all the tax breaks and support that they could get.

Until Colin became ill. Initially assessed under Incapacity Benefit, Colin was able to receive an income and contribute to his family for six years. But in 2008 Labour brought in a new sickness benefit, tougher than the old one, and the 2010 Conservative and Liberal Democrat Government decided to transfer all of the old Incapacity Benefit claimants onto this new ESA. Scared of being labelled a fraud, Colin felt unable to give an accurate account of his illness and its impact on him. Even so, he had been ill and unable to work for six years.

Colin's ESA assessor decided that he would experience a recovery that would see him able to return to work in three months' time.

Some six years later, Colin has still not recovered. The switch to ESA and the introduction of a time-limit on how long contribution-based benefits can be received for means that Colin no longer receives any benefit. Because his wife works, Colin doesn't meet the means-test for income-based ESA. He is no longer claiming ESA, because he fears being assessed as capable of work-related activity. This would require him to comply with activities as set by an employment support adviser; activities that research has shown makes many sick and disabled people more ill. Understandably, Colin does not think that it is worth risking his health when he would not receive anything in return.

Consequently, Colin is still ill, years after he was told he was likely to be able to return to work within weeks, but he no longer makes any financial contribution towards his family.

Like Colin, James – whom we met in a previous chapter – had been on Incapacity Benefit for several years, and like Colin he had found that the assessments for IB were largely okay. The assessors were able to comprehend the difficulties that James' mental state created, and make appropriate judgments on his capacity for work. But over the years following the replacement of Incapacity Benefit with ESA, the assessments became harsher and the assessors, from James' perspective, became colder and more judgmental.

At the end of one such ESA assessment, James felt miserable, humiliated and exhausted. After being placed in a benefit group that required him to engage in work-related activity, despite being assessed as unable to work, James became more and more ill as he tried to comply with the requirements made of him; requirements that he simply wasn't capable of meeting. Eventually, he was re-assessed and the activity requirements were removed.

James is now working towards being able to do some part-time work with support from his church. Effectively, he is back where he started, on a benefit without conditionality. But he was only allowed to go back there after he had made his health worse by trying to participate in work-related activity. He should never have been required to prove his need in such a way in the first place.

This is the system that sick and disabled people face. Sometimes, the assessment seems okay at the time, but the assessment report, once received, suggests a significant misunderstanding on the part of the assessor. Other times, it is horrible from start to finish, with disabled people reporting that their assessors were patronising, refused to accept evidence, or would not give them time to explain fully. Sometimes the recorded information is simply wrong, to the extent that people think that they've been sent someone else's assessment report. One assessor was suspended for a year after producing a highly misleading report.[1]

The Work and Pensions Committee, a body of MPs who scrutinise the work of the DWP, received nearly 4,000 individual responses when they carried out a consultation on disability assessments, on top of responses from organisations. Most government consultations are pleased to get 100 responses in total. One of the most consistent themes in these submissions was the inaccuracy of disability assessment reports.[2] One lady explained that, "Apparently I walk my dog daily, which was baffling because I can barely walk and I do not have a dog!" Another wrote how the assessor claimed she "arose from the chair without any difficulty" when in fact, "I was in bed the whole time (she [the assessor] let herself in) and I only have the one chair in the room and she was sitting in it. She said that I had no difficulty reading with my glasses yet I do not wear glasses to read."

Like James, many find that their health gets worse as they struggle to comply with benefit requirements, until eventually they are made ill enough to be allowed to receive benefit without any such conditions.

Employment and Support Allowance

We saw in Chapter 6 that the replacement of Invalidity Benefit with Incapacity Benefit resulted in fewer sick and disabled people getting the benefit, and that those who did still get support got less money. Most of those who were refused access to the new benefit were not able to go out and get work. The new benefit was too harsh, and it was criticised for being unrealistic in that it did not take into account how people's specific circumstances could exacerbate the impact of their illness or disability.

But the political mileage lay in claiming that too many people were on sickness benefits, not too few. The narrative of welfare dependency, scroungers and malingerers was being trumpeted by politicians from both Labour and Conservative parties. The public followed the politicians, perhaps assuming that those taking money away from needy people knew what they were doing, and that therefore those needy people weren't really needy in the first place.[3] The converse, that politicians either didn't know what they were doing or that they did know and went ahead anyway, is an unpalatable thought – but one that is necessarily true.

So the Labour Government, keen to appear tough on welfare and restrained in spending, brought in a new sickness benefit that was even harsher than Incapacity Benefit. This new benefit, ESA, used a similar assessment to IB but with a higher threshold for what would count as too sick or disabled to work. A new benefit group was formed within ESA, the Work-Related Activity Group (WRAG), for people deemed too sick to work but still able to carry out work-related activity. This intermediate group, as well as being required to take part in prescribed activity, received less money than the confusingly-named ESA Support Group (in which people were not required to engage with employment support). Both ESA groups, however, received more money than standard jobseekers.

When the Coalition government came into power, it was already clear that ESA was not working and needed improvement. High proportions of claimants were successfully challenging their fit-for-work decisions, whilst those in ESA WRAG received little if any meaningful support towards getting into work. Many sick and disabled people were suffering severe distress as they were told that they were capable of work when in fact they were not, and were consigned to lower levels of benefits and stricter conditionality requirements. The independent reviewer commissioned by Labour told the government that ESA was not working well enough to be extended to people already on Incapacity Benefit. The new government over-ruled this advice, and rolled ESA out nationwide. The resulting backlog of assessments and appeals caused significant stress and hardship to sick and disabled people, and in the end all routine reassessments had to be pushed back by two years.

The Work Capability Assessment

A key reason that ESA struggles is the points-based system that it uses to assess capacity for work. The Work Capability Assessment (WCA) used by ESA defines a person as fit or unfit for work based upon how much difficulty is experienced in carrying out a given list of activities. The activities assessed include such things as lifting objects that are small and up to 1kg in weight, or larger but essentially weightless (e.g. a cardboard box); understanding or conveying simple messages (such as the presence of a fire); or coping with a change to a schedule. Points are given based on how much help someone needs to achieve a task, with more points indicating more disability.

The assessment process rests on an assumption that difficulties arising from any given impairment affect only a small number of activities, perhaps severely, without affecting any others. It also assumes that the severity of a person's work-related disability depends upon the severity of their impairment, and on nothing else. For example, visual impairment is expected to cause difficulty with reading and with walking in unfamiliar places, and someone with a higher degree of visual impairment is more disabled (at work). The assessment assumes that visual impairment does not cause difficulties with other activities or materially affect a person's ability to work in any other way. So a person is unfit for work if their visual impairment is severe enough, and not if it isn't. There is little to no possibility of picking up points on other areas – your sight doesn't impact your ability to sit in a chair, for example.

In essence, the system is set up for a politician's understanding of people with sensory impairment, learning difficulties, and loss of limbs or use of limbs – people who may be considered disabled rather than sick. The WCA is designed around the idea of such disabled people who are largely healthy and can, as a broad generalisation, remain in or return to work if they are given appropriate support such as assistive technology, physical adaptations and appropriate tasks. These people have specific tasks which they struggle to perform, in some cases to the extent that they are unable to work, and in general have no problems with other specific tasks. It is a tidy, discrete world where assessments are easy and objective, and disabled people either can do something or can't.

Despite this apparent simplicity and objectivity, the assessment process doesn't work even for these people. The real world isn't simple, and simplistic assessments are harder, not easier, to apply. For example, people with the same severity of visual impairment can have different capacities for work. In particular, older blind people who have been blind from childhood tend to have received a lower level of education, whilst older people who have recently become blind may struggle to learn to adapt to a sightless world. In either case, the computer-based work which many blind people are assumed to be capable of doing may be too challenging, at least without a lengthy training course. In contrast, a young adult who has been blind from birth may be well adapted to their visual impairment, confident in the use of computers and have benefited from a good education. Of course, people's inherent skills are independent from their sight, and some young blind people may find it more difficult to work than others because their natural talents lie in areas precluded by blindness.

All of this assumes that people with static impairments are 'healthy'. In fact, the assumption that someone who is blind, deaf or paralysed does not experience symptoms of chronic illness caused by their impairment is often untrue. Gemma, for example, who is deaf and relies on a hearing aid, plus lip-reading, regularly gets incapacitating migraines from the strain of trying to converse. Blind people report that the extra effort taken up by navigating a world without sight can leave them too worn out to sustain more than part-time work. And wheelchair users can get pressure sores at any time, as the TV presenter Sophie Morgan explained:

> "The reality is that I am more vulnerable than I like to admit.
>
> "Last month for example, I was struck down by a pressure sore. These are common secondary complications of being paralysed, and can occur at any time. I blanched with fear when I discovered it. 'I don't have time', I panicked. 'I literally do not have time to be... disabled'. The pressure sore had to take priority, so all work was put on hold whilst I lay prone for four weeks to relieve the pressure and heal the sore. The fear and dread of having to explain this to my colleagues, business partners and employers was overwhelming. It was almost like telling them would reveal the extent of my disability. My rationale was lost as I found myself terrified that I would lose my job(s). After all who would want to work with someone that could at any point just not be able to work?"[4]

Bizarrely, and despite being centred on the idea of people with mobility, sensory or cognitive impairment, the DWP does not provide accessible assessment centres. Disabled people end up being refused benefit, not because they are well, but because they are too disabled to get to the assessment room. Jaki has been destitute for a year, since being found fit for work when she was unable to attend assessment appointments in either of two inaccessible centres.[5] Journalist Frances Ryan reported that,

> *"For almost a year, she [Jaki] has had only her personal independence payments to live off – barely £300 a month – and the bills are lining up. Debt collection letters flood through the door; Jaki owes £800 to the water company alone. She's lost five stone since her benefits were stopped. The three vouchers she's eligible for from her local food bank were used up "long ago", she says. She is so malnourished that she has developed mild scurvy. Parts of her teeth have broken off because her gums are so weak."*

Jaki attempted suicide on her son's 16th birthday. The loss of her money made her feel that she isn't worth anything. Soon after her suicide attempt, bailiffs came to Jaki's bungalow to collect on debts. They left empty-handed – because there wasn't anything to take.

Chronic illness

The WCA also fails when it is asked to consider a person who has a chronic disabling illness. In fact, it was deliberately designed to exclude many people with chronic disabling illness, as one of its prime goals was to remove one million people – 40% of recipients – from sickness benefits. The WCA was based on the Personal Capability Assessment that had been used by Incapacity Benefit. The biggest difference between the two was the deliberate removal of low-scoring descriptors, thus making it harder, and even impossible, for people with mild to moderate difficulty across several activities to be recognised as too sick to work.

The WCA is incapable of handling the idea that people with physical chronic illness, who often experience diffuse symptoms of pain and fatigue, struggle with every activity, for the simple reason that any activity requires effort, and too much activity makes illness worse. It doesn't allow for any carry over from one activity to another, even though chronic illness tends to cause impairment by limiting the total amount of activity that a person can do, rather than by limiting specific activities. It is designed in a way that makes it unable to manage the fact that a person might be able to carry out every assessed activity but only if they don't, on the same day, carry out any others. Illness is simply not specific enough in terms of what activities it affects.

This failure is compounded by the way in which difficulties stemming from chronic illness are specifically excluded from some descriptors. For example, whilst cognitive dysfunction arising from pain or fatigue can cause difficulties with reading and comprehension, this is actively excluded from consideration under the 'reading' activity. There is therefore no system within the WCA to account for the impacts of common features of sickness such as pain, physical and cognitive fatigue, and nausea.

The WCA also gives no consideration to the importance of being able to work at predictable times. People who need rest breaks at unpredictable times and for unpredictable durations – including resting for months during a relapse – are costly for employers. Indeed, most employers have policies for dismissing employees on health grounds if too much sick leave is taken, with a particular emphasis on many small amounts of sick leave over an extended period as compared to a single, long period of sick leave. We saw earlier how Sophie Morgan fears the consequences of being off sick for a month. But the WCA does not take this into account, other than to treat a person who can, on average, work half the time as able to work all the time. ESA recipients explain,

> "The inconsistency of my illness makes it difficult to keep a steady job. I take on work when I feel well enough but usually relapse within months and have to leave... Employers often do not understand and it is not possible for me to just work when I am well as I need a consistent income and employers need staff they can rely on."

> "I have no idea day to day, or even within a day, how my health will impact on my ability to do simple tasks let alone more challenging ones. I can be too ill for weeks or months or absolutely normal for a week or two."[6]

As a result of this design, what is supposed to be a sickness benefit does not actually assess sickness. Many of those whose illnesses do not fit the function-focused, points-based ESA assessment have instead to rely on two regulations written to catch those who otherwise would fall through the holes in the assessment design. These regulations specify that those whose health would be made worse by work (Regulation 29) or by work-related activity (Regulation 35) should be placed in ESA WRAG or ESA SG respectively. However, the government released new guidance in 2016 to down-grade the weight given to the potential health risks of work or work-related activity, because they felt that too many chronically ill people were being assessed as unfit for work on the grounds that work would make their health worse. After the change, the proportion awarded ESA SG fell from an average of 54% to 38%, whilst the proportion found fit for work rose from 35% to 44%.

> **Box 5. ESA data**
>
> There are currently **1.57 million** people in the ESA Support Group.
>
> **410,000** people are in the ESA Work-Related Activity Group.
>
> In the quarter to June 2018, **42%** of new applicants for ESA were placed in the Support Group.
>
> **20%** of new claimants were placed in the Work-Related Activity Group.
>
> **38%** of people are assessed as fit for work
>
> Around **65%** of decisions that go to appeal are overturned. However, the proportion of cases that go to appeal plummeted in 2013 when an extra bureaucratic step (mandatory reconsideration) was introduced by the government.

Mental illness

The assessment of mental illness struggles with many of the same problems faced by people with physical illness. The assessment relies upon the assumption that most impairments have a discrete impact; that they impact a minority of areas substantially, and the majority of areas not at all, or only mildly. But like physical illness, mental illness can cause moderate problems across a wide variety of areas; or a person may be able to complete an activity fine on one day and not at all on others; or again, a person may cope with a certain amount of activity in a day, but reach a limit and be unable to continue with any activity past that point. The WCA does not consider this, nor the true impact of unpredictable capacity on a person's ability to work from the perspective of a prospective employer.

Before the 2010 general election, a coroner had raised concerns with the DWP that the assessment process failed people with mental illness or learning disabilities. People with such conditions may be more likely than others to struggle to articulate the difficulties they experience, what they can and can't do and what impact an activity has on them. Chad, for example, explains how, in his partner's assessment, "The assessor stated in her report 'no signs of sore hands' 'no signs of repeated washing' 'was well groomed' 'was well dressed'. Anyone with a brain cell knows mental health isn't always visible, and OCD isn't all about excessive washing of the hands! OCD is known as a secretive disorder at the best of times and people in that profession should know better when it comes to mental health."[7]

Three years later, in 2013, a panel of judges made the same finding – that the WCA discriminates against claimants with mental illness, who are likely to under-represent the severity of their incapacity for work; and that the DWP should make more effort to get supporting evidence from claimants' medical teams and other carers or family members. Similar recommendations have come out of DWP reviews of deaths – mostly suicides, but also including heart attacks and malnourishment – of claimants following ESA fit for work decisions. In the reviews, the DWP was repeatedly warned about the problems with their policies and procedures and given recommendations on how to make ESA safer for claimants, but the DWP has repeatedly failed to implement them.

> **Box 6.** Harms caused by ESA
>
> More than **2 in 5 people on ESA** have made a suicide attempt at some point.
>
> ESA is associated with **200 additional suicides per year** and 90,000 additional cases of mental illness.
>
> **9 in 10 people** in the Work-Related Activity Group are anxious about being there.
>
> **8 in 10** in ESA WRAG don't feel ready to take part in work-related activity.
>
> More than **8 in 10** felt anxious about the activities they were required to do or about being sanctioned. Fewer than 1 in 10 didn't feel anxious.

There was enough concern about the level of suicides related to benefit decisions that a group of academics took up the question. After carefully controlling for other associated factors that might contribute to higher suicide rates, the researchers found that areas with more ESA assessments still show higher-than-expected increases in suicides, self-reported mental health problems and prescriptions of anti-depressants.[8] The researchers found that ESA assessments between 2010 and 2013 were associated with an additional 590 suicides and 279,000 cases of reported mental health problems. The authors concluded that this "natural policy experiment… may have had substantial adverse consequences for mental health".

Is the WCA fit for work?

The WCA has to make two judgments: firstly, whether or not someone is fit for work; and secondly, if someone is not fit for work, whether or not they are fit for work-related activity. But the WCA does not define what it means to be capable for work. Its precursor benefit, Incapacity Benefit, was supposed to be designed around a framework of 100 typical jobs, comparing people's abilities to the requirements of these jobs.[9] But there is no evidence that this work-based rationale was ever developed.[10] When ESA was designed, it simply picked up Incapacity Benefit's assessment and made it tougher. So whilst ESA and the WCA assume that the various activities used in the assessment are an accurate reflection of capacity for work, there is no proof. In fact, such evidence as there is suggests that the WCA substantially overestimates capacity for work.

Employment support providers report that many of those sent to them as having been assessed as fit for work are demonstrably unfit and that consequently they are unable to offer any useful support.[11] Government-appointed expert panels used in a review of the WCA found that multiple accommodations would have to be put in place before someone assessed as fit for work could actually work.[12] But these are accommodations that a typical employer may not choose to put in place when a job candidate capable of performing all of the job tasks without change, adjustment or assistance is available for hire. And the DWP's own research reports have repeatedly found that people assessed as fit for work largely don't move into work, whilst those people who do manage to return to work do so predominantly because their health has recovered: people who report being in good health two years after being awarded sickness benefit are 22 times more likely to be in work at that point than those who are still in bad health.[13]

Similarly, ESA lacks an evidence base for the distinction it makes between fit for work-related activity and unfit for such activity. It is not just work that is undefined, but work-related activity as well. Consequently, there is no definition or explanation of how a person who is too ill or disabled to be able to engage in work is supposed to be able to engage in activity that is related to work. The result is that people who can't work can be told to attend training and work placements which, in practice, are only differentiated from work by the fact that they are not paid.

People are not placed in ESA WRAG on the grounds that they are likely to recover in a short time frame, or that they could work if given the appropriate support or re-training. Instead there are seemingly arbitrary criteria that do not act as a good proxy for the level of disability (people can be severely disabled and not qualify for ESA SG) or the ability to work (people can be able to work in the right circumstances, and still qualify for ESA SG). Someone who can't walk (or self-propel a wheelchair) 50 metres in a reasonable timeframe can get ESA SG, as can someone who can't transfer from one seat to another. But someone who has epileptic seizures multiple times a week cannot be awarded ESA SG on this basis, even though frequent seizures would make work unreasonable and impractical due to fatigue, recovery time and hazard risk.

A major problem is that the WCA doesn't split people into different benefit groups in a way that actually relates to their ability and needs. The WCA makes assumptions based upon the severity of an impairment, without asking what it takes to get such a person into work. A person who needs a power-chair, because they can neither walk nor self-propel a wheelchair, can go straight into ESA SG. But such a person may actually want the support of job brokers and occupational therapists to help them obtain both work and the in-work adjustments that they would need. People who could work with support don't get the type of support that they need, regardless of which benefit group they are placed into, whilst people who can't work can be assessed as fit for work or work-related activity and consigned to minimal incomes with the threat of sanctions if they do not take part in mandated activity.

A much simpler and more appropriate outcome would be to say that people who can work sustained, regular hours if they are given support are placed into a benefit group in which they receive an adequate income and

9. EMPLOYMENT AND SUPPORT ALLOWANCE

are asked to work with a job broker to find, get and keep a job if, and only if, the support they need is already fully in place. Such support includes physical and technological changes to the workplace, altered and flexible hours, modified jobs, in-work personal assistance and help at home and with commuting. If that support were not provided or available, then there would be no requirement to look for work or engage in work-related activity, for the simple reason that there would be no point. People who cannot work regular hours would be recognised as too sick or disabled to work, and given adequate levels of financial support to enable them to participate in society in other ways.

As MPs pointed out in 2014:

> "The flaws in the existing ESA system are so grave that simply 'rebranding' the WCA by taking on a new provider will not solve the problems: a fundamental redesign of the ESA end-to-end process is required, including its outcomes, and the descriptors used in the WCA. This will be time-consuming and complex but the redesigned ESA assessment process needs to be in place by the time a completely new contract, involving multiple providers, is tendered in 2018."[14]

A new assessment has yet to be designed.

The difference that support makes

Olivia is a Spanish language and English Literature student who has hemiplegia, a form of cerebral palsy. On a university placement year in Spain, Olivia worked as a language assistant in a school. The programme only asked for ten hours a week, as students were encouraged to develop their Spanish in other ways such as travel and socialisation. Other students took on private work as well as the classroom teaching, but Olivia was unable to do this. She was experiencing problems with the splint for her left ankle, and this led to bursitis in her right hip, which meant that she was constantly tired and aching. Ten hours a week was all she could manage, but it was difficult for her friends to understand; fatigue just doesn't sound that serious.

Back in the UK, Olivia returned to catered halls. Having meals prepared and washed up, and her lectures much physically closer, helped her to manage her pain and fatigue whilst continuing with her Spanish degree.

She benefits from the Disabled Student's Allowance and university funding, which provides her with funding for taxis, a laptop with voice recognition software and an ergonomic chair. Olivia is also given extra time in her exams, because when she is writing (with her right hand), her left hand tenses up, and she has to take time out to stretch and relax it. She can't work for too long, because of the pain and fatigue; to manage it, she has to stretch her hands, legs and hip several times a day, and she can also need to take time out to lie on the floor.

Olivia is unsure what she will do when she finishes university. It is possible that her bursitis will go away, as is usual for cases of bursitis, and with good quality splints she can walk reasonably well. But she cannot guarantee this, and she knows from fellow hemiplegics that wear and tear problems start to show in those in their early 20s and will only increase from there.

Olivia hopes to continue living in the area where she is at university, because the NHS is much better there, at least as regards to Olivia's needs, than in the county where she grew up and her parents still live. In her home county, physio is difficult to get, and comes in six-week blocks; in her university county, she can book sessions as and when she needs them, in a manner that is much more flexible and tailored to her needs. She also has a specialist cerebral palsy consultant at the hospital near her university. Consequently, Olivia's choices regarding where to work and live are constrained by the quality of healthcare.

Olivia is likely to need to claim benefits when she leaves university. Her experience of living in a flat, rather than halls, during university showed her that she would struggle to cook, wash up and clean – any household task that requires standing or moving around whilst using one's hands and arms would be difficult and exacerbate her pain and fatigue. In terms of work, Olivia knows that she can be limited in hours, to as little as ten a week, as her experience in Spain showed. But her experiences don't fit well with ESA and the WCA. Olivia could easily end up in a situation where she is unable to earn enough to provide for herself, let alone manage her health, yet not disabled enough to get government help.

The adequacy of sickness benefits

Since the introduction of the first true sickness benefit, Invalidity Benefit, reforms to sickness benefits have been marked by retrenchment and restriction of eligibility. Tests have become progressively harder, benefit levels

9. EMPLOYMENT AND SUPPORT ALLOWANCE

have been reduced and the activity requirements placed on people too sick to work have increased. Claimants repeatedly depend upon recourse to the appeals system to correct poor decisions and to reverse the effect of sanctions.

In the short-term, a minimal subsistence-level income may be enough. But in the long-term, people unable to work or who will take a long time to get work need to be able to participate in society. Humans are social beings, and we do not lose our need for society just because we are unable to work. Without an adequate income, individuals become isolated, and this in itself – even if finances are adequate for physical needs, which on benefits is often not the case – can cause illness.

It is because higher costs accrue over longer time periods that sickness benefits have historically been set at higher levels than unemployment benefits. Indeed, when Conservative MP Keith Joseph had, in the early 1970s, to choose which benefits to up-rate by how much, it was because the sick and pensioners are out-of-work for long periods that he chose to raise their benefits over those of jobseekers. Whether it is because a person needs time to recover from an illness or because advocacy and liaison with employers is a time-consuming process, even those sick and disabled people with some (future) capacity for work will still be on sickness benefits for prolonged periods of time. They need the higher level of benefit to cover the types of costs that are inevitable in the long-term. For this reason, ESA WRAG, as well as ESA SG, used to come with a higher level of benefit than standard jobseekers. But this has since been cut, by nearly £30 per week, to a level identified by research as destitution.[15]

ESA and the WCA fail to enable an assessment of the keystone of their reason to exist – chronic sickness – and bear no relationship to the amount and type of work a person is able to do, or what support is needed to allow that to happen. Sick and disabled people face financial insecurity, never knowing when they will be summoned for reassessment that might decide they are fit for work, or for activity which, if they fail, will see them lose the money they need to live. The sickness benefit system makes many people even more sick, often adding to or worsening existing health conditions, and driving them further away from being able to work. Lawrence Bond, who had "extensive long-term health problems, including breathing difficulties and reduced mobility", died from a heart attack a few months after being assessed as fit for work.[16] He was on his way home from a Jobcentre appointment at the time, having attended despite "clear physical distress", out of fear of being sanctioned for non-attendance. Elaine Morall, who had been in and out of intensive care, died alone in her unheated flat after being found fit for work and sanctioned for not attending a jobcentre appointment when she was in hospital.[17] Chris Gold, left with serious health problems after a stroke, died starvation-thin only days after an ITV report highlighted his benefit delays and fit-for-work decision.[18] Stephen Braithwaite died from an accidental overdose of painkillers after sustaining broken ribs during an epileptic seizure; he also suffered from liver and lung disease, had mobility problems and had recently been found fit for work.[19]

None of these people should have been considered fit for work. No sensible work capability assessment would have concluded that these people were healthy enough to be required to work and ineligible for State sickness benefits.

Instead of this failed system, a holistic approach should be used to assess what, if any, work a person could do; how much, when and where; and with what support. Assessments need to explicitly consider a person's health and their ability to sustain activity, and this element at least needs to be carried out by a doctor. Reassessments of people with permanent or quasi-permanent illness or disability should occur on timescales measured in years that reflect the need for stability, space and security, rather than the current timescales that are measured in months. More importantly, benefit levels should be adequate for a decent standard of life. The practice and experience of other countries, particularly our European neighbours, show that this is not just desirable but practicable.

NOTES FOR CHAPTER 9

1. **Pring J** (21/06/2018) 'Fit for work' assessor suspended for describing examination that did not take place DISABILITY NEWS SERVICE
2. **Work and Pensions Committee** (2018) No dog, can't walk: tales from the PIP and ESA FRONT LINE LONDON
3. **O'Grady T** (07/11/2017) How politicians created rather than reacted to negative public opinion on benefits London: London School of Economics
4. **Morgan S** (05/07/2017) The hidden pressure of working with a disability NEW YORK: HUFFINGTON POST
5. **Ryan F** (24/05/2018) The disability system is blocking people like Jaki from their benefits – literally LONDON: THE GUARDIAN
6. **Benstead S and Nock E** (2016) Replacing Employment and Support Allowance Part One: support needs of people with chronic illness LONDON: EKKLESIA

9. EMPLOYMENT AND SUPPORT ALLOWANCE

7. **Work and Pensions Committee (n 2)**
8. **Barr B, Taylor-Robinson D, Stuckler D, Loopstra R, Reeves A and Whitehead M** (2015) 'First do no harm': are disability assessments associated with adverse trends in mental health? A longitudinal ecological study JOURNAL OF EPIDEMIOLOGICAL AND COMMUNITY HEALTH ONLINE FIRST DOI:101136/JECH-2015-206209
9. **Baroness Cumberlege** (21/04/1994) Social Security (Incapacity for Work) BILL HL DEB VOL554 C325
10. **Baumberg B** (2018) "Legitimacy is a balancing act, but we can achieve a much better balance than the WCA": a better WCA is possible. p 65 LONDON: DEMOS
11. **Work and Pensions Committee (2013)** Can the Work Programme work for all user groups? LONDON
12. **DWP** (2013) Evidence based review of the Work Capability Assessment: a study of assessments for Employment and Support Allowance LONDON
13. **Becker E, Hayllar O and Wood M** (2010) Pathways to Work: programme engagement and work patterns Findings from follow-up surveys of new and repeat and existing incapacity benefits customers in the Jobcentre Plus pilot and expansion areas RESEARCH REPORT 653 LONDON: DWP.
See similar findings in: **Ashworth K, Hartfree Y and Stephenson A** (2001) Well enough to work? Research Report 145 LONDON: DWP. **Stafford B et al** (2007) NEW DEAL FOR DISABLED PEOPLE: THIRD SYNTHESIS REPORT – KEY FINDINGS FROM THE EVALUATION RESEARCH REPORT 430 **London: DWP.**
14. **Work and Pensions Committee** (2014) Employment and Support Allowance and Work Capability Assessments First Report of Session 2014-15
15. Research with members of the public established £70 per week for non-housing costs as the threshold for destitution. Between 2016 and 2020 Jobseeker's Allowance and (since 2017) ESA WRAG have been set at £73.10 per week. Because some of this money has to go towards rent and council tax benefit recipients are left with less than £70 per week for their non-housing costs. **Fitzpatrick S, Bramley G, Sosenko J, Blenkinsopp J, Johnsen S, Littlewood M, Netto G and Watts B** (2017) Destitution in the UK YORK: JOSEPH ROWNTREE FOUNDATION
16. **Fenton S** (20/01/2017) Man died on his way home from Job Centre 'after being found fit to work'. LONDON: THE INDEPENDENT
17. **Jordan B** (07/11/2017) Heart-rending: mum who died alone in the cold with her hat and scarf on LIVERPOOL: RUNCORN AND WIDNES WORLD
18. **ITV** (24/10/2017) Man died 'in hunger' while waiting for Universal Credit just days after ITV INTERVIEW
19. **Finch E** (13/03/2018) Shocking death of sick man who lost his benefits LONDON: ISLINGTON TRIBUNE

10

Employment Support

Ken was a model student during his GCSEs – 100% attendance, 14 A-A*s. But at A-levels his behaviour changed. He started to sleep in late and often skipped college. His attendance dropped to 30%, and his grades were no higher than Cs and Ds. This poor performance, however, failed to stimulate him to improve his time-keeping, and nor did his teachers' pointed jokes about strangers in the classroom have any effect. He continued to be haphazard in his attendance and work.

Ken managed to make it to university, and the lower levels of contact time at university compared to sixth-form meant he didn't have to massively change the way of life that he had got into. He slept erratically, often going to bed late and getting up even later. His timetabling was fitful – some appointments he missed, others he turned up half an hour early. Lectures were optional. But as his final year didn't have any exams, only coursework, his irregular lifestyle didn't matter.

Moving onto a Master's, the problems caused by his lifestyle started to become serious. Ken began to lie to cover his tardiness. There were certain research skills classes he had to attend if he were to get his Master's, and if he missed too many, he would not be allowed to participate in future sessions – which could make getting his degree difficult. His excuses for not turning up became increasingly convoluted and extreme – like the time he told the session organisers that he couldn't attend because his flatmate had fallen down the stairs, and he was taking her to hospital. It wasn't true.

Ken was aware of his lack of responsibility, self-discipline and self-control. At various times over seven years he had spoken with medical professionals about the erratic nature of his sleeping habits, but they considered there to be nothing wrong beyond usual teenage and student habits. So Ken believed them – what else could he do? Yet he still didn't change, even though his behaviour so clearly impacted his life; even though he believed it was a personal attitude and behaviour problem only, which ought to be amenable to change.

Finally, during his Master's year, Ken found a GP who did more than tell him to change his habits. This doctor gave him a booklet on Cognitive Behavioural Therapy which, at the back, contained screening questionnaires for various conditions that could superficially look like a mild depressive disorder. For Ken, it was an epiphany. For the first time, someone had believed that Ken might actually have a physical disorder rather than a weak character.

It turned out that Ken has a sleep cycle disorder. Unlike most people, whose body clocks are slightly longer than 24 hours and calibrate themselves to daylight hours every day, Ken's body clock is not only significantly longer, it doesn't react much to environmental cues either. It just keeps chugging on, following its own schedule, regardless of sleep hormones and light levels. This makes his condition untreatable and unmanageable. Nothing will make him sleep earlier than his body has decided it wants to; not melatonin, not sleeping tablets, not ongoing sleep deprivation. And nothing will make him wake before his body has decided it is time; not bright lights, not caffeine, not stimulants, not screaming alarm clocks.

The condition is so overwhelming that when his phone alarm goes off, Ken takes out the battery, hides it and returns to sleep – without ever remembering it when he wakes up later. Alarm clocks get hurled across the room until they break, and he still doesn't wake up. Medically, he is in a state of 'sleep drunkenness', where his body acts on its own behalf without his conscious awareness.

But that is not all. Ken can just about push himself through a week of sedatives and stimulants, but his body isn't actually changing its sleep/wake cycle and the consequence is that at the end of the week he is a mess of sleep deprivation, sedation and stimulation all rolled together. Fighting the fatigue raises his blood pressure and heart rate, putting strain on his heart and increasing the risk of long-term ill effects such as heart attacks. The sleep/wake cycle is all-encompassing; it affects many bodily systems including appetite, which means Ken also struggles to eat as he is often sick.

The loneliness can be overwhelming. When Ken is awake during the day, his friends are at work. When he is awake at night, his friends are asleep. He missed his grandfather's funeral because he slept through it. Twice he has fallen asleep whilst cooking. Many times he's stepped into a road to cross it when a car was coming, so fogged with sleepiness that he was oblivious to its approach. He can't plan more than two or three days ahead, because his sleep/wake cycle isn't regular enough for him to know beyond that when he will be awake and when he will be asleep.

Ken isn't lazy. He has an unmanageable and untreatable disorder that blocks him from everyday life. Attempts to participate just make him worse. He doesn't need to be taught how to schedule or time manage, nor correct a workshy character – despite his then undiagnosed difficulties, he persisted with his education, and wants to study for a PhD if he can find a university that is willing to accommodate his needs. Ken's problem is firstly that he has a sleep/wake cycle disorder, secondly that society is not set up to help him, and thirdly that although he cannot sustain work, he cannot get the benefits he needs either.

From the outside, he looks like a typical benefit scrounger – healthy, capable but lazy. But on the inside, he is so far from being workshy that instead of needing to learn how to work, he is having to learn how to refrain.

Even with a diagnosis, Ken still struggles with guilt, as do many with chronic illness. Thoughts would repeat over and over in his head: "If I just tried a little harder, kept going a little more, pushed that bit longer – then somehow I'd magically get better." What actually happens is that he predictably gets worse. It can become a vicious cycle which many people with chronic illness experience: manage one's physical health appropriately, and then feel guilty for not working hard enough; work too hard, crash, take a rest; feel marginally better, feel guilty again, start pushing one's self again. It's an ongoing push-crash-push-crash fuelled by a society that insists that if you're not working, you're not worth anything.

The help that Ken needs is not training on time keeping, motivation or a structured lifestyle. Ken cannot work in the open labour market because of the variability and unpredictability of when he is able to work, and his need to be able to adjust everything fully around his sleep/wake cycle. If support were provided for him, Ken could take part in society on a better footing. He could do some work, whilst also managing his health in a way that didn't cause long-term problems. But at the moment, there appears to be no interest in providing the sort of flexibility that he needs. The government claims to want chronically ill or disabled people to be able to do some work, at the same time as taking away the support that is needed to do that work.

10. EMPLOYMENT SUPPORT

Ken is unable to get the Support Group of ESA, because none of the rules for going into that group apply to Ken. Yet his incurable and unmanageable illness means that he isn't going to be able support himself through paid work. If he were in ESA SG, he could use the additional money he would receive to provide the reasonable adjustments he needs for himself.

If Ken's benefits were adequate, he could pay to use trains rather than coaches for long-distance journeys, which would help him manage his drowsiness as trains are faster. He could use taxis when public transport is not adequate. He could pay the delivery charges on ordering food to his house, so that he doesn't have to try to shop during the day when his body is telling him to sleep – the lack of night buses means that he is not able to get to the supermarket when he is awake at night.

But Ken can't get the support he needs, either financially or practically. He is stuck in a no-man's land, a twilight world, cut-off from society and failed by his government.

Employment Support: what doesn't work

When ESA was brought in, it came with promises from the government that they would significantly improve the employment support provided to people whose ill-health or disability makes work difficult. This would mitigate the impact of fewer people getting sickness benefit and many getting a reduced rate, by getting more sick and disabled people into work, where the restricted benefit would no longer impact them. The new WRAG within ESA was supposed to be an innovative measure that would challenge previous 'can't do' assessments, save sick and disabled people from abandonment, and provide people with the support that they needed if they were to be able to work.

This ESA WRAG was different from JSA in that it was, at that time, worth an additional £30 per week, and because claimants could not be required to search for work, apply for jobs or take up work – they had, after all, been found to be too ill or disabled to work. The group was different from the previous Incapacity Benefit, and from ESA SG, in that it received less money than either of these two groups and in that, unlike those groups, claimants were required to engage in activity under the risk of sanctions if they failed to fully comply.

However, it quickly became apparent that the government had not fulfilled its promise to provide increased levels of support. The support on offer was nothing more than what standard jobseekers could get, and made no effort to consider the barriers to work caused by illness or disability – issues such as being unable to commit to given hours, needing to work reduced hours and from home, requiring physical or technological adaptations, or needing a second person alongside as support. No thought appears to have been given to maximising disabled people's skills and abilities, or addressing the impact of commuting, domestic tasks or caring duties upon the remaining capacity for activity of people who start with very little.

Instead, sick and disabled people are offered courses on CV writing, interview skills, confidence building and other job-search skills which ignore the real issues. CV courses can't hide the impact of ill-health on one's career; what does help is people, as and when they can, engaging in voluntary, community or hobby-related work, which they can then demonstrate to prospective employers. Self-confidence comes from success and social participation; confidence-building courses can temporarily replicate this, but it doesn't last, and self-esteem in any case has little-to-no impact on future success.[1] Job search skills might be enough for most non-disabled people, but sick and disabled people need job brokers – specialists who will work with them and prospective employers to find jobs.

The 2010-15 Government introduced a new employment support programme, the Work Programme, which it outsourced to private contractors. One disabled participant in this programme explained how:

> "[The Work Programme provider] has just stuck me and other ESA 'customers' in groups with people on JSA. We are made to attend courses on CVs and interview techniques, but nothing is done at all to help me find work or to provide any disability-specific support or advice. I end up more exhausted, confused and anxious because I have no real idea what is going on, and I don't see how any of this is benefitting me or getting me back to work."[2]

James, whom we have already met, discovered that whilst his first Work Focused Interview as part of his Work-Related Activity was okay – the whole time was spent discussing his medical history, so there was no time left to discuss the activities he would be required to do – the subsequent interviews got progressively worse. At the second, his interview was held in a public room, separated only by a thin board from the Jobcentre attendees on either side. Everything he said, and everything they said, could be heard by those around.

10. EMPLOYMENT SUPPORT

James felt himself to be under a barrage of attack, as the adviser fired suggestion after suggestion at him: he should get involved with charity work, he should get active, he could do this, he ought to try that. Here's a good one for you, you like the outdoors don't you? You can spend your time – unpaid – cycling around looking for fly-tipping and then notifying the fire service.

James explained that he already was involved in charity work at his church, on his own initiative. The work was great for him because it was supportive, interesting and allowed him to start using his art degree again. It was the type of work that could bolster a CV and start a career. But the adviser didn't listen and wasn't interested. James got the impression that she just wanted to tick boxes and get him doing whatever the DWP said he should do, not what was good for him. Church volunteering didn't fit what they wanted, and it wasn't something he had been told to do, so it didn't count. Unpaid and unskilled work for national chains, like shelf-stacking at Poundland, was much more useful, according to the DWP.

James was eventually reassessed and placed into ESA SG. He found it a huge relief – but it shouldn't be that way. There shouldn't be such a relief that it's 'Not me, not this time,' and nor should people have to make themselves more ill than they already are just to prove that they really are too ill to work. Sick people should have confidence that they will be met with fair treatment and justice, but they're not getting it.

The help that James received from the Jobcentre was no use. There was no intention of considering his specific case. There was no recognition that he already had regular volunteering. Even worse, there was no recognition of what type of volunteering would be most effective or what would best utilise his pre-existing skills. It was simply assumed that the problems James faced were ones regarding time keeping and the desire to focus on the job in hand; and this assumption is applied to all unemployed people, regardless of the real reason that they are out of work.

In contrast to the government's hope that mandated activity would raise the aspirations of sick and disabled people, what it actually does is make people less able to work than before. The activities, advice and courses provided are "neither personalised nor supportive" and the threat of sanctions leaves people "fearful, demoralised and further away from achieving their work-related goals or participating in society than when they started".[2] It is no surprise to disabled people that three in five of those required to join the government Work Programme report that their health is made worse:

they are being told to participate in unhelpful, inaccessible and even actively harmful activity under the threat of financial sanctions if they don't. There is no reasonable choice: either health or vital income is sacrificed. The result is that, contrary to the government's expectations, people who have spent two years on the official Work Programme are actually further away from, not closer to, work than they were when they started.[3]

> **Box 7. Outcomes of the Work Programme**
>
> **Job outcomes achieved within 12 months by people who started the Work Programme in 2016:**
>
> ESA recipients assessed as likely to improve within 3 to 6 months: 15.6% get work within 12 months of starting on the government's Work Programme.
>
> ESA recipients expected to improve in 12 months: 8.3%
>
> ESA recipients expected to be no better in 12 months, but have volunteered to take part in the Work Programme: 10.7%
>
> ESA recipients who were previously on Incapacity Benefit: 3.9%

The government expected that, in the absence of any employment support, 22% of those ESA recipients assessed as likely to recover soon would get into work. When it developed the Work Programme, the government therefore expected that the private contractors who would support these sick and disabled people would get substantially more than 22% into work; otherwise, there would be little point paying for the programme. But the most recent results show that on average 15.6% of the 'healthiest' ESA claimants (people expected to improve in three or six months) actually got work in their first 12 months on the Work Programme.[4] Either the Work Programme made things worse, or ESA recipients are more severely disabled than the government realised – or both.

The likely answer is both. Most ESA recipients who move into work do not think that the Work Programme had an impact. Many are people with short-term illness or injury, who were always going to recover and return to work.[5] They therefore represent not chronically sick or disabled people getting work, but sick or injured people returning to health. At the same time, most Work Programme participants report that the programme makes their health worse, and government data supports this finding.

10. EMPLOYMENT SUPPORT

Even the best employment programmes, which combine specialised job brokers with experienced medical staff, struggle to get as many as one in four participants into paid work, and that is after providing much deeper and more extensive support than anything the UK Government has ever come close to offering.[6] By now, the persistent failure of governments across time and country to get sick and disabled people into paid work should be a clear indicator that the large majority of these people simply aren't, and aren't going to be, able to work. There is a limit to what an updated CV can do when the over-riding barrier is a lack of capacity for work.

The result is that people in ESA WRAG are often left in untenable positions: on destitution-level benefits; subject to sanctions if they don't take part in activities that won't help; and never getting the type of support that might help. Despite over 85% of ESA WRAG recipients still being out of work 12 months later, the government cut their benefits from April 2017 to the same level as jobseekers (the majority of whom are in work within 12 months), and barely above destitution. People have been sanctioned for missing DWP appointments in order to go to a hospital appointment, or told not to take medication that causes drowsiness because then it would be their own decision to make themselves unavailable for work. Jobcentre staff may expect people to attend courses than run 9-5 every day for two weeks, when a person who could manage that would be fit for work; or to attend courses that are held in places miles from a person's home, with no available parking and no nearby public transport links.

One person described this as being "forced into looking for a life that I want but have no chance of having", with the consequence that "I seriously feel I may kill myself because being sick, having next to no money, no life, no future, no cure, constant pain and constant disapproval and rejection defeats me."[7]

Abandoned to bad attitudes?

The government and other right-wing commentators continue to express concern that people who are awarded the Support Group of ESA are "completely detached from the labour market", "completely written off" and "parked" without any support to move towards work.[8] People in ESA SG, unlike those in ESA WRAG, do not have to engage in any work-related activity in order to receive their benefit. They receive benefit solely on the grounds that they have been assessed as too ill or disabled to work.

But because these people do not have to engage in activity, they are much less likely to meet with an employment adviser for support to find work. Labelling someone as unfit for work, even when based on the harshest work capacity test in the developed world, is assumed to mean cursing them to a lifetime of unhealthy indolence and immoral dependence.

But when Ken received his diagnosis, it was life-changing and liberating. For him, it was freedom and an escape from damaging behaviours; escape from the expectation – even a command – to be like everyone else. Ken was not able to follow society's usual advice on how to live and behave responsibility, because to do so was bad for his body and health. But without a diagnosis, he did not know that, and so he continued to strive to behave what he thought was responsibly. In fact, responsibility was to listen to his body as regards what it could and could not do, and in that way to preserve and manage his health as best as possible. Working against his body only stores up future ill-health through the strain on his metabolic and cardio-vascular systems. But until he knew not only that there was something wrong with him but what it was, all he knew were harmful socially-imposed rules where the punishment for failure was guilt, and the reward for obedience was physical illness. For Ken, a diagnosis is not an excuse to be lazy, but permission to refrain from self-harm.

Those who receive the Support Group of ESA, where there are no sanctions and a higher, though still inadequate, level of benefit, report that this group enables them to spend time managing and if possible improving their health, developing their work skills and receiving support from suitable charities and other specialised organisations. As one chronically ill person said, "The best job coach I have had is the neurophysio I have waited for for 12 years!" Another explained how,

> "It's only really getting into the Support Group that gave me that freedom to focus on what I wanted to do and not to have to put all my energy into jumping through pointless hoops and cope with the stress and anxiety of not knowing whether I was going to be referred to sanctions every month... It didn't just happen to me, lots and lots of my peers and friends were set conditions... It's really ruined people's lives. People have just lost that kind of foothold that they had in terms of taking part in society or maintaining an activity that enabled their wellbeing or gave them some hope for the future."[9]

The government insists that putting people into ESA SG is abandoning them. In contrast, sick and disabled people find that ESA SG provides a secure environment for them to explore what works and invest in measures that do increase their employability, for example by taking on some voluntary or community work, or developing a hobby. Such activity allows individuals to test their capabilities, whilst retaining the flexibility to adjust work levels in response to any changes in health, and without the threat of losing financial support. There is none of the harmful pressure to perform to a certain standard and by particular times, as there inevitably is with paid work. Alternatively, sick and disabled people may focus on their family, friends and community; participating the best way they can in what is often the only reasonable way they can. Consequently, for sick and disabled people, ESA SG helps them to manage their health well and, to the extent that such a feat is possible, move towards work; whilst ESA WRAG goes one step further than parking – it actively drives people away.

With time and help, and suitable available jobs, some sick and disabled people can and do get work. But the ironic outcome is that people assessed as 'more' disabled end up receiving more and better support than those considered 'less' disabled, because this more disabled group get the finances, freedom and, if they're lucky, quality of (charitable) support that they need if they are to move in to work. Early results, in research that the DWP has not repeated, found that the supposedly more-disabled members of ESA SG got work at marginally higher rates than ESA WRAG, at 10% vs 9% respectively.[10]

Government attitudes

The government believes that the predominant factors keeping sick and disabled people from work is not their illness or disability, but their attitudes and behaviours, and the attitudes and behaviours of their carers and medical teams. Consequently, their suggested remedies are all about changing the attitudes and behaviours of sick and disabled people, including through "self-care and a return to normal activities, often including work," or about teaching GPs that work is, in general, good for people – something that GPs are well aware of.[11] What the government forgets, if it ever knew, is that bad work can make people ill, and working whilst ill can make people more ill.

We have already seen that "a return to normal attitudes, often including work" was exactly what made Ken's life intolerable and physically harmful.

Behaving like a healthy person was the exact opposite of what he should do. Nor is he the only one; for many sick and disabled people, learning to live within their limits and to prioritise health over social conformity and societal expectations is exactly what they should and need to do. Suggestions that all they need is self-care and normal activity is either callous or grossly ignorant, and in such a situation it is not clear that ignorance is not callousness too.

Consider Natalie, whom we first met in Chapter 2. Natalie has been diagnosed as having Emotionally Unstable Personality Disorder. She is doing everything right. She is forcing herself to function and refusing to give in to the desire to stay in bed and cut off contact with people. She is throwing all the energy she has into going to the gym three times a week, when she'd rather be in bed watching Netflix or sleeping, because exercise is supposed to help. She's attending college and staying there all day, and she's being careful not to drink too much coffee because that just makes things worse. She's doing her best to cook and eat three meals a day even though cooking is the last thing she wants to do. Stir fry meal deals are all she can manage without dissolving into a panicked, overwhelmed and tearful mess, but at least she is trying.

She is trying everything, and yet her depression is not lifting. It is stubborn, overwhelming and exhausting. Her horizon has shortened to one hour at a time, because even thinking of getting through one day at a time is too much. Even the idea of opening her post is too much. She feels herself slipping and is frightened of needing hospitalisation again, and even more frightened of being back in the place where she doesn't want hospitalisation because she wants to end her life. But her case isn't urgent so it will be a while yet before she can see her consultant just to discuss a medication change. 'Self-care' and a 'return to normal activities' are doing nothing for her, yet this – bar basic Cognitive Behavioural Therapy – is all the government offers.

The Conservative Governments of 2015 and 2017 have been very clear that they believe that work is a health outcome (and not just a side-product of being well enough to work) and even that work can be "extremely beneficial to someone's health and act as an enabler to recovery".[12] For people with incurable illnesses and disabilities – as those on ESA typically are – this is nonsense. Work of any type is not going to reverse a degenerative disease, reset a misfunctioning immune or autonomic system or alter someone's genes. People with severe long-term mental illness report that for them this mantra can be catastrophic.[13]

Where work does help is in providing six boosts to mental wellbeing: income, time structure, social contact, collective purpose, status, and activity.[14] It is not work per se that supports people's self-esteem and mental wellbeing, but their access to these six, and in particular the five non-financial, benefits of work. Pensioners, stay-at-home parents, non-working partners and students are not all rendered ill by being out of work; and nor is work a cure-all for those who are sick or disabled. Work is merely a proxy measure, and not always a very good one: despite the poverty, stress and state intrusion experienced by those on benefits, low-level, high-strain jobs are even worse for people.[15] The government should focus directly on the six benefits, rather than acting as if work is uniformly good and uniformly achievable.

Mandated healthcare

The government's approach to support and the tenor of its arguments suggests that it is seriously considering requiring people to accept certain medical care in return for their benefits, just as it requires certain work-related activity. This is not a new approach – the pre-2010 Labour governments were already developing mandatory Condition Management Programmes – but its expansion by Conservative-led governments cannot be laid at Labour's door. David Cameron, whilst Prime Minister, directly commissioned research into compelling those with obesity or drug addiction – conditions which he deemed to be 'long-term yet treatable' – to attend treatment programmes, in return for benefits.[16] Unsurprisingly to sick and disabled people, the reports concluded that what these people needed was less mandation, not more.[17]

The Government seems to think that, because musculoskeletal and mental health problems are the biggest causes of work-related disability, then people on ESA must predominantly be suffering from treatable depression, anxiety or lower back pain. But as we discussed earlier in this book, it is not the condition or type of condition that matters when assessing disability, but the severity of the condition. People on sickness benefit due to depression or back pain are the people at the severest end of the spectrum, where treatment has often been multifactorial and futile, and medicine has run out of ideas to offer. They typically have other conditions which may exacerbate the common conditions and make standard treatments at best useless and at worst harmful. They are people in crippling pain or soul-destroying depression, who would do anything to get better and often have tried, at great expense to themselves, a large range of treatments that even the NHS doesn't think are worth the money.

Self-care, 'normal activity' and low-level physiotherapy or cognitive behavioural therapy are simply not going to help people who are far past the point of being mild. Unsurprisingly, government trials found that very few people on ESA were eligible for basic physiotherapy, but this has not stopped the government's plans. The government is continuing to explore and extend the potential for people perceived to have merely common conditions, such as back pain and depression, to be referred to treatment by their employment support advisers. Such referrals may, like referrals to other work-related activity, be mandatory with the threat of sanctions for non-compliance.

The implication of the government's approach is that sick and disabled people cannot be trusted to know or do what is best for themselves, but must instead be told and controlled. It is an approach that infantilises and patronises disabled people as less than adult, simply because they have an illness, injury or impairment; as though they are inferior people, who should not be given the right to self-determination until such time as they have made themselves able to work.

The ethical implications of mandated activity for sick and disabled people are not small. Many people with chronic illness or disability can be harmed by too much activity, the wrong type of activity, or carrying out activity in the wrong way. Most of those required to take part in the Work Programme found that it made their health worse. And contrary to government expectations, people who have spent two years on the Work Programme are not closer to work at the end, but more ill and further away from being able to work. The Work Programme, far from working, made things worse.

Even skilled occupational therapists, the only professionals trained in both health and functional capacity, can be over-optimistic about a sick person's abilities. Pam attended a specialist three week course on pain management, in which she had daily sessions with physiotherapists and occupational therapists. At the end of the course, she was invited to set some goals for the next three months and plans for how to achieve them. Pam over-estimated what she could achieve in that time and made herself so ill through her desire to work and the pressure that she put on herself to

10. EMPLOYMENT SUPPORT

continue that she ended up attempting suicide. But the occupational therapist had only queried her optimism gently; she did not advise Pam to lower her goals to ones more likely to be achievable without harm. If a trained and experienced professional cannot always identify when a patient is overreaching herself, how can an employment support adviser be entrusted with the same role?

It seems that the government is unaware of the severity of illness and disability experienced by people who qualify for sickness benefit. Appropriate policy cannot be designed and implemented, or disabled people's rights adequately provided for, for as long as the government is unaware of the nature of incapacitating illness, injury or impairment experienced by the people whom it is trying to help.

The Work and Health Programme

The level and scope of conditionality on sick and disabled people was increased in 2018, when the failed Work Programme was replaced with the Work and Health Programme. Where previously any conditionality could occur only after the WCA, now it applies before the government has made a decision on whether or not a person can participate in such activity, in the form of a Health and Work Conversation (HWC) prior to their WCA. If they do not attend, they will be sanctioned until they do, plus a sanction for a fixed length of time after taking part. The government has said that people unable to take part in such an activity will not be required to, but it has not said how these people will be identified before they have been assessed.

The idea of the HWC is for sick and disabled people to set a short-term goal and plan with the employment support worker, or work coach, how to achieve that goal. But work coaches are not medical professionals, occupational therapists or specialist job brokers. They are not qualified to help sick and disabled people to identify, set or work towards work-related goals, let alone health-related goals. Work coaches cannot identify what type or amount of work a sick or disabled person could do, nor what aids or adaptations would make work possible; consequently, they cannot work with employers to carve out job roles either for disabled people generally to apply for or a job for the specific disabled people with whom they are working. They cannot diagnose the medical problems experienced by a person and therefore cannot make appropriate referrals to healthcare services; and they cannot identify the cause of functional problems, and therefore cannot suggest remedies. Work coaches are fundamentally unable to make safe recommendations to sick and disabled people on what work-related activity they can and should do.

The government is keen to merge the healthcare and employment services, insistent as it is upon the idea that healthcare professionals should prioritise work and that work should be used as a marker of recovery. For several years the government has been planning to install DWP work coaches in GP surgeries, but patients and benefit recipients have objected. Paula Peters, a disabled campaigner, explained,

> "There is a blurring of the lines between healthcare and the [DWP] and it's wrong. We are already having to watch everything we say to doctors, we treat every appointment as a work capability assessment in case it's used against us... You put a mental health patient who is distressed, who is not well, and pile the pressure on them, they are going to relapse. They might harm themselves.

> "We have lost so many disabled people already to these schemes, how many more are we going to lose before doctors say 'I didn't become a doctor to get involved in schemes like this'?"[18]

GP surgeries are places for confidential discussion of health matters, in safety and without pressure, with someone whose job is to help the patient improve their health; they emphatically should not be places where sick people will feel any pressure or coercion to return to work before they are ready or to make work a priority over their health. GPs and other healthcare professionals should be given the freedom to advise their patient on what is best for the individual, and not use generalities to overrule specific needs. Sick people need to be able to trust their GPs and not worry that their doctor has become a DWP stooge, or that recovery is going to be defined not as an improvement in health but on whether or not they have returned to work.

Well aware of these concerns, the government is not openly placing Jobcentre work coaches in GP surgeries. Instead, in a somewhat duplicitous move, the government has introduced 'patient coaches'. The job title implies a healthcare professional whose interest is in helping people to improve their health and wellbeing, with no expectation that this will involve paid work. Indeed, health coaches already exist within the NHS, whose job role is to help sick people learn to prioritise their health and to improve their health-related quality of life. But patient coaches are the opposite. Far from being healthcare professionals, they are DWP work coaches just with a different name and working in a different place. Instead of prioritising health over work, patient coaches are all about returns to work, regardless of the severity of the individual's illness: GPs are told to refer anyone, however ill and far from being able to work, to patient coaches. The DWP has also told GPs not to tell their patients who the patient (work) coach is or where they have come from.[19]

Health should always come before work, but the government wants healthcare decisions to be based not on patient wellbeing, but on whether or not they facilitate a return to work.[11] They are considering fast-tracking treatment for people in work over those not in work, as if unemployed people can justifiably be treated less well than people with jobs to return to. They have told GPs to consider refusing to sign more than one sick note until a person has been to see the patient (work) coach, even though seeing a patient (work) coach is supposed to be voluntary. This sort of work-based prioritisation and pressure should never be applied, and has no place in the healthcare system.

Sick and disabled people are already afraid of being spied upon by the DWP.[20] People have been told that if they are well enough to attend a GP appointment (to get a sick note) then they are well enough to go to a Jobcentre appointment. Now the Jobcentre is in the GP surgery. A single malicious phone call to the DWP leads to 18 months of every inch of one's life being scrutinised, overseen and pulled apart in the search for fraud – including not just the benefit recipient's bank accounts, but those of friends and family. Supermarkets will hand over CCTV footage not just to the police for crime prevention but to the DWP to catch benefit recipients out.[20] The police will hand over information about people on protest marches.[21] It is no wonder that sick and disabled people fear to even do some light gardening in case a neighbour is watching, or feel that they have to justify everything that they do to everyone they meet.

The DWP argues that video footage and social media posts are only used in extreme circumstances, implying that no-one except frauds need to fear. It's a similar argument to their insistence that few people receive benefit sanctions. "But that ignores a key psychological truth," says psychiatrist Dr Jay Watts:

"One does not need to have done anything wrong to feel that one has done something wrong. You know that feeling one has of getting caught out when going through airport security? That need to 'perform' innocence, even though you know that you don't have a kilo of cocaine in your hand luggage? It is this, a thousand times worse, 24 hours a day, seven days a week for claimants, whose homes and leisure time are being invaded in unprecedented ways."[22]

We are left in a situation where the DWP has substantially increased the amount of conditionality placed on sick and disabled people, whilst offering little more than the flawed idea that Jobcentre or Work and Health Programme advisers will provide basic levels of healthcare and advice on health management. The support that sick and disabled people need – such as a stable and adequate income or the upfront provision by the government of the adjustments that they would need in a workplace – has not been offered. All that has happened is that sick and disabled people face more pressure to try to get back to work, from people who lack the requisite expertise, under the threat of sanctions and without there ever being any recognition of the actual barriers that keep a sick or disabled person from work.

What works

It does not have to be this way. Sick and disabled people have made clear what support they need if they are to find work. They need a job broker, to liaise with an employer on their behalf to create or carve out a suitable job; an occupational therapist, to advise on and, crucially, make available the aids and adaptations they need; access to in-work support workers and British Sign Language interpreters, including at interviews; access to education, training and voluntary work with all the same support measures as for work and work search; and consideration of the impact of personal care, domestic tasks, family responsibilities and commuting on the capacity available for paid work. They need enough money to enable them to participate in society, and freedom from the sanctions which largely serve only to cause stress and poverty and to enforce participation in inappropriate activity that then prevents people from carrying out useful activity. Most importantly, they need recognition that they too have the right to family life and rest and leisure.

10. EMPLOYMENT SUPPORT

With the right support and investment, some disabled people do get into work, including into mainstream employment. Eli, for example, has epilepsy that is largely controlled, but he still has a few fits a year. He is not allowed to drive, but overall he is not so disabled as to be unable to work. However, because of his fits he does have to have more sick days than most people. When a fit comes on, he has to be able to leave what he is doing immediately and go to a safe place. A job that required frequent or prolonged interaction with other people would not be suitable, and nor would a job using machinery. He needs to be able to leave his work immediately and unpredictably.

After a fit, Eli is exhausted. He has to take the following day off work in order to recover. If he doesn't, the fatigue he experiences triggers another fit. It's very important for him that he gets enough rest and sleep in order to manage his epilepsy. His medicine also makes him drowsy, which can make work difficult.

He would benefit from being paid disability leave, rather than the current situation in which he cannot get any sick pay for the days he takes off after a fit, and he needs an employer who does not treat his sick leave as a cue for disciplinary measures. The employer must be able to manage workflow around Eli, and not put pressure on him to work when he needs to rest. Eli also needs understanding colleagues, who will not feel uncomfortable around him or be upset that he is allowed to take sick days without disciplinary action when they cannot. Special treatment from employers towards sick and disabled employees can cause resentment amongst healthy colleagues, when in reality it is simply about making work as accessible to sick and disabled people as it is to healthy people.

In contrast, Gemma is struggling to find work because of her profound deafness. She can't use a phone at all, and struggles with written English because it is not a natural language for her – it is difficult to learn a language you cannot hear. Lip-reading causes her severe migraines. She is essentially debarred from jobs that involve client interaction, as many entry level jobs do; and she cannot do work that requires writing or any more than basic reading in English, because it is not a language in which she is fluent. And because of her poor education as a child, combined with growing up before computers became mainstream and her difficulty with English, she has found that any computer-based task is usually beyond her skill level.

She is trying, with training courses and mini-jobs and extensive job search, to get a permanent job, but she hasn't yet found one. Employers are put off because she is deaf, and don't give her the opportunity to work with them to provide a suitable, safe job for her (contrary to typical expectation, she is safer in noisy environments than many hearing people are, precisely because her deafness means that she is accustomed to looking out for non-verbal alerts). No support is provided for her in terms of British Sign Language interpreters for training, work experience or voluntary work, and the Access to Work scheme, which is supposed to fund support above what employers can be required to do, has proved too slow to be of any use for job interviews. Gemma can work part-time, but only if the government cares enough to do anything useful about it.

The government, when consulting on its ideas for getting sick and disabled people into work, cited Jamie as an example of a disabled person who successfully obtained paid work. But when Channel 4 recruited Jamie, a wheelchair user, to a one year internship, it was as part of a deliberate policy to recruit more disabled people. This is not the same as employing a new staff member despite their disability. If recruiting disabled people requires special policies, it shows that disabled people are not competing on an open basis and level footing with non-disabled people.

A report on conditionality for disabled people said that,

> *"The most striking case among disabled people of a successful transition from welfare into sustained employment was enabled by both the exercise of discretion and ongoing support by a sympathetic Jobcentre adviser who chooses to disregard the threat of sanction, and the long-term unconditional training and support simultaneously provided by a third sector homelessness organisation."*[23]

The current approach means that, "by the time you've attended these Work Programme courses you're so demoralised and demotivated and kicked around so much that you lose the will to carry on." But where conditionality is removed and necessary support at work is provided, a small number of sick and disabled people do move into work.

What these examples show is that employers and the government are the ones who make the difference in whether or not disabled people capable of some work are employed. Eli and Jamie are in work not because of any special merit or worthiness on their own part relative to other disabled people, but because an employer agreed to make the necessary adjustments

10. EMPLOYMENT SUPPORT

and bear that cost. Equally, Gemma is struggling to get work not because she has a bad attitude or isn't trying hard enough, but because employers are not willing to accommodate her. When the Jobcentre managed to help a disabled person into work, it was because the standard conditionality was not imposed whilst a third-sector agency provided key long-term support. It is, therefore, far more the responsibility of the government to make it financially and practically viable for employers to take on disabled staff than it is the responsibility of the disabled person to demonstrate work habits outside of paid work.

Sick and disabled people have the right to decent, remunerative employment; the same as anyone else. And in the absence of such work or the ability to take part in such work, they have the right to an adequate standard of living through other means. But it is the government that sets the rules of the labour market – the maximum hours someone can work per day and week; how long they can work without a break; minimum pay; acceptable managerial control and pressure. And it is the government that sets the rules of the benefits system – how much activity someone has to engage in; what activity is required; the level of benefits paid; and the severity of and triggers for sanctions. In this game of life, the UK Government isn't fulfilling its side of the contract, but is instead leaving sick and disabled people to struggle in a harsh work and benefits environment.

Other countries, such as a number of Western European and Scandinavian countries, invest significantly in vocational rehabilitation and support. Claimants only enter long-term disability pensions when all attempts at support have been exhausted and found unsuccessful. The UK, in contrast, is known internationally for its poor rehabilitation and employment support. The latest employment support programme, the Work and Health Programme, replaced the Work Programme in 2018. It is supposed to be so good that it can fully mitigate the impact of reducing ESA WRAG from £102.15 to £73.10 per week. But it consists of little more than the suggestions that sick and disabled people should be mandated to engage in basic level healthcare and activity management by staff who are trained in neither medicine nor occupational therapy.

For people with traditional disabilities who are capable of stable, predictable work on at least a part-time basis, the responsibility of those who can work to actually do so is not what needs to be focussed on. The government's ongoing focus on motivation, confidence and behaviour ignores the real issue: that people with disabilities are costly to employ, whether on an upfront or ongoing basis. They need jobs that are adapted to them, removing roles that the disabled person cannot do and altering expectations as necessary. They need the workplace and workstation to be adapted to them, and some need support workers on hand at all times.

What these people need is not to discuss health-related plans with Jobcentre staff, but to discuss the work they want to and can do with specialist job brokers, who will liaise with employers to create or carve out such suitable jobs, and with occupational therapists who can identify and provide the necessary support. The government must provide money upfront and in time for disabled people to be able to start a new job on an equal footing with non-disabled people, confident that the assistance, aids and adaptations that they need will already be in place. If job brokers and adjustments are competently provided by the government, employers will be much more confident about taking on disabled staff.

Most people who return to work from sickness benefits do so because their health improved; this is a recurring theme in the DWP's own research papers. The government's focus should therefore be first on improving health, not on inadequate or irrelevant work-related measures that make health worse. And improvements in health should be sought by increasing funding to the NHS and allowing doctors to refer patients to the best medical care, not by limiting access to only the lowest forms of care, or basing treatment on whether or not it will return someone to work.

For chronically sick people, the severe limitations on their ability to carry out any activity, let alone a predictable amount at predictable times, must be recognised. It is not practicable to insist that these people work or try to work. Until a significant improvement in their health occurs, there is no value or reason for activities that allegedly keep them close to the job market. There is time enough for that – through productive activities such as voluntary work, training courses or the development of hobbies – once a person is well enough and is likely to see an adequate recovery to allow at least part-time work. For sick people, what they need is the time and space to manage their health and participate in society in other ways. The stress of juggling health and work or of living in poverty and insecurity will only make them worse, defeating the government's alleged purpose of enabling everyone to live fulfilling lives and giving security to those who can't work.

10. EMPLOYMENT SUPPORT

NOTES FOR CHAPTER 10

1. **Warrener M, Graham J and Arthur S** (2009) A qualitative study of the customer views and experiences of the Condition Management Programme in Job centre Plus Pathways to Work Research Report 582 LONDON: DWP. **Baumeister RF, Campbell JD, Krueger JI and Vohs KD** (2003) Does high self-esteem cause better performance interpersonal success happiness or healthier lifestyles AMERICAN PSYCHOLOGICAL SOCIETY VOL 4 ISS. 1

2. **Hale C** (2014) Fulfilling potential? ESA and the fate of the Work-Related Activity Group London: Mind. For the negative effects of sanctions on health finances and other factors see also **Dwyer P, Jones K, McNeill J, Scullion L and Stewart A** (2018) Welfare Conditionality Project: Final findings – Disabled people WELFARE CONDITIONALITY PROJECT

3. **Moran M** (2017) The 2015 ESA trials: a synthesis Ad-hoc Research report 49 LONDON: DWP

4. **DWP** (2018) Work Programme national statistics. DATA UP TO DECEMBER 2017.

5. See for example: **Hales J, Hayllar O, Iyaniwura C, and Wood M** (2008) Pathways to Work: the experiences of existing customers. Findings from a survey of existing incapacity benefits customers in the first seven pilot areas. Research Report 527 LONDON: DWP. **Sejersen T, Hayllar O and Wood M (2009)** Pathways to Work: the experiences of longer-term existing customers. Findings from a survey of four to seven year incapacity benefits customers in the first seven pilot areas Research Report 586 LONDON: DWP

6. **Schneider J, Slade J, Secker J, Rinaldi M, Boyce M, Johnson R, Floyd M and Grove B** (2009) SESAMI study of employment support for people with severe mental health problems: 12-month outcomes. HEALTH AND SOCIAL CARE IN THE COMMUNITY VOL 17 ISS. 2, PP. 151-158 DOI: 10.1111/J.1365-2524.2008.00810.X

7. **Hale (n 2)**

8. **Pickles C, Holmes E, Titley H and Dobson B** (2016) Working welfare: a radically new approach to sickness and disability benefits. LONDON: REFORM

9. **Dwyer et al (n 2)**

10. **Barnes H, Sissons P and Stevens H** (2011) Employment and Support Allowance: Findings from a follow-up survey with customers. Research Report 745 London: DWP. **DWP and Department for Health (2016)** Improving lives: the work health and disability Green Paper. London

11. **Bollag U, Rajewaran A, Ruffieux C and Burnand B** (2007) Sickness certification in primary care – the physician's role. SWISS MEDICAL WEEKLY VOL 137 PP.341-346. **Macdonald S, Maxwell M, Wilson P, Smith M, Whittaker W, Sutton M and Morrison J** (2012) "A powerful intervention:" general practitioners' use of sickness certification in depression. BMC FAMILY PRACTICE VOL 13 ISS. 82

12. **DWP & DH (n 10)**

13. **Benstead S** (2017) Replacing Employment and Support Allowance – Part 3 Dignity and Support: a new sickness benefit. LONDON: EKKLESIA

14. **Jahoda M** (1981) Work, employment and unemployment: Values, theories and approaches in social research. AMERICAN PSYCHOLOGIST VOL 36 PP. 184-191
15. **Chandola T and Zhang C** (2017) Re-employment job quality health and allostatic load biomarkers: prospective evidence from the UK Household Longitudinal Study. INTERNATIONAL JOURNAL OF EPIDEMIOLOGY DOI: 101093/IJE/DYX150
16. **Black C** (2015) An independent review into the impact on employment outcomes of drug or alcohol addiction, and obesity: call for evidence LONDON: DWP
17. **Black C** (2016) An Independent Review into the impact on employment outcomes of drug or alcohol addiction, and obesity LONDON: DWP.
Adams L, Tindle A, Ponomarenko A and Coburn S (2017) Drug and alcohol proof of concept evaluation, and wider approaches to supporting clients with a dependency London: DWP . Aznar C, MacGrgor A and Porter L (2017) Views of claimants: qualitative findings of the Dame Carol Black review Research Report 937 LONDON: DWP
18. **As quoted in Gayle D** (02/03/2016) Activists angry at scheme to embed job coaches in GP surgeries. LONDON: **The Guardian.** See also **Roberts N** (08/03/2016) Protesters criticise scheme that puts job advisors in GP practices. GP ONLINE
19. **Bloom D** (13/11/2018) Jobcentre chiefs withdraw 'deceitful' guidance for GPs to help people off benefits. LONDON: THE MIRROR
20. **Watts J** (31/05/2018) No wonder people on benefits live in fear. Supermarkets spy on them now. LONDON: THE GUARDIAN
21. **The Independent** (24/12/2018) Police force admits passing disabled anti-fracking protesters' details to DWP LONDON.
Pring J (14/02/2019) Tory conference police force admits sharing information on protesters with DWP. DISABILITY NEWS SERVICE
22. **Watts (n 20)**
23. **Dwyer et al.** (n 9)

11

Personal Independence Payment

In the last two chapters we have looked at the help available to people whose sickness or disability limits their capacity for work. We have seen that the assessment for determining who can work is deeply flawed and unable to result in a reliable or valid assessment of capacity for work. People who are required to engage in job search or work-related activity do so under the threat of financial sanctions, without any of the support that they actually need, whilst being made unable to take part in activity or health management that would be useful. The UK thus fails sick and disabled people twice: firstly by not enabling those who can work to actually be in paid work; and secondly by not providing an adequate income for those who lack the opportunity or ability to work. This has become worse since the 2010 general election, because the test for work capacity has become harsher, benefit levels have been reduced, activity requirements have increased and there is still no meaningful support for work or other socially useful activity.

In this chapter we look at the disability benefits which are paid to people because their disability causes extra costs on top of standard daily living costs. The original extra-costs benefits, Attendance Allowance and Mobility Allowance, were replaced in 1992 with the single Disability Living Allowance (DLA) for those under pension age. But the 2010 Coalition Government thought that DLA was too generous and gave support to people who did not need it, so they created a new Personal Independence Payment (PIP) for working-age disabled people. Bizarrely, there are now three extra-costs benefits: DLA for children and those pensioners who were already in receipt of DLA as working-age adults; PIP for working-age adults, and Attendance Allowance for pensioners. There is still no mobility allowance for pensioners.

The government's justification for PIP depends upon the accuracy of their claims regarding the scope and adequacy of DLA. This chapter will therefore start by considering the development of DLA, and its strengths and flaws, to provide a background against which to compare the government's arguments and justifications for PIP.

A need for change

Disability Living Allowance (DLA) was introduced in 1992, in response to campaigning and evidence from disabled people that its two precursors, Mobility Allowance and Attendance Allowance, were inadequate. DLA was therefore designed to reach more disabled people, and to give more support to the people it reached. It did this by introducing three payment rates for the care component (replacing the two rates of Attendance Allowance) and two rates for the mobility component (replacing the one rate of Mobility Allowance). DLA was created for children and working-age adults; pensioners had to continue to use Attendance Allowance, although a person in receipt of DLA at the point they reached pension age could continue to receive DLA until their needs changed.

A new assessment system was brought in for DLA, as the previous medical examinations had fallen out of favour. Medical exams were criticised for being able to provide only a snapshot view by a stranger, which brought little to no additional value to the assessment process compared to the personal knowledge of the individual and the long-term clinical observations and care of his or her healthcare team. Tony Newton MP, a Conservative cabinet minister at the time, said that he was, "convinced… that it should be possible to determine a sizeable proportion of claims without the need for a special medical examination."[1]

In addition, DLA would place more weight on the collection and use of evidence from claimants' carers and medical staff, including "their GP, health visitors, district nurses, relatives or other carers". Mr Newton went on to say, "We believe that this will also give us a better picture of the circumstances than the snapshot of a Department of Social Security [now Department for Work and Pensions] medical examination". The government said that, "We intend to place the emphasis firmly on self-assessment and on supplementary evidence from those in contact with the claimant, giving proper weight to the judgment of those in the best position to know the effect that a claimant's condition has on his or her life."[2]

DLA struggled to assess many chronic illnesses because, "the assessment process is grounded both structurally and informally in a stereotypical notion of disability, i.e., conditions manifesting visible, static and relatively permanent signs or symptoms, of a level of severity that does not vary unpredictably across individuals."[3] This is the same problem we saw with ESA. Also like ESA, the assessment struggled because the regulations tried to separate illnesses into either mental or physical origin, even though in reality many illnesses cannot be divided in this way.[4]

People with a chronic physical illness were the most likely to have to appeal their original decision to get a correct award. Those with mental illness struggled because they were excluded from some criteria: people who could not make use of their physical ability to walk outdoors due to severe mental illness were excluded from the higher rate award of the mobility component; whilst to get the care component, individuals with mental health conditions generally had to prove a need for "continual" supervision, which was harder to get than the corresponding physical health threshold of needing "frequent" assistance. This bias against mental illness was one of the reasons given by the 2010 Government for replacing DLA for working-age adults with PIP.

DLA had faced other challenges. Initially, the mobility component could not be claimed for children under five years old, on the grounds that a disabled child is little less mobile than a healthy child at that age. This was successfully challenged by Disability Alliance, who were able to show the negative effects on development when children are not given mobility aids at a young enough age.[5] Similarly, individuals who had severe visual impairment could not initially claim the higher mobility rate, until the RNIB challenged this.[6]

Domestic tasks have never been assessed. DLA considered 'bodily functions' which included 'breathing, hearing, seeing, eating, drinking [and] walking'. It excluded those areas considered as 'domestic duties'. In Judge Denning's words, a bodily function is those things which "an ordinary person – who is not suffering from any disability – does for himself. But they do not include cooking, shopping or any of the other things which a wife or daughter does as part of her domestic duties."[7] This exclusion of necessary domestic tasks means that the disability extra-costs benefits have never been adequately comprehensive. Many people whose costs arise from needing to pay for someone else to do their shopping, cleaning, laundry or other necessary activities are totally reliant on the one domestic task that is included: the ability to cook a meal. Costs arising from higher utility bills, special diets or higher clothing costs are also excluded.

Even if people didn't need social care, or didn't have to use some or all of their DLA to pay for social care, DLA still did not come close to meeting the additional costs of living experienced by disabled people.[8] Less severely disabled people received no or very little benefit, yet on average they experience disability-related costs of around £200 per week. Very severely disabled people and people with sensory impairments typically received higher awards, but their extra costs are higher still, again leaving them with shortfalls of over £200 per week.

Although the number of people receiving DLA had increased over the years, as the government said, this was not due to an unwarranted softening of criteria or lax standards. The increase in people with physical illnesses and disabilities receiving DLA was entirely consistent with demographic trends that mean there are more people with physical disabilities now than in 1992. The increase in people with learning disabilities and mental illness reflected an earlier under-appreciation of the severity of disability experienced amongst these people groups, plus the increasing survival into adulthood of people with learning disabilities.[9]

These concerns and evidence regarding DLA meant that when the 2010 Coalition Government suggested that DLA needed to be reformed, they were simply saying what sick and disabled people and their representative organisations had been saying for years. Those with chronic illness or disability, and their representative organisations, wanted to see wider eligibility and more generous payments, in line with the available evidence on need.

But this was not want the government intended.

A cut by any other name

When the government decided to replace DLA with a new benefit, their rationale was that it was "time to bring disability benefits into the 21st century", because "we need to ensure that the benefit reflects the needs of disabled people today, rather than in the 1990s."[10] Maria Miller MP, then

11. PERSONAL INDEPENDENCE PAYMENT

Minister for Disabled People, said that the new benefit would be clearer and easier to understand, more consistent, and better able to respond to changes in society, attitudes and equality legislation. It was framed as an "opportunity to improve the support for disabled people and better enable them to lead full, active and independent lives."

As with the introduction of ESA, Personal Independence Payment (PIP) was introduced in the context of an alleged need to reduce spending on social security. It was again argued that benefits were increasing too fast, with the implication that many of the latest recipients were not truly deserving. The government wanted the new benefit, PIP, to reduce spending compared to DLA by 20%. This 20% decrease would fall only on working-age adults and not on the children and pensioners who were also in receipt of DLA, and made up around half of the caseload. Disabled people therefore experienced the new benefit as a cut in support, with half of DLA recipients getting a reduced award or no award at all when re-assessed for PIP.

The government's intention for PIP included 'better targeting' of extra-costs benefits. It was expected therefore that some people would receive more support than if DLA had been kept. A key part of this was the government's intention to increase the support available to people with severe and enduring mental health problems. The 20% cut was only a net cut: people with physical disabilities would on average lose more than this. The contradiction between claiming that DLA was too generous in part because increasing numbers of people with mental illness were receiving it, and claiming that people with mental illness weren't getting enough support, appears to have gone unnoticed by the government.

Despite being designed to cut support, PIP has not in practice had much impact relative to what was expected if DLA had been kept. For the most part, it has simply rearranged who gets what support, shifting support from physically to mentally ill and disabled people. The impact has been somewhat unpredictable, particularly if trying to understand how people with different impairments are affected. The net effect seems to be a shift of approaching half of people who would have had a medium-level award under DLA, with twice as many getting a lower award under PIP than a higher award.

By giving the appearance of being cost-neutral, the implementation of PIP has masked the actual severity of the government's intentions as well as the impact on those who have lost support. The government has subsequently enacted a number of changes to reduce PIP awards, including an attempt to reduce support for people with mental illness – a change which has since been overturned by the justice system as discriminatory, and which ran directly counter to the government's stated intention of improving support for these people.

> **Box 8. PIP & DLA award rate data**
>
> **1.5 million** people currently receive at least some level of PIP.
>
> **45%** of new claims for PIP are given an award. This is similar to the proportion of claimants under DLA who were given awards.
>
> Of those who are in receipt of PIP, **65%** receive both components. **31%** receive only a Daily Living award, and **4%** get only a Mobility award. **28%** get the highest award for both components.
>
> Under DLA, **81%** got both components. **11%** got only a daily living award, and **8%** received mobility only. **16%** got the highest award for both components.
>
> **48%** of people transferred to PIP get less on PIP than they did on DLA. **52%** of these (**25%** of DLA reassessments) get nothing.
>
> **40%** of people transferred to PIP get more on PIP than they did on DLA.

Bad assessments

The assessment process for PIP has returned to the flawed, snapshot medical exam which was so lambasted by John Major's Conservative Government. Most claimants now have to have a face-to-face assessment, and the decision-making process relies heavily on the assessor's opinion. A consultant may say that a loss of PIP "could lead to increased complications, hospitalisation and risk of mortality"; the DWP merely responds that doctors can't comment on a person's functional ability.[11] In addition, PIP has introduced an unsuitable points-based methodology akin to the one used for ESA. The alleged simplicity of a points-based system is, in practice, more difficult to administer due to the complexity of human illness and disability.[12] Thus the problem with ESA, that it assumes discrete impairments, is replicated in PIP.

The unsuitability of the points-based assessment is exacerbated by reports that assessors are making things up, with the consequence that disabled people are inappropriately assessed as not qualifying for benefits. The disability journalist John Pring has collated nearly 300 such cases, including one lady, Vanessa, who was awarded £5,000 in compensation after her inaccurate assessment report and the subsequent rejection of her claim left her suicidally depressed.[13]

When Megan received her assessment report, she found that the assessor had repeatedly written that the difficulties she said she experienced were inconsistent with her medical condition; in essence, that she was lying. Her assessor, a paramedic, had never heard of her main condition (hypermobility Ehlers-Danlos Syndrome), and made no reference to the likely impacts of her fibromyalgia. He completely ignored the effects that a third, then undiagnosed, condition had upon Megan, even though this one caused some of the most severe problems.

Until you receive such a report for yourself, it is hard to describe what it feels like. You can argue that a stranger's opinion should not materially impact your perception of yourself, but it doesn't work. It's not just that assessors have significant power and authority to change claimant's lives. It is also that these flawed reports give the impression that the assessor believes the claimant is a liar, and it is difficult not to take on some element of shame, humiliation and self-attack from such an assessment. Megan became, along with other such sick and disabled people, a member of the undeserving poor; a deliberate malingerer making up her symptoms so that she didn't have to work; one of those people who needed poverty to teach them moral aptitude.

It took Megan two years to appeal this decision, by which time she had accrued £6,000-worth of back payments. In the process, she was variously assessed as getting zero points; two points each on four daily living activities; and four points each on two daily living activities. She also went from zero points on the mobility component to 12.

A group of people with the rare condition trigeminal autonomic cephalalgias (TAC) have reported that they have experienced assessors:

> "making false statements about TAC; reaching conclusions that directly contradict those of neurological specialists; refusing to accept documentary evidence about their conditions; failing to record key evidence told to them during assessments; and altering what they are told by the claimant during the assessment."[14]

One gentleman with this condition, who struggled to bathe because heat triggers neurological attacks, was told it was "his choice to avoid having a bath due to trying to avoid having an attack". Assessors use 'personal choice' to mean that they consider a person to have made an unnecessary choice to avoid doing something that he or she can in fact do. Usually it is used to argue that someone could mobilise themselves if they would use a walking stick or manual wheelchair, but that they have chosen not to because they feel embarrassed. In this case, the assessor was not arguing that bathing as usual would not have any impact; she was arguing that the high likelihood and severity of seizures triggered by bathing were not a valid reason for not bathing.

The government doesn't collect data on how people's PIP awards vary from one assessment or appeal to the next, though this would be highly useful. But the available information suggests that widely varying assessments are the norm, not the exception. The government's claim that PIP would be objective and consistent is simply untrue.

Cutting mobility

When the government brought in PIP, it said it wanted to increase support for people with mental illness or disability. But because it also wanted to cut support overall, any increases for people with mental illness had to be funded by reductions for people with physical illness. This was done by cutting the support for people who struggled to walk. Under DLA, appeals against adverse decisions had resulted in the establishment under case law of 50m as the threshold for being considered virtually unable to walk. Accessibility guidelines are based around this 50m, with Blue Badge spaces being provided within 50m of the facility they serve, and seats in pedestrian areas being no more than 50m apart.[15]

Under PIP, the government effectively reduced this definition to 20 metres, by shifting people who could walk between 20m and 50m from the higher mobility rate to the lower, a loss of around £35 per week. The government anticipated that, as a consequence of the lower threshold, around 600,000 people would lose their entitlement to the higher rate of mobility payments.[16] By October 2016, more than half of the 254,200 who had received the higher rate of the mobility component under DLA and been reassessed under PIP had lost it.[17]

This doesn't just mean a substantial drop in income. Many people who had qualified under DLA as virtually unable to walk had used some (for basic mobility scooters) or all (for powerchairs or cars) of their higher DLA mobility award to rent a car, mobility scooter or powerchair from the

11. PERSONAL INDEPENDENCE PAYMENT

charitable Motability scheme. When these people were transferred to PIP, anyone who was assessed as able to walk over 20m lost their access to this scheme, because the lower rate of benefit for those able to walk 20-50m did not cover the cost. 51,000 people had lost their Motability vehicles by October 2016, reaching 900 per week as the roll-out of PIP covered more and more of Great Britain.

At the time of the original consultation on PIP, the Bristol Disability Equality Forum wrote to the government to voice its concern that there appeared to be a flawed assumption on the government's part:

> "that all disabled people with mobility impairments will have the use of a car... This assumption means that, for example, someone who 'Can move up to 50 metres unaided but no further,' will score 8 points [enough for the lower PIP mobility award] because '50 metres is considered to be the distance that an individual is required to be able to walk in order to achieve a basic level of independence such as the ability to get from a car park to the supermarket.' Yet 8 points will not pay for the Motability car that they would need to be walking from, to meet this assumption..."[18]

Nor does it help the person who, having walked from the car to the supermarket, is unable to return to their car, let alone do their shopping.

Many disabled people rely on the Motability scheme to access work, get to medical appointments and achieve independence. Thus the loss of access to a car could have knock-on effects that include disabled people being unable to work, or alternatively having to rely on the more expensive taxi scheme under Access to Work (the government-funded Access to Work scheme will pay for taxis, minus the equivalent public transport cost, for people it has verified as unable to drive, walk or use public transport).

David is one such example.[19] He struggles to walk due to Becker muscular dystrophy. Because of his difficulties, he was previously awarded the higher rate mobility of DLA, all of which plus more went on renting a suitable vehicle from Motability. But when he was assessed for PIP, the tighter criteria combined with a faulty assessment of his abilities meant that he lost the money he previously used to rent a car from Motability.

David is employed, and drives 30 miles to work. When he lost his car he had a choice: he could ask the government-funded Access to Work scheme to pay for a taxi for him to get to and from work, at vast expense; or he could purchase his own adapted car. He opted for the latter, which cost him all of his family savings and put him into debt. His assessment decision was overturned, but it is too late – he has already put money into a car to replace the one he should never have lost. He took a principled decision not to put the government to the cost of daily taxis, and as a result is now in debt for the first time in his life.

The loss of a car or the money to cover travel costs doesn't just impact work and social participation. The MS Society found that MS sufferers who had lost their higher rate mobility payments under PIP ended up needing more care from the NHS.[20] Two in five had increased their use of GP services whilst two in three reported that their health had been made worse. Many ended up housebound or heavily restricted in how often they could go out, because they no longer had an accessible car to go out in. The extra money of the higher compared to lower rates of PIP and DLA makes a substantial difference not just to being able to access more, better or different therapies than are available on the NHS, but also for buying enough basic necessities like food and heating.

The Bristol Disability Equalities Forum went on to say, in a later consultation specifically on the change to a 20-metre threshold for the higher rate mobility award:

"Furthermore, we believe the 20 metre rule to qualify for the highest rate of the new benefit, Personal Independence Payment (PIP), will leave many of those with the greatest needs without vital support and trapped in their own homes. Such circumstances will result in Disabled people dropping out of work and education, increased poverty and isolation, and increased costs in other areas of government spending – most especially, health and social care and unemployment benefits.

"This is not pure speculation, there is clear evidence provided through Department of Health research that isolation alone is very expensive by resulting in substantial increases in anti-depressant prescribing, hospital admissions and increased demand for residential care...

"Nowhere has there been any consideration as to where people who can do further distances if they rest in-between are going to be able to sit down, how long they will need to recuperate, the surface people will be walking on, the kerbs they will have to navigate nor the weather which, in this country, is renowned for being both wet and unpredictable."[21]

Again and again in responses to the DWP consultation, it was pointed out that the 20m threshold is contrary to case law on what it means to be "virtually unable" to walk. And in the real world, where pavements can slope up, down and towards the road, and where there are steps, uneven flagstones and tree roots and branches, the ability to walk 50 metres on the flat, once, whilst not carrying any shopping or handbags or coats, is really not very helpful at all.

In contrast to the Government's decision to give less money to people who could walk 20-50m, disability organisations had been asking for a top-up rate for those unable to walk at all. The Joint Committee on Mobility for Disabled People had recommended that a third, higher, rate be added to the mobility component.[22] This third rate would be for those who are fully unable to walk, such as those with full spinal paraplegia or multiple limb loss. These people have additional costs, such as a requirement for specialised vehicles, which are less likely to occur amongst those who retain some, albeit limited, ability to walk. The Motability scheme requires additional up-front payments, starting from £2,500, to rent a vehicle that can be driven by a wheelchair user, whilst someone looking to purchase a powerchair suitable for full-time use would expect to pay several thousand pounds. However, the government instead chose to reduce payments for those with the ability to walk between 20 and 50 metres, and to refuse the request for increased support for those who are completely unable to walk.

Taking away aids

Because PIP didn't initially take away as much support as the government wanted, the DWP subsequently sought for other ways to make cuts. They decided that people reliant on, but able to manage with, aids or appliances for four of the daily living tasks assessed under PIP are not really disabled. The government therefore suggested that such people have minimal needs and minimal costs, and should be excluded from PIP. Following a consultation, the responses to which rejected the idea that such people have minimal disability, the DWP decided to reduce the points given to two of the four activities. They estimated that 640,000 people would be affected with an average loss of £36 per week each, meaning that most of the people affected will either drop from the higher rate of the daily living component to the lower, or will cease to qualify at all.[23]

The government presented its argument in the form of two hypothetical examples. One was of a gentleman who experienced COPD, a lung condition which causes breathlessness and, in severe cases, oxygen deprivation. The DWP described this hypothetical person as needing to use aids when washing, dressing, cooking and using the toilet, and considered that aids for these four activities would be cheap. They assumed that those would be all the difficulties, and all the costs, that such a person would experience.

However, they neglected to consider the other costs that such a person would be likely to experience, or what the difficulties experienced by this hypothetical gentleman said about his disability in other areas. Someone who gets breathless with the relatively gentle activity of dressing even whilst sat down, or who struggles to get on and off a toilet, will find it difficult to perform a range of other, more intensive and time-consuming activities. These include shopping, tidying, cleaning, laundry and basic household maintenance. They may find that they get cold easily, so need to spend more on heating; or that they drop food down themselves, so need to spend more on laundry. Similarly, a lady with arthritis – the other hypothetical example – who needed the same adjustments to the same activities would likely have problems with the same non-assessed activities.

Fiona, for example, experiences many difficulties because of her blindness that are not covered by PIP. She can't afford many of the aids available to help blind people in their daily lives, and this puts many of even the simplest tasks beyond her abilities. She can't cook for herself, because she can only identify a hob by the heat it is giving off, and if something is spitting in a pan she cannot tell if is spitting only within the pan, or if it is going to spit hot fat onto her – or even if it is on fire. Nor can she tell when her food is cooked, or what temperature a hob or oven is at, or even precisely where the hob is. Fortunately, the activity of cooking – once one has excluded the need to be able to move around the kitchen, bend down to an oven, reach up to a cupboard and carry large or heavy items – is considered in assessing a person's need for support with daily living tasks, and so Fiona can score some points on this activity. However, whether she is assessed as unable to cook, able to cook with assistance or able to cook with aids she doesn't have is up to the individual assessor.

In shops, Fiona can't identify fresh food from food that is going off, particularly where meat is ageing or fruit is bruised. She is vulnerable to cheats and to defective products; her dad, also blind, once bought a tin of paint that was cracked and had leaked. No-one, whether shop staff or fellow customer, attempted to stop him from buying it. Fiona herself has resorted to standing

11. PERSONAL INDEPENDENCE PAYMENT

in shop doorways, blocking the paths of other customers in order to get their attention to ask for help in finding the items she needs. Being unable to see, she cannot identify which tin or cardboard box or carton contains the beans, cereal or juice that she wants.

When getting herself dressed, Fiona cannot tell which of her clothes go together, nor – unless they smell – whether they are clean. She might be able to identify large tears, but can't identify let alone repair small ones. Living with her parents, she relies upon them to tell her when she needs to change her clothes into something clean or more appropriate before going out. The alternative options – of washing clothes frequently just in case they're dirty and of buying clothes more frequently to replace those that might be worn out, or that are worn down through being washed more frequently – mean higher laundry costs and higher clothing costs.

But these issues are apparently irrelevant – because even today, Fiona's wife or daughter could do them for her.

PIP was deliberately designed to exclude all these activities which Fiona and the DWP's examples would have struggled with. When it was recommended to the government that the activities considered under PIP should be extended, the DWP's argument in response was that,

> "The assessment is not designed to take into account every area of daily life, but to look at a range of activities which, as a whole, act as a proxy for overall level of need. We are confident that the activities included in the final assessment will provide an accurate indication of levels of need and will award appropriate priority in the benefit as a result..."[24]

To subsequently claim that certain people are not disabled enough, on the grounds that the only criteria they fit look, superficially, quite mild is mere sophistry. The DWP quite deliberately chose not to include criteria that would reveal the extent of a person's disability and extra costs, and is now claiming that those costs don't exist because they didn't show up on an examination that didn't consider them.

It is important to realise that an aid or appliance never removes a disability, it merely alleviates it in one area. A long-handled brush for washing is not going to help with getting things out of a floor-standing cupboard or oven. It is not going to change the fact that the reason non-disabled people don't use a long-handled brush to wash their feet is because reaching down to the feet is easier and more thorough than using such a brush. Many aids cause their own problems, 'sharing out' the disability around the body but never really removing it. Crutches, walking sticks and manual wheelchairs regularly damage joints and muscles that were never designed to bear that task.

A good aid can make a big difference, but good aids are not guaranteed. The crutches, and occasional wheelchairs, handed out by the NHS are the most basic models, rather than the ergonomic designs that put less strain on shoulders and elbows. Olivia, who has hemiplegia, has found that whilst it is her left side that is affected by the hemiplegia, more recently it has been her right side that has been problematic. She experienced several years in which the splints made for her left ankle, whilst well cast, were made by underpaid and under-skilled factory workers. The bad splints substantially impeded Olivia's ability to walk well, placing strain on her right leg. The result was bursitis in her right hip, a painful swelling of the fluid-filled sacs (bursa) that cushion the joints. Normally a short-lasting condition, Olivia has had bursitis for over two years. The pain in her hip causes further stiffness, pain and fatigue in her right side, compounding the problems in her left.

Bad splints cause other problems, including blisters and raw skin. One carbon fibre splint that was re-worked to make it more skeletal became so brittle that carbon fibres constantly flaked off and rubbed the skin raw. It was necessary to get a new splint, but getting an appointment with the adult NHS services was difficult. Olivia had to ask her GP to phone up for an appointment, because she wasn't allowed to make a self-referral. She asked if the team could look at her badly-made plastic splint, as well as the flaking carbon fibre one, but when at the appointment the team looked at the plastic splint first – and then refused to look at the carbon fibre one, for which the appointment was originally made. She was told that they could only address one issue at a time, and that she would have to go back to her GP for another referral to address the problems with the carbon fibre splint.

Similarly, prosthetic limbs cannot be assumed to function as well as a living limb. BLESMA, the British charity for ex-service men and women who have lost limbs or use of limbs, explained that:

> "There will be times when the adaptation or aid cannot overcome the impairment or health condition, e.g. when stump problems prevent an amputee wearing a prosthetic limb or occasions when they break down or malfunction. The imposition of financial penalties on people who endeavour to manage the impact of their impairment would be unfair...

> "Exercise can have a significant impact on the stump; break-down of the skin, soreness and changes in stump volumetrics impact significantly on even the most 'prosthetically mobile' amputees and can prevent the prosthetic being worn. Amputees' gait can have a detrimental effect on other parts of the body, such as the hips and back, causing significant pain. Standing and walking on one day, such as the day of the assessment, might be completely out of the question the next due to the impact on the stump or other parts of the body."[25]

Mental health

In 2017, the government implemented emergency legislation to prevent people with mental illnesses from accessing the higher mobility payment. Using emergency legislation meant that the government did not have to pass the legislation through the usual parliamentary debate and voting. The government made this change on the grounds that people who struggle to get around outdoors due to severe mental illness should not be getting, or do not need, the same amount of financial support as people who struggle due to physical illness or disability.

The government claimed that such outcomes went against the original policy intent. But in fact, increasing financial support to people with severe mental illness was one of the government's few positive justifications for introducing PIP. Their subsequent emergency legislation gives the impression that the government is more interested in finding any rationale for making cuts than it is in making just or fair assessments of need – even when that rationale contradicts its previous statements of intent.

Some Conservative MPs went so far as to say that mental illness was not a true disability and that benefits should only go to "really disabled people", not to people with incapacitating mental illness – and somewhat ironically citing dialysis patients as 'really disabled', given that many dialysis patients have to go to appeal to get an award.[26]

In contrast, the Conservative MP Heidi Allen told the government that it should accept a Tribunal ruling on this matter, and that it should review the whole PIP process because "it is not fit for purpose at the moment."[27] Disabled people pointed out that the desire to increase awards to mentally ill people who struggled to get around outside was a key reason cited by the government not only for replacing DLA with PIP, but also for cutting the award given to people with physical disabilities.

In December 2017, a high court judge ruled that "the 2017 regulations introduced criteria... which were blatantly discriminatory against those with mental health impairments and which cannot be objectively justified."[28] Because the new regulations were discriminatory and went against the original policy intent, the DWP did not have lawful power to make them without a proper consultation. The DWP has decided to conform with the ruling and has reversed the 2017 regulations, with the intention of reviewing decisions made during the period of change to bring them in line with the original and now re-instated criteria. As of writing, this has yet to happen. People with severe mental illness are forced to continue to wait for the money rightfully owed to them, whilst the amount owed increases each week that the correct award rate is not paid.

A breach of rights

Extra-cost disability benefits have never been adequate for reaching every disabled person who has more than trivial extra costs, or at giving sufficient benefit to cover all of the extra costs experienced by those who do qualify. At the time that PIP was introduced, disability benefits needed expanding, not shrinking. Too many people either couldn't access the benefit at all or couldn't get enough support to overcome the barriers that kept them from living as full citizens on an equal footing with non-disabled people. Disabled people on average had costs of £200 per week above what they could get from DLA, and DLA had been shown to be failing to fully account for someone's disability.

The change from DLA to PIP has meant that many activities are no longer considered, such as getting up and down stairs, mobilising around the home and getting into and out of bed. A need for supervision in order to remain safe, or for assistance during the night, is also no longer considered. Other activities where a person needs help have never been considered by either benefit, such as cleaning, laundry, basic house maintenance and shopping. Costs such as higher utility bills and specialist or more expensive food also continue to be ignored.

Because of these exclusions, disabled people are dependent on being able to demonstrate need in those activities that the government has included if they are to get the support they need to live full and independent lives. They might have many other needs, and associated costs, but PIP has no provision for this. Indeed, it was a deliberate decision of the government to rely on the 12 chosen activities as a proxy for all other costs. Yet the government has chosen to since reduce support to around 600,000 people who need aids and appliances in daily living, on top of the 600,000 who lost support because of the reduction in mobility awards when PIP was first brought in. The net change in people on PIP in October 2018 compared to if DLA had been kept was expected to be minus 400,000, because some people get more under PIP than under DLA, but in fact dropped by only 200,000 to 2.0 million. However, the fact that there is a net negative change on a benefit that was never adequate in the first place means that PIP is regressive.[29]

The introduction of PIP has meant that, instead of progressing in the matter of disabled people's human rights, the government has gone backwards. This new benefit uses the same type of assessment that has failed in ESA, and fails to take account of the real extra costs of living and how and why they are incurred. By removing or reducing the money that sick and disabled people rely on to cover the extra costs they experience, the government has made society less accessible and increased their dependence upon other people being willing to carry out activities for or with them without payment.

The frequent changes to PIP, designed to reduce award rates, makes for an uncertain environment for disabled people. There is already insecurity as disabled people can get very different outcomes at reassessment or appeal without their health or abilities changing. With the government also changing the rules and guidelines for PIP as it goes along, people who qualified at one assessment can find that again, with no change in their abilities, they don't qualify at the next. The government keeps moving the goalposts on what counts as 'disabled' in what context, but isn't doing so with any reference to the extra costs that disabled people actually experience or the kinds of support that they actually need. This merely adds to the overall injustice of the benefits system.

Whilst disabled people agreed that DLA needed reform, what they were asking for was more support, not less; for example, in increasing the access to lower rate mobility for people who could walk distances between 50m and 200m, and increasing access to higher rate mobility for people who could walk but who had other difficulties getting around outside. PIP therefore is a retrograde step: it re-introduces flawed medical assessments; it copies ESA's flawed points-based system; and it reduced the amount of support that many disabled people could receive, without increasing it for all who were under-served by DLA. At the same time, the government's main justifications – that the benefit was too generous and subjective – are not borne out by the facts. In fact, Megan's case, which is not at all unusual, shows clearly that PIP is neither objective nor consistent. An objective and consistent assessment would not vary so widely in the conclusions it reached.

NOTES FOR CHAPTER 11

1. **Mr Tony Newton,** Conservative Secretary of State for Social Security. Disability Living Allowance and Disability Working Allowance Bill, HC DEB (21/11/1990) VOL181 CC311-53
2. **Mr Nicholas Scott,** Conservative Minister for the Disabled. IBID
3. **Hammond C** (2002) A poorly understood condition: Disability Living Allowance and people with CFS/ME. SOCIAL POLICY AND ADMINISTRATION VOL 36 ISS. 3, PP.254-274
4. **Harris N** (2000) Social security law in context. OXFORD: OXFORD UNIVERSITY PRESS
5. **Howard M** (1994) Too young to count: the extra-mobility related costs of children under five. DISABILITY ALLIANCE
6. **Royal National Institute for the Blind** (2006) Taken for a ride. LONDON
7. **R v National Insurance Commissioner ex p Secretary of State for Social Services** (1981) 1 WLR 1017
8. **Smith N, Middleton S, Ashton-Brooks K, Cox L and Dobson B with Reith L** (2004) Disabled people's costs of living: more than you would think. York: Joseph Rowntree Foundation.
Scope have released more recent research on disabled people's extra costs. However, their approach is less transparent, does not account for severity of disability, and does not make clear whether it takes into account disability-related costs that do not occur because the person cannot afford them. Scope estimates that disabled adults experience extra costs of an average £583 per month above what they can receive in benefits. One in five experience extra costs of £1500 per month.
John E, Thomas G and Touchet A (2019) The disability price tag 2019 LONDON: SCOPE.
9. **Campbell S, Anon, Marsh S, Franklin K, Gaffney D, Anon, Dixon M, James L, Barnett-Cormack S, Fon-James R, Willis D and Anon** (2012) Responsible reform: a report on the proposed changes to Disability Living Allowance. SPARTACUS NETWORK
10. **Maria Miller MP, Minister for Disabled People** (2010) Foreword to Public consultation: Disability Living Allowance reform. LONDON: DWP
11. **Anon** (16/10/2018) The result was zero points for everything. WOW VOICES
12. **Meershoek A, Krumeich A and Vos R** (2007) Judging without criteria? Sickness certification and disability schemes. SOCIOLOGY OF HEALTH AND ILLNESS VOL 29 ISS. 4, PP.497-514 DOI: 10.1111/J.1467-9566.2007.01009.X

11. PERSONAL INDEPENDENCE PAYMENT

13. **Pring J** (21/12/2017) Court orders Atos to pay disabled woman £5000 over dishonest PIP assessment. DISABILITY NEWS SERVICE
14. **Pring J** (09/03/2017) PIP investigation: Claimant group tell MPs of 'systemic malpractice' by assessors. DISABILITY NEWS SERVICE
15. **Department for Transport** (2005) Inclusive Mobility LONDON
16. 428,000 fewer people will receive higher mobility under PIP compared to DLA However, around 200,000 will be newly eligible for reasons other than physical mobility, so the total losing out due to changes to the physical mobility criteria will be over 600,000.
17. **Muscular Dystrophy UK** (15/03/2017) Over 900 Motability vehicles being returned a week under PIP reform, say Muscular Dystrophy UK LONDON
18. **Bristol Disability Equality Forum** (2012) Response to second consultation on PIP BRISTOL
19. **Gale D** (07/04/2017) Dad Dave Petitions: "Keep PIP Promises, Penny". DISABILITY UNITED
20. **Wetherley L and Erez R** (2018) PIP: a step too far. LONDON: MS SOCIETY
21. **Bristol Disability Equality Forum** (2013) Response to consultation on the 20 metre threshold BRISTOL
22. **JCMDP** (2011) Inquiry into proposal to replace DLA with Personal Independence Payment: Response from the Joint Committee on Mobility for Disabled People LONDON
23. **DWP** (2016) The Government's response to the consultation on aids and appliances and the daily living component of Personal Independence Payment LONDON
24. **DWP (2012)** The Government's response to the consultation on the Personal Independence Payment assessment criteria and regulations LONDON
25. **British Limbless Ex-Service Men's Association** (2012) Response to consultation on second draft of PIP LONDON
26. **As quoted in Stone J** (14/03/2017) DWP 'tells disability benefits assessors to discriminate against people with mental health conditions'. LONDON: THE INDEPENDENT
27. **As quoted in Simons N** (27/02/2017) Tory MP Heidi Allen tells government not to cut mental health disability payments. NEW YORK: HUFFINGTON POST
28. **Mr Justice Mostyn** (2018) RF v Secretary of State for Work And Pensions [2018] PTSR 1147 [2017] EWHC 3375
29. **DWP** (2018) Personal Independence Payment: Official Statistics to July 2018 LONDON

12

Social Care and the Independent Living Fund

At the end of Chapter 5, we saw that the large institutions in which disabled people used to live were beginning to be closed in favour of much smaller residential units. Although these housed groups of people in the single digits and gave individuals their own bedrooms rather than large dormitories, the fact remained that these were closer to the old institutions than they were to the goal of individual disabled people living in their own homes. Nor had large institutions gone away. People with learning disabilities or mental illness were still at risk of being labelled as 'challenging', a term which acts like a passcode for local authorities to be allowed to forcibly place these people in private hospitals, often many miles away from their home and family. And it continues to be entirely normal to expect older disabled people to live in residential homes, with usually only a bedroom to themselves and perhaps a private toilet, but shared living spaces and little to no choice in what they eat.

The goal of a modern society should be that sick and disabled people have access to the same choices as everyone else. When it comes to choosing schools, workplaces, where to live, when and what to eat, what to wear, when to go to bed and many mundane and normal lifestyle decisions, sick and disabled people should not find that their choices are constrained, let alone segregated, compared to the general public. The rights to an adequate standard of life, family life, decent paid work, community participation and leisure time should be equally available to all. Social care should be about more than merely making sure that sick and disabled people get fed at some point or that on most days they get to have a wash or use a toilet instead of a nappy.

12. SOCIAL CARE AND THE INDEPENDENT LIVING FUND

Funding cuts

Funding for social care has been falling in real terms since 2010, as part of wider cuts to funding for local councils. Councils lost 40% of central government funding between 2010 and 2015, representing a loss of 25% of their total income.[1] The councils that received the most money from central government – the ones that have the biggest gap between what their residents need and what they can raise through Council Tax and business rates – have suffered the most, and have had to cut their spending on services by 33%, compared to 9% for the least grant-dependent councils. Almost all of the reductions in spending on disadvantage has occurred amongst the 20% most deprived councils.

> **Box 9. Impact of cuts on adult social care**
>
> **The impact of the cuts on adult social care in England has been devastating:**[2]
> Funding from central government to local authorities fell by 40% from 2009 to 2015.
> Spending on social care in 2015/16 was only a little smaller than in 2010/11, but would have been substantially higher had it kept pace with demographic change.
> In 2018/19, local councils planned to reduce social care spending by a further 5%. Social care funding had already fallen from £21.5bn in 2010 to £14.5bn in 2018.
> Half of local authorities used some of their council reserves to go towards social care in 2017/18. At current rates, 10% will have run out of reserves by 2020/21.
> The steepest cuts have occurred in home-based and day care.
> Private residential and nursing home providers are closing down or handing back contracts in almost 1/3 of local authority areas.
> The number of adults receiving social care in England fell from 1.7-1.8mn in 2010 to 860,000 in 2017.
> In 2017/18, 1.3 million adults requested social care. 2/3rds of working-age disabled adults and half of disabled pensioners are refused social care.
> Two-thirds of councils have had service providers close or hand back their social care contracts since 2010.

Adult social care is the largest element of local government's spending, meaning that it is difficult if not impossible to protect social care from the impact of substantial income drops. Between 2011/12 and 2015/16, councils have experienced a £5bn funding gap in adult social care.

As the Conservative peer Lord Porter explained:

> "Even if councils stopped filling in potholes, maintaining parks, closed all children's centres, libraries, museums, leisure centres and turned off every street light they will not have saved enough money to plug the financial black hole they face by 2020."[3]

ADASS and the Local Government Association reported that:

> "With social care and waste spending absorbing a rising proportion of the resources available to councils, funding for other council spending drops by 66% in cash terms by the end of the decade; from £24.5 billion in 2010-11 to £8.4 billion in 2019-20. This is the equivalent of an 80% real terms cut. And of course, these "other" universal services are those which play a key role in supporting an individual's general wellbeing, such as libraries, leisure and transport."[4]

Whilst the government says it gave social care an extra £2bn per year between 2012 and 2014/15, this has not been enough to meet the increasing numbers of disabled people in the UK. Half of the additional £2bn cited by the government was a redirection of money from the NHS to social care, in an attempt to reduce pressures on the NHS. This redirect, part of the Better Care Fund, was initially supposed to improve both health and social care through closer integration of the two, but the focus of the fund has since been changed to reducing emergency admissions. The Public Accounts Committee described the Better Care Fund as "little more than a ruse", giving an appearance of additional funding without actually doing so.[5] Other money allocated by central government to social care came from savings from the New Home Bonus; but the Local Government Association note that if the expected savings of £0.8bn are not met, "it is not clear what the implications may be for the money earmarked for adult social care."[6]

One-off additions of money may temporarily save some councils from collapse, but give councils and care providers no certainty for the future.

12. SOCIAL CARE AND THE INDEPENDENT LIVING FUND

Councils have to plan as though they will be unable to afford normal levels of service and will have to cut back on social care. Disabled people similarly have to plan how they will cope with less support than they need. When a government subsequently decides to give a little more money towards these needs, it doesn't undo the stress and administration that went before. People need certainty that their rights will be met, rather than being dependent upon what amounts to random central government charity.

The Conservative-run council of Northamptonshire has already gone bankrupt, whilst many others say that the "worst is yet to come" with "truly unpalatable" choices to be made between social care, Sure Start centres, libraries, rubbish collections, and road repairs even if councils raise council tax and bring in new fees and charges.[7] This is despite a near-halving in the numbers of people who receive social care. In Liverpool, the situation has become so poor that, in the words of one Guardian journalist, "So constrained are funds that those in need of care cannot enter the system until someone else leaves."[8]

The cost of cuts

Because of central government cuts, councils simply don't have the money to do what central government demands of them. Councils are increasingly having to review care packages with the aim primarily of reducing costs rather than identifying need or maintaining rights.[9] In Merton, a council document outlining spending cuts includes plans to review all social care packages in order to make cuts of between 5% and 15% for various impairment groups and levels of need.[10] Southampton Council has contracted the private provider, Capita, to carry out social care reviews with the result of an average 7% cut.[11] Again, it is the most deprived areas that are having to reduce spending on social care, whilst the most well-off – those with the least need – have actually managed to increase spending.[12]

In many areas, PIP daily living awards are taken into account when assessing how much support a council will pay for, despite the recipients needing this money to pay for other disability-related needs or top-up basic necessities. Councils only provide social care on a means-tested basis, which goes against the principles of the NHS and extra-costs benefits – that disabled people should not be doubly penalised by disability, once through the disability itself and the second time by having less disposable income after spending on disability-related costs. Councils increasingly expect family members to provide the care that a disabled person needs, but this often puts substantial pressure on relationships, finances and the carer's own health. Marriages can break up, families fall apart and carers experience breakdowns in their own health. The capacity to cope with even minor crises is lost.

Only one in four social care recipients report that the social care they receive always supports their day-to-day living, whilst two in five say that their social care is so inadequate that it is never enough for day-to-day needs.[13] Half of recipients say that they need, but don't get, help with maintaining their physical health and a healthy diet. More than half of those needing social care don't get enough hours, and many with deteriorating conditions never get an increase in hours. Consequently, what looks like an acceptable maintenance in the status quo is actually a reduction in support relative to need.

The lack of social care leaves people isolated, and restricts some who would otherwise be capable of working from doing so.[14] Two-thirds of social care recipients say that care and support is very important if they are to be able to engage in work or training, including voluntary work. A lack of social care has led to people having to give up their jobs or education, as well as wider desires for community participation.

Edith is a chartered accountant who has MS, and needs assistance getting in and out of bed. Her care agency recently stopped delivering services to her, due to staff shortages. The local council is trying to find a replacement, but the only option she has been offered would make her life impossible: getting out of bed at 9:30am, half an hour after she is meant to start work; and going back to bed at 6:45pm, five minutes after she would get home from work. If no care is found, she'll have to go into a care home – or give up her job. As Frances Ryan, a disabled journalist, says:

> "Suggest that a non-disabled person live like this and there would rightly be outrage. And yet someone like Edith, with her whole life ahead of her, is expected to waste her days in bed or a care home. It's reminiscent of attitudes to disability that were said to have died out before Edith and I were even born: that people with disabilities are 'not normal,' and as such don't need a career, social life or family."[15]

There is a high turnover of care staff, meaning that care recipients constantly have to endure complete strangers coming in to assist with intimate activi-

12. SOCIAL CARE AND THE INDEPENDENT LIVING FUND

ties such as bathing and toileting. Recipients also have to spend more time explaining what needs to be done, which takes away from the already-limited time for actually doing the necessary tasks.

Social care recipients report going without washes, proper food or sleep, with knock-on consequences for health. One person explained how the cuts to social care mean that:

> "I'm getting more and more sores, yeast infections because I can't wash as regularly as I should be able to. And it's embarrassing, because I'm incontinent."

Another said:

> "I'm existing. I just survive. I'm lucky if I get two baths a week. I don't get hot food or drinks Monday to Thursday. I'm lucky if I manage to eat at all. I often don't get undressed and sleep in my clothes because it's easier. I sleep on a two seat sofa downstairs so that I will make it to the loo. My house is not wheelchair accessible so I often have to crawl to the loo. This is not a life."

This has poor consequences for health: more than one in six have missed crucial medical appointments, and one in four have needed hospital treatment due to inadequate social care.[14] Between 2010 and 2016, returns to hospital within a month of discharge increased by nearly 20%, due both to patients being discharged before they're ready (to make way for other patients) and to lack of support at home.[16] This included a 25% increase in readmissions within one day of discharge.

And whilst elderly hospital patients increasingly occupy hospital beds that they don't need because they lack social care at home, working-age disabled adults don't always even get to stay in hospital. One young woman, given an eviction notice from her care home just days after she made a complaint about physical abuse, ended up in hospital with blood poisoning – only to then find out that not only was she now evicted from the care home, but the hospital also was evicting her because she no longer had septicaemia.[17]

Cuts to social care and healthcare have been linked to an increase in mortality amongst older adults and babies.[18] Deaths from falls amongst the elderly increased by 107% between 2008 and 2016, even though the population over 85 increased by only 19% in that time. In 2015, infant mortality increased for the first time in ten years. Disinvestment leading to failures in both health and social care sectors was pinpointed as the most likely cause of the additional 30,000 deaths that occurred in 2015 compared to what was expected. And in the 2017/18 winter, the first six weeks of 2018 saw an additional 10,000 deaths compared to the average in the same period over the previous five years, despite being unusually mild.

The NHS, which has also been asked to make significant cuts to its expenditure (under the name of 'efficiency savings') has pointed out that its savings could only be made:

> "provided we take action on prevention, invest in new care models, sustain social care services, and over time see a bigger share of the efficiency coming from wider system improvements."[19]

This is not occurring. The cumulative impact of cuts to social care and to the NHS, as well as to extra-cost and out-of-work benefits, are substantial and will only increase the burden on the NHS and social care. By reducing the services available, individuals who could have maintained mild or moderate care needs had they been supported are likely to escalate to substantial or critical care needs, costing far more in the long-run than if preventative support had been available. This is not just an economic cost; it is a moral injustice, leaving people to suffer and deteriorate, excluded from society and unable to achieve a basic dignity and standard of life. As the charity Leonard Cheshire Disability said:

> "There are some things none of us should have to experience in modern Britain... We believe that being left trapped in your home for days on end without vital support and human contact, or forced to stay in bed until 11am and go back to bed at 8pm are among them. Many disabled people tell us this is a daily reality for them."[20]

The Independent Living Fund

In 2010, 1.7mn adults received social care, including 19,000 who received additional money through the Independent Living Fund (ILF). This latter fund was for people who had the most severe disabilities. It had been set up as a way to keep the most disabled people in their own communities by providing additional money on top of what the local government could afford

12. SOCIAL CARE AND THE INDEPENDENT LIVING FUND

in the way of social care. It was an independent discretionary trust funded by the DWP but managed by a separate board of trustees. The trust was set up in 1988, and in 2010 it supported around 19,000 people at a cost of £320mn.

The ILF was originally supposed to be a temporary measure whilst legislation was developed for community-based care and a review was undertaken into social security support for disabled people. That review led the way for the development of DLA to replace the inadequate Attendance and Mobility Allowances. The ILF also replaced a little-known fund, the Domestic Needs Allowance, which was never publicised and therefore claimed by very few people.

The ILF was due to be disbanded in 1993, but campaign work convinced politicians of its ongoing worth, and a new version of the fund was set up. The fund continued to be available only to the most needy: recipients had to be in receipt of the highest care component of DLA, receive social care services worth £340 per week and have savings of less than £23,250. However, this created some problems in poorer areas of the country, where councils were not able to afford to give people with high needs enough support for them to qualify for ILF funding. This meant that some severely disabled people in poorer areas lost out twice. Uptake of the ILF also depended upon the approach of the local council: councils that set out to help people claim ILF saw high claim volumes, whilst those that didn't provide support plateaued out at a relatively low level. Other problems occurred when there was conflict between a person's local council, the ILF and, if relevant, Access to Work about which body funded which particular bit of help.[21] And because the ILF was not a statutory body but a discretionary trust, recipients did not have statutory protection as they do under the Care Act 2014.

The Fund trustees had to ensure that their spending was compliant with the powers and obligations of the Trust Deed, and in particular that their spending stayed within each year's budget. As disability in the UK increased in absolute numbers, so the demands on the fund increased, and the Trustees had to limit new claims in order to keep within the fund obligations. From 2008 the trustees became increasingly restrictive in whom they would support, focusing primarily on the two priority areas of existing recipients and people in at least 16 hours of work a week. But in 2010, the year's budget had all been allocated by June, and the trustees had to close the fund to new applicants until 2011. Before it could reopen, the 2010 Coalition Government undertook a review of the fund and found it to be unsustainable as it was. Rather than increasing the funding, they closed it permanently to new applicants, although existing recipients continued to receive ILF whilst the government determined what to replace it with.

The government decided that the ILF would be closed completely from 2015, and the funding given to local authorities. The closure of the Independent Living Fund, which attracted much criticism from disabled people at the time, was done in order that the money could be released to local authorities and distributed by them in accordance with local need. The government claimed that this resulted in a fairer system for people who previously had not had access to the monies in the ILF, particularly because the ILF had been closed to new users.

Consultation respondents asked that the money be ring-fenced so that it could only be spent on social care, and in particular on ILF recipients, but the government's position on ring-fencing was that it prevents local authorities from meeting local statutory needs in a flexible and responsive way.[22] They preferred to leave spending choices up to the local authority, even though local government was already severely constrained by a 40% cut in the funding it received from central government. In contrast, a major benefit of the Independent Living Fund was that it was centralised: if a person moved house, their budget came with them without them needing a reassessment or risking losing out under a postcode lottery.

The closure of the ILF has exacerbated the lack of funding for social care. In some areas, over half of previous ILF recipients have lost care hours, even though their needs have not changed.[23] This varies by local council, making the receipt of social care even more arbitrary, even though an individual's care needs do not vary depending upon where they live. Some people have had to move into residential care because they could no longer get the social care that they needed at home. Because councils already require sick and disabled people to contribute money towards their care, including PIP, people who lose some of their social care generally can't get round it by paying for private top-ups. Disabled people report that they feel that they are being treated "worse than a dog" because "at least dogs get taken for a walk every day."[24]

Ongoing institutions

The closure of large institutions from the 1960s sadly did not result in a citizenship-based model of support. Disabled people were primarily moved from large (NHS) institutions to small (local authority) ones, which still failed to meet the goal of equal living in the community. Many of those who needed the most support were simply transferred straight to private hospitals, without the opportunity to try community living. For the rest, the under-funding of local authorities, combined with the lack of a national social-care service, meant that even the poor standards of the NHS institutions were difficult to maintain when passed on to local authorities.

Instead of the personalised support that can work so well, what many sick and disabled people experience is that support remains paternalistic and imposed from above; sick and disabled people are told what is good for them and are expected to be content with that. Disagreement, particularly by people with learning disabilities, mental illness or autism spectrum disorders, can be written off as challenging behaviour.[25] Such a label implies that the person has a behavioural disorder, thus pathologising them; and rests upon an assumption that the person is too immature or ignorant to know what is best for themselves or to understand the good that is being shown them, thus infantilising them. In contrast, a personalised support approach encourages professionals to view the individual as an equal; as someone who is expert by experience rather than qualification.

Families report that, instead of early support to get them through problems or crises, too often their disabled family member is placed in a group home or school. With the disruption of normal routine and family life combined with institutional inflexibility, problems could escalate. The disabled person may feel ignored, imposed upon and even bullied; the care provider sees someone who is ungrateful, uncooperative and unnecessarily difficult. The disabled person is frustrated, bored and lonely; the staff can only tell them to accept what they get. When a person is faced with such unsympathetic bureaucracy and rigidity of thought we should neither be surprised if they get upset nor use it as a reason to remove even more independence from them. Instead, it should be taken as an indicator of a break-down in support from the provider's side.

When the local authority group-based care struggles to support a disabled person, many end up further pathologised as they are sectioned under the Mental Health Act. Local authorities have no financial reason to challenge this, because such pathologisation of normal fears and frustrations means that the cost of care is transferred to the local NHS. In such places, their care moves from being funded by the local authority to being funded by the local NHS Clinical Commissioning Group.

The Assessment and Treatment Units to which people with challenging behaviour are transferred are supposed to be just that: places for assessment and treatment, in order to discharge people back into community within 18 months. But instead the average duration spent in an ATU is 5.5 years.[26] Residents can expect some form of restraint on a monthly basis, whether sedation, seclusion or face-down prone restraint. Sir Stephen Bubb, the lead author on two reports into the government's progress on closing ATUs since the Winterbourne View scandal of 2015, says:

> "There are deaths of people in these institutions, some of them unexplained. We know there are significant problems and there will be at some stage another scandal, and yet we know what we need to do. The idea that in the 21st century you lock people up, you restrain them, you use prone restraint, you hold them down, I think is disgusting, it is barbaric and it is unacceptable, and it needs to be made unlawful."[27]

Beth, who has autism and severe anxiety, has been kept in a seclusion room since the start of 2017; she spends more than 23 hours of each day in that room, and has not been outside since January 2018.[28] She has food delivered through a hatch; the same hatch at which her father has to kneel to see her. She is just 17 years old, and she has nothing to do. She isn't even in seclusion because of her own needs, but because the hospital where she is kept doesn't have enough staff. She has developed diabetes; she self-harms and has started talking to imaginary friends. She could be supported to live in the community at far lower cost than the current £13,000 per week, but that would mean a transfer from the NHS – which has that sort of money – to the local council – which doesn't.

If at any point a person is deemed to need higher levels of security, then their support funding moves to NHS England. The person is often transferred even further away from their home and family. Some of these hospitals, such as Winterbourne View, have been the subject of substantial criticism for their abusive practices, yet distressingly the families affected reported that Winterbourne View was still one of the least bad services they had received.[29]

Because of a failure to support families when or before a crisis occurs, disabled individuals get shunted into a system of increasing institutionalisation, at increasing cost, increasing distance from home and increasingly inhumane treatment. Because the funding switches from council to NHS and local to national NHS, there is no incentive for lower-level care providers to prevent escalation. Yet if the funding had been available to support disabled people and their families right from the start, families would not have been stretched past breaking point; disabled people would not have their independence and control taken away from them; and the financial cost of support wouldn't reach six figure levels per person per year. Thus the lack of competent personalised support in the community leads to a process of increasing inflexibility and institutionalisation which only serves to further exclude vulnerable people from society.

> **Box 10. On-going institutionalisation**
>
> **3,500** learning disabled people still live in institutions, run or funded by the NHS.
>
> More than **3,300** working-age disabled adults live in care homes for the elderly.
>
> In March 2015, there were **2,395** people in ATUs. In September 2018, it was **2,315**. The number of children in ATUs has increased from **110** to **230**.

It is frustrating for disabled people to know how they want their life to be and what support is needed to get there, but to be faced with professional systems that do not seem to allow their staff to listen or make discretionary choices. People who have been considered to have challenging behaviour can successfully and safely live in the community, if they are listened to and given the support that is relevant to their needs, abilities and interests. People who are happy, secure and content tend not to lash out from fear or anger, and do not need physical or pharmaceutical restraint. People who have been assessed as always needing 24-hour care due to their behaviour can, with the right support, live on their own in their own homes, have their own social and community life, and successfully go out to work without ever showing any signs of their allegedly unalterable challenging behaviour, as these stories show:[30]

> *"Edward, who had been living in residential care for many years, with at times very challenging behaviours, was supported to move for the first time into his own home. We bought a 2-bed bungalow in a location and context ideally suited to his needs. We recognised his anxiety levels would be significantly increased by these changes. So we selected a team of 5 workers, all of whom had known him well for over 10 years, to support him and ensure that he was with people he trusted and was familiar with. His*

challenging behaviour has since diminished considerably. In the past his behaviours meant that he only left the care home once a fortnight. Now he goes out most days, sometimes by bus and attends a gym and work activity on a weekly basis. He is clearly more secure, confident and flexible."

"Mark came to us from a traditional service and he had a reputation for challenging behaviours. We were told by the commissioner that he required close supervision and 1:1 support in his previous day service. In a short time we were able to ascertain he liked cars by the fact that he spent a lot of time around staff's vehicles. We found him a role in a local car yard where he worked alongside other staff maintaining the cars in the yard. Mark was supported to develop roles he valued and skills that enhanced his sense of self and confidence. Staff at the yard were supported to understand how to support him, which led to the development of friendships and relationships. Within 6 months, he did not require staff support at all and he worked there for many years with no sign of the 'challenging behaviours' we were warned about."

Contrast this with Isabelle and Ian's experiences. Isabelle's parents had always felt that something was different with their daughter, but it wasn't until she reached GCSE age that they found out what: she had Asperger's Syndrome. Isabelle was being bullied at school and needed extra tuition, which, following her diagnosis, social services were willing to provide through group evening classes. But her difficulties at school, family problems at the time and the impact of years of undiagnosed Asperger's resulted in a mental breakdown. Isabelle was sectioned for most of a year, during which time she went through periods of hyper-mania, extreme depression, hallucinations and confusion.

Whilst still legally a child, Isabelle's Asperger's diagnosis helped her to get access to additional education and social activities. But as an adult, that attention and support disappeared. The residential homes which Isabelle has lived in since adulthood have not provided the social interaction and meaningful activity which Isabelle, like anyone, craves. They are also many miles away from her family. Isabelle is aware of her social difficulties, but this only adds to her frustration that she cannot seek a career, live by herself or even make friends. This frustration coupled with her reduced social awareness can lead to complex and challenging behaviour, which over time has deteriorated and, as her brother describes it, has almost become more autistic.

12. SOCIAL CARE AND THE INDEPENDENT LIVING FUND

In her current home, Isabelle has not received any care beyond the basics of food, cleanliness and so on. Her brother, Ian, considers that the disinterest of the residential staff in Isabelle's social and intellectual needs has contributed to her unhappiness, frustration and autistic behaviour. With nothing to do, Isabelle has retreated into her room, away from the other residents. Ian has described how Isabelle has retreated into herself just as she has retreated into her room, because those caring for her do not go beyond her physical care.

Ian used to work in a college for autistic adults before it was turned into a day centre. Many of the teaching staff were made redundant and invited to reapply for their jobs but with a 30% salary cut. This led to a whole team of new staff who, although having good intentions, were nowhere near as qualified or even interested as the previous staff members. Lessons soon became little more than holding activities and many service users started to regress rather than improve.

The area manager who had made this decision had previously been the manager of a dog food factory and was hired for his financial abilities rather than any empathy with autism. The few times that Ian met the new manager, he found the manager to be patronising and apathetic towards the service users. Profit was being put before people, and the consequences were appalling. Without denying the importance of finance, the quality of life for service users is of paramount importance and should be the first priority in the provision of care.

For those living in residential settings, their basic rights are substantially lower than those enjoyed by people living in their own home. People living in residential homes receive care and support as part of a package: if they leave, their care necessarily changes; if they stay, they can't change their care. There is no choice or control over who provides what support or when. Legislation requires that the person be neither a tenant nor an owner occupier, and consequently they don't have the rights or personal control of either. They can be moved to a different bedroom and restricted from certain areas; they have no choice over who else is resident there; they can't insist on more suitable or better quality furnishings, and nor do they even have the right to bring their own. One person reported that:[31]

> "Although I am in a care home, I receive no attention other than being washed and dressed. I am left to walk myself to the toilet even though I've had falls in this care home before. I have food put in front of me that I

can't see, can't cut, and can't balance on cutlery. Staff take it away again saying: "Oh you must not be hungry today." I prefer a sandwich, but even though my family have specified this, I'm served a hot meal that I can't be independent with, and give up after struggling with a couple of mouthfuls."

Another, Glyn, explained how:[32]

"My wife Kristin was diagnosed with Relapsing Remitting MS 16 years ago and has had Secondary Progressive MS for four or five years now. She is also a type 1 diabetic and is on a diabetic pump...

"Because the care home she's now in has limited staff she's sometimes left in bed until after 11am. Sometimes she's left on her own, and if her catheter bypasses she's left sitting in wet. Because of limited staff they frequently have to rely on agency nurses who've got no idea how to use Kristin's pump and/or insulin. She once ate dinner at 7pm the night before, they forgot her breakfast and then the lunch feed was late so it was 1.45pm the next day before she got anything to eat.

"I'm completely falling apart - I check and double check everything that's done."

Personalised care

The best social care is personalised care which meets five principles: it supports people to play a full part in their community; it is organised around the needs and capabilities of the person receiving social care; it considers the care recipient to be an equal partner in determining what support is provided and how, with the providers being accountable to the receiver; it is based on long-term relationships, where the staff do not turnover very often, and providers do not pass the receiver on to someone else during more difficult times; and support is sourced in a way that utilises the resources of the local community.

Simon Brisenden explained that:

"We need to be clear what we mean by independence. We are not talking about being able to do everything for yourself. Neither does it imply cutting oneself off from the assistance of others. For what matters is not whether you do something with or without the help of others, but that it gets done under your direction. Being independent simply means that you have some control over your life, and that you do not live by the routine of others...

12. SOCIAL CARE AND THE INDEPENDENT LIVING FUND

> *"Independent living is used in a practical and common sense way to simply mean being able to achieve our goals. The point is that independent people have control over their lives, not that they perform every task themselves. Independence is not linked to the physical or intellectual capacity to care for oneself without assistance; independence is created by having assistance when and how one requires it."*[33]

The UK Government has argued that it wants to increased disabled people's independence by reducing their dependence upon formal, state-provided care.[34] But independence is not about whether the support a person receives is self-support, informal support from friends or family or formal support from the state. Independence is about having control over what support is provided, when, how and by whom. When assistance from another person is necessary, reducing state support does not make the person more independent, but less so. Formal state support is provided as of right by people who are paid to provide support. Informal support, on the other hand, relies upon the good will and availability of people who may well have their own jobs to go to, lives to live and health needs to take care of. By reducing social care, the UK has made disabled people more dependent, not less so.

Although there was considerable drive in the 1960-80s from disabled people for greater inclusion and citizenship, some campaigners feel that there has been a loss of momentum, power and passion in more recent years. Initial goals of disability rights have given way to political processes that favour efficiency, best value (usually lowest cost) and the perception of choice over a more basic and objective consideration of access to human rights. Much of the best practice that is available is seen in small, locally-focused groups driven and led by personal or family need, but these messages aren't getting back to those in charge of the money and decision making. The large-scale market-driven providers which the government currently favours rarely show the values-driven support that is found in small-scale, community-driven organisations. This system has been eloquently described:

> *"[sick and disabled people] were in trouble if they didn't like the services commissioned on the basis of block-contracts. Even when individual care packages became the norm, [it was] not an easy process to change these as people's lives unfolded, and it was remarkable how similar one care package was to another. It was like having a personal shopper whose*

boss had already signed contracts with the stores they liked best and had negotiated Groupon type deals that stipulated things like 'only applies to X range' and 'not redeemable on weekends'."[35]

Currently, the funding that is available through social care does not provide the kind of flexibility that sick and disabled people need and want. Although some (usually physically) disabled people receive money directly to spend on purchasing their own social care services, rather than the direct provision of services, this is not the same as disabled people being able to personalise their care and share in the decision making. Instead what happens is that disabled people are required to use the money they receive to directly employ their own support team, whilst the nature of the support they can purchase is strictly specified.

Councils have sought to reduce their costs by pushing the cost of managing employees onto disabled people themselves – a skill set which few disabled people have, and a burden that they do not want. The extra time and effort required to manage one's own staff often detracts from the opportunity to engage in family, social or work life. At the same time, the control of being an employer in this way does not come with an equal control over what sick and disabled people want to control – where, when, how and on what they spend the money that they are given for their care needs. This results in an all-or-nothing choice, which leaves many people having to choose between the challenges of being an employer (in order to get some level of control) or having no control at all.

Yet it is quite possible to provide true personalised care. There are examples across the country of organisations set up to serve sick and disabled people, often on a small and local scale and in response to a personal need. These organisations, by listening and giving control of services to disabled people, come up with ways of providing support that actually work. Places like Bradford and Dorset have restructured their commissioning process in a way that now allows disabled people to design their own support framework and choose their own support worker. The service providers retain control of the management costs, lifting this onerous burden from disabled people who neither need nor want to be direct employers. Creativity and flexibility is encouraged, rather than being prevented by the use of fixed support plans and hours-based contracting.

To spread such successful services across the country requires a change in political thought. Politicians must reconsider the principle of subsidiarity –

who has the right to make what decisions. Should support be provided by the state in a constrained manner, akin to having a voucher for a pick 'n' mix machine which contains only six varieties of sweets? Or should it be more like giving someone the money they need and the freedom and support to choose where and how they spend it? It is these latter systems that see people who have previously been labelled as challenging and expected to live in private hospitals for the rest of their life instead live freely in the open community, engaging in their local social life and going out to work.

Social care now and in the future

The UK has never fully got rid of its old institutional model of care for disabled people. The consequence is that many disabled people still live in institutions, typically in smaller groups than in previous decades but with a substantial minority, often the most vulnerable, held in private hospitals that have been the subject of major abuse scandals. Disabled people are often viewed as unable to make the best judgments as to their own needs and abilities, and are expected to always be grateful for the support they do get, even when it isn't what they want and poorly matches what they need. The support that is there, whether at home or in a residential home or in a hospital, is inadequate and leaves disabled people who need social care with little to no independence, and often no quality of life either.

Care for disabled people does not have to be provided in this way. There are many success stories where service providers have listened to disabled people and then provided the type and level of support that is actually wanted. Often, once the time and effort has been put in, and there is a commitment to genuine long-term, stable care, it turns out to be cheaper than the harried, high-turnover support that disabled people currently suffer. The result of these appropriate forms of care is that many people who previously were labelled as unable to ever live in normal society now live in their own homes, socialise with their own friends and family, and take part in voluntary, community and paid work. Disabled people should be enabled to fulfil their basic rights, rather than treated as stock to be managed as cheaply as possible. The transformation when disabled people are listened to rather than frustrated and abandoned is both a reason to celebrate and a cause of shame, that when alternatives exist the vast majority of disabled people are still viewed and treated as second-class people.

NOTES FOR CHAPTER 12

1. **Smith NA, Phillips D, Simpson P, Eiser D and Trickey M** (2018) A time of revolution? British local government finances in the 2010s. LONDON: INSTITUTE FOR FISCAL STUDIES

2. **The King's Fund** (2015) The King's Fund verdict: how serious are the pressures on social care? LONDON. **Butler P** (12/06/2018) Adult social care services on brink of collapse, survey shows. LONDON: THE GUARDIAN.
Local Government Association (LGA) (2016) Adult social care funding: 2016 state of the nation report. LONDON.
NHS Information Centre (2009-18) NHS and Adult Social Care Data: Community Care Statistics: Social Services Activity.

3. **Porter G as quoted in Sharman L** (26/11/2015) Spending Review: Warning that councils at financial tipping point. LONDON: LOCAL GOVERNMENT ASSOCIATION

4. **Written evidence from the Local Government Association and the Association of Directors of Adult Social Services** (PEX 22) to the Health Select Committee

5. **Committee of Public Accounts** (2017) Integrating health and social care. LONDON

6. **LGA** (n 2)

7. **Butler P** (27/06/2018) English councils warn 'worst is yet to come' on cuts. THE GUARDIAN

8. **Maguire P** (05/02/2017) System is 'close to failure' as PM's council raises tax for social care. LONDON: THE GUARDIAN

9. **Butler P** (12/06/2018) Adult social care services on brink of collapse, survey shows. LONDON: THE GUARDIAN

10. **Merton Centre for Independent Living** (2018) Choice control and independent living: putting the Care Act into practice. Merton. MERTON COUNCIL GENERAL FUND REVENUE BUDGET AND COUNCIL TAX STRATEGY

11. **Pring J** (22/09/2016) Council 'pays Capita to cut care packages'. DISABILITY NEWS SERVICE

12. **Lloyds Bank Foundation and New Policy Institute** (2018) A quiet crisis: local government spending on disadvantage in England LONDON

13. **Grayston R** (2015) Disabled people's experience of social care: findings from the Better Care Project 2014-15. LONDON: SCOPE

14. **Care and Support Alliance** (2018) Voices from the social care crisis: an opportunity to end a broken system once and for all.

15. **Ryan F** (10/05/2018) Now disabled people face a kind of internment. Just ask Edith. LONDON: THE GUARDIAN

16. **Grayston** (n 13)

17. **CSA** (n14)

18. **Morris J** (2018) Emergency readmissions: Trends in emergency readmissions to hospital in England. LONDON: THE NUFFIELD TRUST AND THE HEALTH FOUNDATION

19. **Pring J** (14/06/2018) Young woman evicted from care home while critically ill in hospital. DISABILITY NEWS SERVICE

20. **Green MA, Dorling D, Minton J and Pickett KE** (2017) Could the rise in mortality rates since 2015 be explained by changes in the number of delayed discharges of NHS patients?

12. SOCIAL CARE AND THE INDEPENDENT LIVING FUND

British Medical Journal Journal of Epidemiology and Community Health Vol 71 Iss. 11 DOI:101136/jech-2017-209403.
Campbell D (07/04/2018) More elderly are dying after falls as care crisis deepens. **London: The Guardian.** Taylor-Robinson DC, Bradshaw J, Wolfe I, Weeks A, Barr B and Whitehead M (2018) Death rate continues to rise for poorest infants in England and Wales. **British Medical Journal.**
Hiam L and Dorling D (2018) Rise in mortality in England and Wales in first seven weeks of 2018. British Medical Journal 360:k1090 DOI: 101136/bmjk1090

21. **NHS** (2014) Five year forward view
22. **Leonard Cheshire Disability** (2016) The state of social care in Great Britain in 2016: our call for urgent action on social care London
23. **Watch L** 2015 In celebration of the closure of the Independent Living Fund Disability and Society Vol 30 Iss. 9, pp. 1434-1438 DOI: 101080/0968759920151091150
24. **Freud D** (23/06/2014) Hansard House of Lords cWA126
25. **Ekklesia** (03/07/2018) 'Postcode lottery' for disabled people since Independent Living Fund abolished. London
26. **Inclusion London** (2016) One year on: evaluating the impact of the closure of the Independent Living Fund London
27. **Duffy S and Sly S** (2017) Progress on personalised support: results of an international survey by Citizen Network Sheffield: Centre for Welfare Reform
28. **Kelso P** (2018) 40 people died in 'barbaric' secure hospitals the government pledged would close. London: Sky News
29. **Bubb S as cited by Kelso (n 26)**
30. **Birrell I** (07/10/2018) A teen with autism is locked in solitary confinement and being fed through a hatch. Have we really moved on from Bedlam? London: iNews
31. **Duffy S** (2013) Returning Home: piloting personalised support. Sheffield: Centre for Welfare Reform.
32. **Duffy and Sly** (n 25)
33. **CSA** (n14)
34. **CSA** (n14)
35. **Simon Brisenden** (1989) Charter for personal care. Disablement Income Group
36. **Committee on the Rights of Persons with Disabilities** (2016) pg14. Inquiry concerning the United Kingdom of Great Britain and Northern Ireland carried out by the Committee under article 6 of the Optional Protocol to the Convention: Report of the Committee. United Nations CRPD/C/15/R.2/Rev.1
37. **Squire A and Richmond P** (2017) No place like home: The economics of independent living. Sheffield: Centre for Welfare Reform

13

General benefits

So far we have looked at three key ways through which governments may support sick and disabled citizens to live full, equal lives: sickness benefits, extra-cost benefits and social care. But sick and disabled people don't only claim disability-related benefits. Many also need the other benefits which people on low incomes claim. These include child benefit, housing benefits, council tax benefits and the new Universal Credit. These have all been included in the post-2010 Governments' cuts to welfare. The government says that it has protected disabled people from welfare cuts, but even if the various disability benefits had been protected, this claim wouldn't be true.

In this chapter we look at these other benefits and consider how cuts to these benefits have impacted sick and disabled people.

Housing the poor

Lucy used to live in a two bed flat in Camden, near to the vitally important specialist hospital that she visited almost weekly, and keeping the second bedroom for her overnight carers and the storage of the many bandages she needed to control and care for her skin condition.[1] Her condition, epidermolysis bullosa, meant that her skin separated from the underlying tissues and caused widespread blisters and significant pain. Internal tissues would also blister, leaving the equivalent of third-degree burns. Her family could only touch her, to give her a hug or to hold her hand, after hours had been put into carefully wrapping Lucy up in protective bandages. She had to eat 4,000-5,000 calories a day to match the energy her body put into repairing itself, but food could rip her throat.

13. GENERAL BENEFITS

Lucy was already making up £90 per week for her rent because the maximum housing benefit she was allowed was too low. Labour had introduced a rule in 2008 which limited private tenants' housing benefit to the price of the middle-most property for a given area and their qualifying property size. A couple or individual over 25 got housing benefit based on the market rent of one bed properties, whilst those under 25 were limited to the price of a room in a shared property. Disabled individuals like Lucy, who received a care award of DLA, could get housing benefit up to the limit for a one bed property. But there was no recognition that Lucy needed a two bed property.

A tribunal ruling in 2011 meant that Lucy became eligible not just for the one bed rate, but for the two bed rate because she needed a second bedroom for an overnight carer. But the 2010 Coalition Government had already reduced the limit on housing benefit from the cost of a property at the 50th percentile down to one at the 30th percentile. The drop from the 50th to the 30th percentile was so large that, even though Lucy was now eligible for a larger property, she was left even worse off. The 30th percentile for a two bed flat was less than the 50th percentile for a one bed, and Lucy lost a further £60 per week.

Through the intervention of a housing charity and her MP, Lucy was eventually found a one bed property in King's Cross – affordable, but now her carers had to sleep in the lounge and there was nowhere to store the dressings she had to buy to manage her medical condition. Lucy's health had deteriorated with the stress and financial poverty and she did not pick up again. Two years later, in January 2015, she died.

The government's position on housing benefit is that the changes were made in order to restore a fair balance between taxpayers and benefit recipients, so that those paying tax are not excessively subsidising the lives of those who claim benefits. The reduction in benefit paid to people in the private rental sector, which meant that they were limited to the price of the bottom 30% of the rental market (down from 50%), was designed both to re-establish fairness between taxpayers and benefit recipients, and to encourage landlords to charge lower rents and thereby reduce the excesses in the housing market.

But landlords were already reluctant to let to benefit recipients before 2010. Prior to 2008, a landlord could make it a condition of tenancy that the recipient arranged for Housing Benefit to be paid directly to the landlord. From 2008 the introduction of the Local Housing Allowance (LHA) restricted the level of housing benefit that could be paid (to the bottom half of the market), and also changed the payment of benefit so that it went directly to the recipient rather than to the landlord. There was concern from landlords, benefit recipients and welfare agencies alike that individuals in need of housing benefit may struggle to keep up with their rent payments, because other urgent needs – food, heating, electricity – might crop up first.

The LHA was introduced at time when the housing bubble meant that many people were priced out of home ownership and therefore dependent on private rent. This meant that there was high competition for private tenancies, and landlords could refuse to let to benefit recipients without risking an empty property; there was always a non-claimant ready to take the property. Consequently, benefit recipients were finding it increasingly difficult to find a property to rent – not only did it have to be in the bottom 50% in terms of price, but it was also necessary to find a landlord who was willing to rent to LHA recipients in the first place.

> **Box 11. Failing housing policy**
>
> **29%** of the population claims housing benefit.
>
> **28%** of properties in the private rental sector are inadequate.
>
> Housing benefit for private sector tenants covers less than the bottom **30%** of the private rental market.
>
> By 2020, housing benefit for a two bed property won't cover the rent for a property at the 25th percentile (bottom quarter of houses) in **83%** of areas.
>
> Only **20%** of landlords are willing to rent to benefit recipients.

The post-2010 governments then made a series of change that reduced housing benefit relative to the rental market. The most significant was to change the cap on benefit from a price equivalent to the middle of the housing market (for a given area and house size) to the price of the bottom 30% of the market. In comparison, whilst not everyone who qualifies for housing benefit actually claims it, 29% of the population does claim housing benefit. In some areas, more than 30% of people are in receipt of housing benefit; all of these, plus poor people who are eligible but not claiming, or people who are just over the threshold but still struggling, are competing for the same 30% of properties. It is inevitable that some people on benefits will be unable to cover their rent using just their housing benefit.

The government then changed the rules on up-rating housing benefit. Where previously it rose in line with house prices, so that it always stayed at the same percentile level, the benefit now only rises in line with Consumer Price Index (CPI). CPI is a measure of inflation which explicitly excludes rises in house prices, which (in the UK's dysfunctional housing market) tend to rise faster than any other goods or services. CPI therefore underestimates the cost of increases in rent, meaning that year-on-year housing benefit will fall behind even the 30th percentile. For example, in the ten years from 1997 to 2007, private rents increased by 70% whilst CPI increased by 20%.

This has since been exacerbated by two further changes: in 2014 and 2015, the government decided that housing benefit was to rise by only 1%, rather than the 2.2% of CPI; and the benefit is not being increased at all between 2016 and 2020. Since April 2011, rents have increased on average by 6.8%, whilst housing benefit has increased by 3.22% – less than half of the actual increase in rental prices.

> **Box 12. Austerity's impact on housing**
>
> **4.5 million households** live in the private rental sector.
>
> 78% of the increase in homelessness since 2011 is because of households losing their private sector tenancy.
>
> **14,420 households** were accepted as homeless between Oct and Dec 2016, up 50% from the same period in 2009.
>
> In Dec 2016, **76,000 households** were living in temporary accommodation, of which **60,000** included children or pregnant mothers.
>
> In May 2018, ¼ of the 79,000 households in temporary accommodation were being paid for through exorbitant 'by the night' lettings. This form of letting has grown by 500% since 2009.
>
> Over **80% of local authorities** have found it difficult to meet their statutory duties to homelessness applicants.
>
> The primary cause of increased demand in the private rental sector is the increasing inability of people to afford a mortgage.

In some areas of London, housing benefit now only covers the rent for the lowest 10% of properties (i.e., 9 in 10 properties cost more than the LHA will cover) and fewer than 1 in 20 of the homes on the market at any one time are affordable, available and decent.[2] 28% of houses in the private sector are 'non-decent'; this includes 9% with damp problems, 16% without central heating and 25% with a band E-G energy efficiency rating, as well as properties in a poor state of repair, all of which place further costs on those tenants who are the least able to afford them.[3] The absolute number of bad private rental properties is also on the increase. Tenants have been forced to compromise on quality, including renting from rogue landlords, living in overcrowded conditions and negotiating lower rent in return for living in non-decent conditions. It is believed that over 2mn people live in houses that actively damage their health.[4]

Tenants report that:[5]

> "The money that we get, the bills comes out of that and we don't have a lot for food. So we both go on sort of like days... weeks where we don't get enough food in for ourselves... We've lived on, and that's the honest truth, at Christmas, we've lived on just tins of soup."

Another explained how:

> "...I got pneumonia twice. I was in hospital for ten days once... I was really ill... because I hadn't put my heating on... when I contract pneumonia it seems to be round about the cold weather, and obviously if you haven't got much money and the bills are high anyway you tend to not put the heating on... I have to reduce me energy bills... I find I do spend a lot of time in bed... if you're asleep, one, you're not using the water, two, you're not using the electricity, you're not using the gas, and then I'm not eating the food that is there."

Shelter reported that claimants are cutting back on essentials, asking for discretionary, temporary help from councils (although government funding for this has been reduced), and borrowing from family and friends to make up the shortfall. Four in ten are falling into rent arrears. Renters are choosing not to report rogue landlords because they cannot risk being evicted. Few move homes, as there is rarely an affordable home to move to.

13. GENERAL BENEFITS

They cannot leave their local area or home because if they do so without finding somewhere to live then they will be classed as intentionally homeless (so the council has no duty to provide a home) and ineligible for many social tenancies which require a connection to the area of several years' standing. Many cannot follow the DWP's solution of moving into work, because they are either already in work or are unable to work due to illness or caring duties. Of those that are seeking work, the inability to move to new areas or to more expensive areas constrains the ability to actually get work by blocking people from living where the jobs are.

Some landlords have reduced rents in order to retain good tenants, or because of the difficulty in chasing the shortfall from individuals who cannot afford it, but this is not viable for all landlords. Instead, 90% of the shortfall created by reductions in housing benefit have been absorbed by tenants reducing spending on non-housing costs, rather than landlords lowering rent.[6] For most landlords, rent at the LHA rate does not cover their costs.[7] The proportion of landlords letting to housing benefit recipients has fallen from 48% in 2010 to 18% in 2016.[8] Shelter predicts that by 2020, housing benefit will be below the bottom 25% of the market in 83% of areas, and households will have lost an average of £50 per week from their housing benefit.[9]

Homelessness has increased as landlords have become less likely to renew or extend Assured Shorthold Tenancies (ASTs) once the initial fixed period has come to an end.[10] People who previously would not have been at risk of homelessness can now find themselves without a home. The end of ASTs is now the biggest single cause of homelessness in the UK, increasing from one in ten in 2009/10 to one in three in 2016/17, as households forced to leave their rented property are unable to find alternative properties. More than a million families may be evicted from their privately rented homes by 2020 because of the increasing gap between rent and housing benefit. This includes over 200,000 households containing one or more disabled people.

Statutory homelessness is up 10% from the same quarter in 2015, and the number of households in temporary accommodation in 2018 was up 60% since its low in 2010. Such accommodation is typically overcrowded and in a state of disrepair with infestations of pests and poor safety standards. Access to cooking facilities is frequently poor, living space is overcrowded, and there are often restrictions on normal life such as having visitors. Because of the housing crisis, 25% of people live in temporary accommodation for more than a year; far longer than the statutory maximum of six weeks.

The Guardian reported in May 2018 that many landlords are making large sums of money by charging councils for temporary, one-night-at-a-time accommodation.[11] Landlords may charge as much as £70 per night for accommodation that is cold, damp and mouldy; infested with cockroaches, mice or other pests; and cladded in a flammable aluminium composite. Caretakers run out of prepaid electricity cards and aren't available at weekends anyway. Shabana, who lives in one of these flats with her husband and children, said:

> "Everything smells of mould and damp. It goes down our noses and mouths. My son has asthma now and I've developed osteoarthritis. It is horrible. It was meant to be temporary but we've been here four years."

The flat is so cold that £100 per week on prepaid cards for electric heaters isn't enough to make it warm.

Councils agreed these lets in an attempt to stop prices climbing inexorably upward, as overstretched councils competed against one another to secure beds for the statutorily homeless people for whom they had responsibility. It isn't their fault that there is a gross undersupply of housing.

Increasingly, people living in temporary accommodation are not even given places near to their jobs or their children's schools. In 2017/18, 1,200 Birmingham families were placed in temporary accommodation outside of Birmingham – up from just 81 in 2013/14.[12] This is hugely disruptive of education, work and social activity. Families are taken from their existing networks, and can't properly settle in new schools, jobs or social networks when they will at some point be returned to their previous home area.

Councils are struggling to find both temporary and permanent accommodation as a consequence of both inadequate supply relative to demand, and the cuts to housing benefit which mean that even the available accommodation is too expensive. Councils are struggling to place households into social housing, due to the lack of homes, and many are instead paying inflated sums to keep people in temporary accommodation in ex-social housing that has since become private rent.[13]

Sir Steve Bullock, an executive member for housing at the umbrella London Councils group, said that:

> "As the London housing crisis has deepened we have seen the boroughs increasingly relying on the private rental sector to meet the rising demand

13. GENERAL BENEFITS

for temporary accommodation including ex-council units. The sad irony is that without the Right to Buy the crisis might have been less dramatic and the units maintained in better condition not to mention lower rents."

And Ahmet Oykener, Enfield council's cabinet member for housing and regeneration, said that:

"Without this [Right to Buy] policy we would have more than 20,000 properties, and if we had 20,000 properties we would have no housing crisis in Enfield and we would be able to house homeless households."

Just like in the Thatcher years, Right to Buy is resulting in poor social tenants subsidising better-off tenants in their desire for home ownership.

In 2018 there were 1.2mn people waiting for a social house, but the true figure is nearer 1.5mn.[14] New rules introduced in 2011 allowed councils to refuse people who have not lived (or sometimes worked) in that area for a long enough period. With typical requirements of two-five years, people who had left one area – perhaps for work, or to find a cheaper property, or because of needing better disability access – and entered another could find themselves debarred from any council waiting list. A similar number of housing benefit recipients are trapped in unaffordable private rent. But fewer than 6,500 new social homes were built in 2018, and only 290,000 became available for new tenants.[15] Only one in three households waiting for a social house get one within a year, whilst one in four wait for over five years.

Freddy, a commercial engineer from West London, explains the impact that these waiting times and location rules have had:[16]

"I grew up here, went to school here, worked here. I have been on the waiting list for a solid 18 years. I've been homeless, private renting, or sofa surfing all that time.

"Not having a settled place makes it hard to do anything, even getting letters delivered so you can get accepted for doctors is hard. I'm in my mid-50s, and at this age I should be looking after my family and relaxing in the job that I've been doing for a long time, but I can't do any of that until I get my own place."

Shelter estimates that there are 1.3mn privately-renting households which, after housing costs, do not have enough money to meet the minimum income standard.[17] Seven in ten private renters do not meet the Living Homes Standard, which is the public's definition of what makes a good home.[18] Most of these people are in work, and form part of the low-pay, low-skill sector. Such people typically are unable to lay any money aside to save for a deposit on a lower-rent property or manage financial shocks. Amongst low-earning private renters, one in three have had to borrow to cover their rent in the previous year.

For these people to be able to live well, and not struggle to scrape enough money together to pay the rent each month, they need genuinely affordable rent. But when the government talks about providing more affordable homes, it doesn't mean what a reasonable person might expect it to mean: something based on what is a reasonable proportion of income to spend on rent, and what that looks like in a given area. Instead, it is defined as 80% of what a landlord would expect to get. If a landlord expects the median rent, then 'affordable' would mean properties at the 40th percentile – when housing benefit in many areas doesn't reach the 25th percentile. It is just another government misnomer to mask the inadequacy of its provision. Shelter recommends instead that affordable, or living, rents should be no more than 1/3rd of the average low-earner's take-home pay in a given area.

The only viable solution is to build more social housing, for genuinely affordable rent. Roger Madelin, who led the regeneration of King's Cross in London and Brindley place in Birmingham, says that the current approach of making private developers pay for so-called 'affordable' homes is "a stupid way of meeting this social need."[19] It is not, he argues, for the private sector to provide for social needs at a high level. The private sector has to make direct profit if companies are to continue to exist. They cannot provide housing at the price that many people need; indeed, the housing crisis is not due to a collapse in house building by the private sector, but a collapse since the 1980s in the public sector. The private sector is at fault only in that it did not do as the government expected, which was to fill the gap left by the public sector.

The Bedroom Tax

The under-occupancy penalty for people in social housing, more commonly known as the Bedroom Tax, was introduced in April 2013. This reduced

Housing Benefit by a fixed percentage based on the number of spare bedrooms above what a person, couple or household were assessed as needing (14% for one spare bedroom and 25% for two or more). 600,000 households were affected, of which the government initially estimated two-thirds included a disabled member. Pensioners who under-occupy their social housing were excluded. Excluding sick and disabled people from the penalty was rejected, on the grounds that this would remove the majority of tenants from the penalty and thereby render it less impactful.

A study in 2015 found that the Bedroom Tax had "increased poverty and had broad-ranging adverse impacts on health, wellbeing and social relationships." Health impacts included respiratory conditions such as pneumonia arising from living in damp, unheated housing; mental health conditions arising from the stress of mounting rent arrears and being unable to provide sufficient food for themselves and their children; and the mental and physiological impact of not being able to sleep well (often due to cold as well as hunger). Social isolation increased as even a bus fare to visit family, or the cost of a cup of tea for visitors, was too much. Adults became dependent upon parents, grown-up children and neighbours for assistance.

Downsizing was rarely an option for people affected by the Bedroom Tax, due to the unavailability of smaller properties, and also the financial cost of moving. For disabled people, this can include the cost of making a new home suitable for their disabilities. Many people affected by the Bedroom Tax did not consider that they were under-occupying; the spare room was used for children for whom they had part-time custody, siblings with different ages and needs, grandchildren, couples who sleep apart for health reasons, or carers. In many cases, the spare room was needed for storing disability-related equipment.

DWP research showed that only 5% of those affected had been able to mitigate the impact of the Bedroom Tax by getting a job or increasing earnings – whilst 3% had lost a job over the same time period.[20] This is unlikely to represent people getting work because of the Bedroom Tax, as opposed to the natural flow of people into and out of work. A lack of jobs or additional hours prevented many from entering or increasing work. Some had made up the shortfall in rent through applying for Discretionary Housing Payments, using up savings or borrowing from friends or family. These are not sustainable options. Many claimants affected by the Bedroom Tax have had to cut back on energy bills, travel costs and food – all essential items.

An additional measure had been suggested, which would be to limit social tenants' housing benefit to the equivalent private sector rent. Because in most cases social rent is cheaper, for most tenants this should not be a problem. However, even the suggestion of such a cap has had serious negative consequences on sheltered and supported housing, which disproportionately provide for disabled people. The cap would devastate the supported housing sector whose rents are naturally higher, including women's refuges, halfway houses (including those for people with mental illnesses) and sheltered housing for elderly or disabled people. Because of the proposals, plans for new sheltered and supported housing had dropped by 85% by August 2017, to 1,350 homes, as schemes were postponed, cancelled or closed.[21] There was already a shortfall of 15% in the provision of supported housing for working-age adults.

The Work and Pensions Committee said that an alternative payment system for sheltered and supported housing is needed, "given the inability of Universal Credit to reflect short-term changes in circumstance."[22] Because UC is paid monthly, and is based on a person's situation on a single specified day of the month, it fails to reflect short-term housing needs of less than one month or changes that occur mid-month. Commenting on the initial plan, David Orr, chief executive of the National Housing Federation, said that plans to reduce funding for such housing "bear no relation to the real cost of providing this type of housing."

The government has since come up with a new proposal: to devolve the funding of short-term housing to local councils, via ring-fenced funding. Such a short-term funding model is a cause of considerable concern to providers, who fear that the money will not be adequate to need (as history shows it rarely is, when functions are devolved to local government). Unlike social security spending, which does not limit how many people may receive it and therefore goes up in times of greater need, short-term housing will have a fixed budget to spend regardless of how demand changes. This means that the more people need help, the less help each person gets. Devolving such functions to local councils inevitably leads to a postcode lottery, with better services provided in richer areas where need is lower. Such a system is inequitable.

Accessibility

In their 2014 report, the *English Housing Survey* found that only 12% of social properties met the criteria for visitability – having all four of the following:

level access; flush thresholds throughout the home; a ground-floor WC; and wide doorways and hallways.[23] These criteria mean only that a property is visitable, not that it is livable: there may not be an accessible shower; the kitchen may not be suitable for a wheelchair user (e.g. surfaces too high, or cabinets prevent legs from getting under the kitchen top); the toilet may be too small. Two thirds of wheelchair users living in social housing are in properties that do not meet the four visitability criteria – which means that they do not meet the occupier's living needs either. Whilst the government cites as evidence in its favour that 93% of homes built since 2001 have downstairs toilets, this is very far from meaning that they are accessible – the toilet may be too small, the corridor off which it stands may be too narrow, and the property itself may be inaccessible because of steps or steep gradients up to the front door.

Including privately rented or owner-occupied homes makes the picture worse: only 6% of all homes are classed as visitable. 84% of houses have two or fewer of the four key features, meaning essentially that they are not accessible. 40% of privately rented homes that aren't fully visitable are adaptable with minor (e.g. a ramp or a flush threshold in a doorway; up to £1000) or moderate work (e.g. widening hallways or installing a ground-floor toilet; up to £5000), whilst 39% cannot feasibly be adapted. 50% of non-visitable local authority and housing association properties could be made accessible with minor or moderate work.

However, landlords' duty to provide reasonable adjustments covers only minor (temporary) adaptations, not those classed as moderate or major (substantial or permanent). Suitable furniture, furnishings, door handles and taps are considered reasonable, as is a change in colour of a surface and a new or different door bell and door entry system. Making a house accessible for a wheelchair user by means of a permanent ramp, removal or change in position of internal walls, widening of doorways and provision of a downstairs wet-room or toilet are not considered reasonable adjustments.

The government is considering bringing into force legislation that would require landlords to permit disabled tenants to makes entrances, hallways and staircases accessible.[24] The cost of this would still be borne by the disabled person, which in practice may render the policy ineffective, and the government has not said when the law will be implemented. The law was written into the *Equality Act 2010* shortly before the general election that saw Labour replaced with a Conservative-led coalition, but the government wants to take more time to consider any problems the law might cause before saying when it will bring the law into force.

Home owners can get a Disabled Facilities Grant from their council to cover the cost of adapting their home to make it suitable, but the system is notoriously slow – too slow for people who have immediate needs. The council won't retro-actively fund adaptations, meaning that disabled people have to choose between spending months in unsuitable housing (or, particularly for the elderly, continuing to stay in hospital) or funding expensive adaptations themselves. The council will also only fund grants up to £30,000, which means that the most severely disabled people cannot get the help they need.

The grants are only available to people who expect to remain in their property for the next five years, which for people with severe or deteriorating health conditions may not be something the person can confidently predict; if they do move out, they are liable for the costs of the grant, which they may not be able to afford. The rise of television shows like DIY SOS, where poor and disabled people have their squalid houses renovated and inaccessible ones made accessible, are in some ways heart-warming – but they should not need to exist. They show the range and depth of need which is not met by government, either local or central, and which people cannot afford to meet themselves.

For permanent wheelchair users living in unsuitable housing, the isolation can be overwhelming, and is often described as being like prison – trapped in one or two ground-floor rooms, unable to get out of the house. The loneliness is described as unbelievable, unbearable, and horrible. Inadequate housing "puts life on hold." Unable to get out of the house, these people cannot go out to work or for social visits; unable to get upstairs, wheelchair users can no longer sleep with their partners; in such limited space, family relationships are put under significant stress and strain.

One lady, in a report by Aspire, commented that, "I don't want the world. I really just want the small things. I want to hold my husband in bed and to not worry about him when I leave him.[25]" Another said, "A house, with adaptations, is all we ask." The process of applying for suitable housing was described as "one long battle that makes you heart-broken, exhausted, more sad." A third person asked, "Why put me through this? Are people who work in housing trying to make my life more miserable? If they could only see how I live each day, a miserable, lonely, horrible existence, if you'd even call it an existence."

13. GENERAL BENEFITS

Aspire concluded that, without significant investment in suitable housing, the consequence is,

> "...people spending years depressed and unhappy living in a room or two of their house, stuck downstairs completely unable to access their bedrooms, or even their children's rooms. It means having to wash at the kitchen sink every day because the bathroom isn't wheelchair friendly. It means people thinking about ending their life or actually attempting suicide. It means people needing an ambulance to come and help them when ill, and an expensive visit to a hospital. It means people ending up stuck in hospital for months on end when their physical health cannot be maintained at home – and costing the NHS tens of thousands of pounds."

Failing to provide for citizens in this way is, as Aspire say, a "national scandal" and means that the UK Government "is failing to implement the *United Nations Convention*" on the *Rights of Persons with Disabilities* which includes accessibility rights, housing rights, and family rights. The lack of adaptations doesn't just make life more difficult for disabled people – it also makes falls and fractures more likely, and increases hospital admissions for cardiorespiratory conditions.[26] Many disabled people face being forced to return to institutionalisation – living in residential and nursing homes not by choice, but by necessity.

The government could make significant steps to change this. There is a national housing shortage, so building significant numbers of houses would have multiple benefits: it would reduce the cost of housing, leaving individuals with a higher disposal income and the government with a lower Housing Benefit bill; and it would stimulate the economy, increasing tax receipts. If all new homes were built to the visitable standard, fewer disabled people would be trapped in their homes and moving house would be both easier and less frequently necessary. Even better, all new homes could be built to the *Lifetime Homes Standard*, which recommends 16 design features that add minimal costs to new homes whilst ensuring that future disability adaptations are achievable for reasonable cost.[27] There is a growing call for such a policy.

Yet the opposite has happened. Central government has cut funding to both local councils and Housing Associations, resulting in neither being able to afford any significant amount of house building. And where houses are built, accessibility standards as well as space standards (which can be key to whether or not a house can be made accessible retrospectively) are now optional, which Habinteg explains means that "local authorities will have the option to set policies for new homes that many disabled people, older people, families with young children and others will find it impossible or difficult to live in. Such homes will be designed in ways that create restrictions to mobility – design flaws that could be easily avoided. Such disabling barriers have major impacts on independence, inequality and health."[28] There isn't even a requirement for an accessible downstairs toilet or that houses be built in a way that makes future conversion to an accessible standard possible. Developers are expected to build a certain percentage of affordable homes when they are given planning permission, but they regularly get these requirements downgraded during the building process, usually under the guise of maintaining a 20% profit margin. The same argument allows developers to get away without building accessible or convertible homes.

The scrapping of these standards was done to make house building more profitable for private developers, but the long-term cost on the country has been ignored. As Habinteg pointed out, the impact on individuals' employment, social lives and independent living can be huge, resulting in costs to the country from reduced capacity for work, mental health issues arising from isolation, and physical health conditions occurring as the consequence of trips and falls.[29] These result in a greater demand on at-home social care, but also on what otherwise would have been avoidable residential care, hospital admissions and hospital stays. Just two nights in hospital or one week in residential care, as a consequence of living in less accessible housing, costs more than the estimated cost of building that house to accessible standards in the first place.

Council Tax

Council Tax arrears rose from £691m in 2013 to £836m in 2014, their highest level in a decade, after the government devolved the provision of the benefit to local government but only gave councils enough funding for 90% of the cost. As with other general benefits, this impacts disabled people too – and disabled people are more likely to be poor enough to need Council Tax benefits in the first place, and therefore be negatively impacted by this change. Because the government also insisted that pensioners should be fully protected, a greater than 90% cut has fallen upon poor working-age adults and their children. Citizens Advice reported a 17% increase in the number of people coming to them to ask for help with Council Tax arrears. In the 2014-15 financial year, half a million more people received court summons for Council Tax arrears compared to the previous year, an increase of 25%. For people who previously would have received full Council Tax Benefit, court cases went up more than 400%.

Universal Credit

Universal Credit has attracted a lot of comment and critique. It has been billed as a radically new form of welfare, but in practice it is just a different way of paying benefits. It takes six benefits – housing benefit, out-of-work benefits (JSA, ESA and Income Support) and tax credits (Child and Working Tax Credits) – and combines them into one new benefit, Universal Credit. As people will only have been on one out of the five non-housing income benefits, in practice UC replaces two benefits per person, i.e. housing benefit and one of the other five.

By combining the out-of-work benefits and tax credits into one payment system, it is easier for benefit recipients to understand how income affects their benefits. Under the previous system, a person's benefits could either be reduced at a fixed rate (e.g., 80p of benefits removed for every £1 earned) or were unaffected until a certain income was reached and then were removed altogether (usually, when a person earned the equivalent of 16 hours at the minimum wage). It was difficult to get hold of information for whether different benefits disregarded an initial amount of earnings, at what rate they would taper off, and whether two or more benefits were tapered at the same time. Rather like the current tax system, which has different allowances and tax rates for different forms of income-related tax, the benefits system had different taper rates for different benefits.

UC simplified this, because people did not have to think about whether they were switching from an out-of-work benefit to tax credit (or nothing), or whether housing benefit was reduced at the same time as their other benefit or tax credit. There is one disregard (for parents or disabled people) and a fixed taper of 63%. However, council tax benefit was not included in UC, which means that it is tapered off on top of the UC taper; and because it was devolved to local councils, there is no national consistency over how much a person can earn before starting to lose council tax benefit or what rate it is withdrawn at. What is a substantial improvement is that there are no longer any cliff-edges, where a person gaining one extra hour of work a week or earning one extra pound goes from keeping all of their JSA or ESA to losing all of it. However, it did not require UC to achieve any of this; the government could have chosen to introduce tapers to JSA and ESA, and to taper income, housing and council tax benefits in sequence and at a universal rate.

UC has two main problems: the inadequacies of the computer system; and the underlying assumptions and policy decisions that don't match up with reality. Because so much attention was given to the problems of developing and delivering the computer system, little attention was given to the actual design and the assumptions it was based on. The project itself was a concept of Conservative MP, and previous leader of the party, Iain Duncan Smith and the think-tank that he set up, the Centre for Social Justice. Further parliamentary debate and nation-wide consultation did not occur. From the poll tax to tax credits, a common cause of major government policy blunders is the failure of the government to speak, let alone listen, to the people at the bottom.[30] The architects and implementers of UC have blundered in the same way.

One of the problems with UC is that it is paid monthly, in an attempt to replicate the monthly paycheck that comes with many (middle-class) jobs (although it doesn't replicate the incomes of middle-class people). It quite specifically cannot cope with people who are paid weekly or fortnightly, and therefore in some months get an additional wage payment. In these months, UC cuts off, and the person has to re-apply in the following month. Yet many people on UC are at the bottom end of the pay-scale, where jobs are paid fortnightly or even weekly: one in four people are not paid monthly, and half of these earn less than £10,000 per year.

Similarly, UC can't cope with people who are paid less than monthly; self-employed people, for example, who may be paid at the end of a project, or who are paid late by the larger businesses they sell to. Nor can it cope with these same self-employed people buying in stock for their business on anything other than a monthly basis. As an added twist, UC treats people as being paid not on the date of their pay-slip, but the actual date that the money enters a person's bank account – meaning that weekends and bank holidays can throw a person's UC even further out of kilter.

UC is paid in arrears, at the end of a month, and the first payment doesn't occur until at least UC is paid in arrears, at the end of a month, and the first payment doesn't occur until at least five (previously six, because the first week received no benefit at all) weeks into the claim. The five-week wait is because of bureaucracy; it simply takes the DWP that long to sort out benefits, and always has. The DWP's failure to streamline its benefits process stems from an assumption that most people will have a month's wages in hand to cover the gap to their benefit payment. In fact, four in five social tenants do not have a months' wages in hand when they sign on for benefits, and 60% of claimants have to make an application for a hardship loan.[31]

The difference relative to previous benefits is that the previous system paid benefits on a fortnightly basis, thus making it easier for claimants to crawl back from any debt incurred during the first five weeks. But UC only pays at the end of each month, and the result is that 90% of tenants start their tenancy in rent arrears and debt as they have to borrow money to live off. When their benefit is finally paid, of course in reality it is then needed to cover the expenses of the next month, until the next benefit payment, and isn't available for repayment of loans. The system thus locks people into perpetual debt, by only ever paying benefit after the need to spend money has occurred. Arrears under UC are both more common and more severe than the previous system, with over 40% of UC recipients in arrears by more than 75% of their rent, compared to fewer than one in ten for non-UC benefit recipients.[32] It takes three months for claimants to start to be able to reduce their rent arrears, whilst arrears not paid off by five months are likely to never get fully repaid. The DWP was warned of this following trial results in 2015 and was advised not to proceed with the built-in delay, but did so anyway. Consequently, financial hardship is all-but universal amongst UC recipients.

Adam, who has lived in the same rented property for 15 years, has been served notice since being moved onto UC.[33] He says that his previously good relationship with his landlord has broken down since having to wait eight weeks for his first payment. The experience has caused his illness to worsen and he feels constantly harassed by the DWP to take part in activities he isn't capable of performing. It would be inaccurate to say that he is barely getting by; he can't really be said to be 'getting by' at all. He is struggling to feed his children even through the use of food-banks, and can't charge his electric wheelchair because he can't afford the electricity. Adam says:

> "I can't continue to cope this way: there was nothing wrong with the old system. I'm around £400 worse off a month. I think the government wants to finish us off, either by driving us to suicide or leaving us homeless and freezing on the streets."

For Chris, the failure of the UC system was fatal.[34] Chris suffered a stroke in 2015 which left him with serious health problems. But he had failed his WCA, and had to claim UC without any top-up and with the requirement to look for work. Early in 2017, Chris spoke to an ITV reporter about what claiming UC was like:

> "I feel like I've been hung out to dry and not eating and that – it just makes you feel ill all the time. Yeah I want to keep the house because I've worked hard for 38 years but it just seems unfair that I've worked all my life to buy a house and now I'm going to end up with nothing.
>
> "But there it is."

Chris's UC payment was delayed. His sister, Heather, reported that,

> "He knew that he was going to lose everything. His house, where he brought the girls up. He knew. He couldn't go to work - he was ill. Just looking at him he looked like a ghost on legs. He was so pale, no fat on him."

Heather said that, if he had received his UC, he would have been able to pick himself up and re-build his life. But Chris never received his UC. He died waiting.

Previously, the combination of receiving several different benefits each paid on its own schedule, plus any earnings, meant individuals had money deposited into their accounts in the majority of weeks. This made it easier for people to budget as they had a more even income over the course of a month, rather than a single lump sum. It is, after all, easier to go without food one day at the end of each week than four or five days at the end of each month. And when payments come in through different mechanisms, then if one goes wrong there is still income from other payments coming in. But under UC, if that one benefit goes wrong and is not paid or is underpaid, everything goes wrong: there is no other benefit coming in. This is much more drastic for families.

UC is based upon a person's household. It is paid to only one adult in a household, and varies depending upon the number of children and any disability within the family. But instead of being based pro-rata on the number of days a person met one of the criteria (e.g., looking after children three days in every week, or being too sick to work for three weeks), it is based on the situation on one day of the month. For people with variable circumstances, as many people in low-paid work and poverty are, this system doesn't work. If a parent cares for children for half of a month, but doesn't have them on the assessment day, he or she will not get the money to cover the costs of those children. If a person's circumstances change frequently – such as having children on one assessment day, and not the next – then the computer system really struggles. It simply wasn't built to handle as many monthly changes as people in poverty experience. UC thus fails to pay benefit in accordance with people's needs, when they need it.

Moira has found reporting a change in circumstances to be very challenging. Moira was pregnant and was supposed to indicate the baby's due date on her online UC record, but it was unclear how she was to do that. She then had a caesarean which made it difficult for her to report the birth in person. The DWP said that they could not pay her until she has a birth certificate, but she is struggling to get an appointment at the council to register the birth, because the waiting list is so long. She's now being threatened with sanctions. Moira says:[35]

> "They were going to sanction me because I hadn't entered the due date online. But nobody knows how to find it on the system, even in the Jobcentre… Don't have a baby on Universal Credit!"

Another woman, struggling to walk following a difficult labour, was forced to take her four day old baby to the Jobcentre to register the birth; no-one else was allowed to register the birth for her.[36]

Unlike work, UC comes with heavy sanctions. At work, a person who is late once may get only a warning. In lower-end jobs, there is often a three-strike rule, meaning a person can only go wrong twice before, on the third time, losing their job. These sorts of jobs do in some ways match UC: the strikes can be for petty things, like sitting down at work, taking too long on the toilet or being late because of queuing through security to get into work. But in the type of work that the government wants UC to replicate, such harsh punishment does not exist. A person would have to be repeatedly late, and late in such a way as to materially affect their performance at work, before a performance review could be called and the person eventually dismissed if he or she did not improve. This is not how UC works, where even if everything else was done perfectly, one mistake or failure in one week brings a four-week sanction.

People in ESA WRAG, some of whom previously could have received the Severe Disability Premium (if they live alone) or the Enhanced Disability Premium (if they became ill at a young age), now won't get either, meaning that under UC they lose out doubly – losing both the WRAG component (around £30 per week, scrapped since April 2017) and the disability premiums. The government has effectively raised the threshold of deservingness for sick and disabled people, where sick and disabled people are now only worthy of support if they are judged ill enough to qualify for ESA SG. WRAG recipients, on the other hand, are increasingly treated the same as any other jobseeker, despite being too ill or disabled to work. One lady was even told by her adviser to look for work of 12 minutes a day, up to 45 minutes commute away.[37]

Through UC, the government has increased dependency. It has increased familial dependency through the policy of paying the entire benefit to one person in a couple. With the benefit paid to a couple and not to the individuals separately, one person's income depends on another person's behaviour. Worse, if one person is in work and the other looking for work, then the benefit is paid to the one who is in work. This puts victims of domestic abuse into a highly vulnerable, dependent state: they no longer have recourse to their own source of money and own bank account. The government says that paying UC into one bank account means that couples can make financial decisions without government interference, but to insist that one member of a couple cannot have financial independence is government interference.

The government has also increased dependency on the job market. The government is relying on in-work conditionality to make claimants get more hours or higher hourly pay. But the job market is a structure that is beyond individual claimants' control. Employers are demonstrably not offering the amount of work at the wages and with the security that individuals need. Putting people into financial insecurity in order to force them to look for better work that isn't there is not the right way for a government to go about improving either the labour market or the living standards and opportunity to thrive of its citizens.

It is not only benefit claimants who are struggling. Jobcentre staff are finding the system difficult. They report that they lack the time and ability to identify claimants who need additional support, and that they aren't confident about making adjustments and applying flexibility. Jobcentres have had to introduce additional resilience training to their staff to help them cope. Because sick and disabled people, as well as people in work and people with young families, are all now part of the system, staff are dealing with much more vulnerable people than before. This is both time consuming and emotionally demanding, particularly in a system that is not set up to deal with such issues.

Hurting the poor

Changes to the benefits system have caused significant hardship for all benefit recipients, not just for the sick and disabled. Rent arrears, evictions and homelessness are all increasing, with councils struggling to house people who have been made homeless. People who can't afford their rent rarely have the opportunity to move; aside from the costs of moving, landlords are reluctant to let to benefit recipients and benefit recipients are unlikely to find properties that are cheaper than their current rent. Consequently, poor people are forced to live in unsuitable conditions.

The situation is worse for sick and disabled people, who are more likely to be in poverty and have more housing needs which limit their choice even further. There are not enough disabled-accessible homes, meaning many sick and disabled people are left to struggle to live in houses that are unsuitable for their needs and for which they are charged more rent than they can afford on housing benefit. Sick and disabled people are less likely to be able to work, and therefore more likely to lack recourse to other sources of income to make up the gap left by the government's benefit cuts. UC is a mess, deliberately designed to fail to cope with reality, as ministers refused to listen to those who could see the problems before UC was rolled out. The overall impact is of people trapped in unsuitable homes without enough money to cover their rent, the support they need or their food and bills. This will only get worse as benefit cuts grow deeper, the housing crisis severer and local councils poorer.

NOTES FOR CHAPTER 13

1. **The Guardian**, profile, Lucy Glennon
2. **Shelter** (2015) Cuts and changes to housing benefit for private renters (LHA) LONDON
3. **Shelter** (2017) Happier and healthier: improving conditions in the private rented sector LONDON
4. **Booth R** (28/01/2018) Bottom of the housing ladder: 'I feel like a squatter in my home.' LONDON: THE GUARDIAN
5. **Moffatt S, Lawson S, Patterson R, Holding E, Dennison A, Sowden S and Brown J** (2015) A qualitative study of the impact of the UK 'bedroom tax.' JOURNAL OF PUBLIC HEALTH DOI:101093/PUBMED/FDV031
6. **IFS** (2015) as cited in Shelter (2018) Shelter briefing: ending the freeze on Local Housing Allowance LONDON
7. **Local Government Association** as cited in Shelter (2018) Shelter briefing: ending the freeze on Local Housing Allowance LONDON
8. **National Landlords Association** (2017) Written Evidence to the Work & Pensions Select Committee LONDON
9. **Shelter** (2018) Shelter briefing: ending the freeze on Local Housing Allowance London.
Policy in Practice (2017) The cumulative impacts of welfare reform: a national picture LONDON
10. **Shelter** (2018) Briefing: Estimates day debate on homelessness LONDON
11. **Wall T** (26/05/2018) Firms make millions out of 'by the night' flats for England's homeless. LONDON: THE GUARDIAN
12. **Demianyk G** (13/05/2018) Exclusive: 2000 Birmingham households moved to B&Bs up to 100 miles away as housing crisis deepens. NEW YORK: HUFFINGTON POST
13. **Barker N** (27/04/2018) Councils spend millions using Right to Buy flats as temporary accommodation. LONDON: INSIDE HOUSING
14. **Foster D** (12/05 2016) Why council waiting lists are shrinking, despite more people in need of homes. LONDON: THE GUARDIAN
15. **Partington R** (22/11/2018) Construction of homes for social rent drops 80% in a decade. LONDON: THE GUARDIAN
16. **Gardner D** (09/06/2018) Why we need a bold new plan for social housing. LONDON: SHELTER
17. **Shelter** (2017) General election – Living rent: the case for living rent homes LONDON
18. **Shelter** (2016) Living Home Standard. LONDON
19. **Madelin R quoted in Booth R** 14/05/2018 Social housing funding system is 'nuts' says top property developer. LONDON: THE GUARDIAN
20. **DWP** (2014) Evaluation of removal of the spare room subsidy. Interim report. Research Report 882 LONDON
21. **National Housing Federation** (25/08/2017) Government plans cause 85% drop in new homes for most vulnerable LONDON
22. **Work and Pensions Committee** (2017) The future of supported housing LONDON
23. **Department for Communities and Local Government** (2013) English Housing Survey: profile of English housing LONDON

24. **Pring J** (22/03/2018) Eight years on government announces plans to bring in access laws for tenants. DISABILITY NEWS SERVICE
25. **Smith B and Caddick N** (2016) The health and wellbeing of spinal cord injured adults and the family: examining lives in adapted and unadapted homes. LONDON: ASPIRE
26. **Garrett H, Roys M, Burris S and Nicol S** (2016) The cost-benefit to the NHS arising from preventative housing interventions. BERKSHIRE: BUILDING RESEARCH ESTABLISHMENT. **Rodgers SE, Bailey R, Johnson R, Berridge D, Poortinga W, Lannon S, Smith R and Lyons RA** (2018) Emergency hospital admissions associated with a non-randomised housing intervention meeting national housing quality standards: a longitudinal data linkage study. BMJ JOURNAL OF EPIDEMIOLOGY AND COMMUNITY HEALTH VOL 72 ISS. 10, PP. 896-903
27. **Goodman C** (2011) Lifetimes Homes Designs Guide. LONDON: **Habinteg** and **IHS BRE**
28. **Habinteg** (2015) Briefing: 7 points about the new Housing Standards 2015 LONDON
29. **Habinteg** (2013) Accessible homes, independent lives London
30. **King A and Crewe I** (2013) The blunders of our governments. LONDON: ONEWORLD PUBLICATIONS
31. **National Audit Office** (2017) Rolling out Universal Credit LONDON
32. **The Smith Institute** (2017) Safe as houses: the impact of Universal Credit on tenants and their rent payment behaviour in the London boroughs of Southwark and Croydon and Peabody LONDON
33. **The Guardian** (08/10/2017) 'I can't even charge my wheelchair': the impact of universal credit delays LONDON
34. **McGrail B** (24/10/2017) Man died 'in hunger' while waiting for Universal Credit just days after ITV interview. LONDON: ITV
35. **Shelter** (n 2)
36. **Hughes C** (20/09/2018) Debt collection agencies contracted to collect so-called Universal Credit debt; Woman forced to attend appointment four days after giving birth; Welcome to Universal Credit hell. THE POOR SIDE OF LIFE
37. **Halewood J** (25/08/2017) Fit for work? Oh do feck off!!! SPEYEJOE2

14

Disability and access

The campaigning work of disabled activists in the 1960s through to the 1980s brought significant changes to the lives of disabled people. A new model of disability, the social model, was developed and proved a powerful tool in both clarifying and campaigning for disability rights. Disabled people successfully campaigned for long-term sickness benefits, extra-costs disability benefits and care in the community. The general environment was made more accessible, and education became more inclusive. Where initial policies did not meet the required standard, such as the first extra-cost benefits that were inadequate for the level of need, disabled people campaigned for new and improved policy. Thus extra-costs benefits, and to some extent sickness benefits, went through a series of improvements.

But despite progress in many areas, significant problems still existed, and more soon emerged. The sickness and disability benefits entered a third iteration (ESA and PIP), which are more restrictive than the second-generation benefits (IB and DLA). Substantial cuts have been made to the social security system generally, building upon the curtailment of the welfare state since the 1980s, and this exacerbates the impact on sick and disabled people of changes to their disability-related benefits. Social care has been drastically cut back. And whilst access in the general environment has improved, it is still far from ideal. Sick and disabled people continue to be excluded from full participation in society because they are unable to get out of their homes, travel or get around public spaces.

Harriet, a wheelchair and mobility scooter user, finds train journeys to be stressful and draining. Although she can book support in advance, it does not always turn up. She can't always risk waiting for assistance to arrive: she

14. DISABILITY AND ACCESS

may have a connection to make, or the train she is still on may be about to depart. On one occasion when she was not quick enough in asking a fellow-passenger for help, the train left with her still on board. It took her two hours to get back to where she was supposed to be.

Harriet has had staff turn up to help, but then go away when they couldn't see her waiting at the doors (Harriet was waiting in the wheelchair space as she struggles to self-propel her wheelchair). It is not unusual for there to be disagreements with other passengers regarding the placement of their luggage, bicycles and prams in relation to wheelchair access. Sometimes passengers stack their luggage around the wheelchair, including on and under the small table provided for wheelchair users to use, or in places that block access to the toilet and to the exit doors. At other times, passengers have to physically stand in the way of electric doors to prevent them from closing before a disabled person can reach them. At unmanned stations, Harriet cannot travel without a train guard to get the ramp for her, yet the Department for Transport and private railway operators are pushing for guard-less trains.

A scare on the underground has put Harriet off from using it at all. Travelling back to Euston, Harriet was unable to disembark at that station because it is not accessible, and so she carried on to King's Cross. But at King's Cross, a smoking train had triggered an emergency alert and the station was being cleared. Some people got back onto the tube they had just left and others went to the tube waiting on the opposite platform, but Harriet could not do either because there were no other nearby accessible stations. The lifts were closed, there were no escalators at that level and Harriet struggles to climb stairs. If she had left her mobility scooter and its battery behind, it could have been hazardous for emergency personnel – not merely as a trip hazard, but also because lithium batteries explode under heat – but she certainly couldn't carry it up stairs.

She only got out of the station through the assistance of a member of the public, who turned back to help her and carried her scooter up the stairs for her. No staff were visible until the ticket level, two levels up, by which time Harriet and her unknown helper were the only two members of the public left on the station. But even then, no staff member made any movement to help Harriet, instead leaving the stranger to carry her scooter up the last set of stairs whilst a staff member began closing the gate across the top, all the time crossly telling Harriet to hurry up as Harriet struggled to pull herself up to the exit.

Public transport

In the 2015-16 Parliamentary year, a Select Committee of the House of Lords convened for the purpose of examining the accessibility of the UK to disabled people. They found that for many disabled people, transport was the biggest issue. Often unable to drive, disabled people are dependent upon public transport to get around – but public transport is largely inadequate. Even modern developments do not seem to consider accessibility a necessary feature: Crossrail's original plan for its route across London included seven stations without step-free access. The Lords responded in surprise:[1]

> "We find it astonishing that, in the development of new rail infrastructure, retaining stations without step-free access could even have been contemplated. The Department for Transport, Network Rail and Transport for London must ensure that there is never again a prospect of new rail infrastructure being planned without step-free access being built into the design from the outset."

But it is not just a failure to consider accessibility in modern stations that is a problem. Many small stations across the UK do not have level access on both – and sometimes either – sides, nor is there an accessible crossing from one side to another. The government has claimed that 75% of journeys by the end of 2019 will involve stations with step-free access, but this ignores the many journeys that haven't been made, or costly detours that have been made, because stations aren't accessible. In fact, only 18% of Britain's train stations are wheelchair accessible, a much more informative and relevant figure for Britain's disabled people. And the DWP has cut the budget for Access for All rail station improvement from £102mn to £55mn over five years.[2]

On top of this, there is rarely, if ever, level access from platforms to train carriages. For whatever design reasons, train carriages are not a consistent height above the platform, let alone flush with the platform – although this is a feat achieved routinely by the Manchester trams and occasionally by underground trains. Some trains are so high above the platform that the resulting gradient of the ramp put in place to allow wheelchair access is too steep for independent use by wheelchair users (the wheelchair would fall over backwards) or the smaller mobility scooters that are permitted on trains (their motors aren't powerful enough).

14. DISABILITY AND ACCESS

The London Underground is worse. The majority of accessible stations are at the far ends of the lines, where they are overground stations. In Zones 1 and 2, the most important for people wishing to get around within London, very few stations are accessible. For example, on the Circle line, a wheelchair user starting at Hammersmith could be confident of getting off only at King's Cross and then Westminster, and possibly at Wood Lane. Paddington has a wide gap between the train and the platform, and Euston Square and Liverpool Street are accessible only from one direction. The remaining 25 stations are greyed out on the 'Accessible Tube Map', or have coloured rings which show that a wheelchair user can change between lines, but can't exit the station there. Overall, excluding overground services, there are only 11 fully accessible tube stations across Zones 1 and 2.

People with mobility problems cannot just turn up at a train station; they have to ring ahead and find out if it is accessible, whether or not it is manned at the time they want to travel, and if not whether there is a guard on the train who can assist. This is as well as having to make a booking for assistance at least 24-48 hours before wanting to travel, which necessarily blocks spontaneous travel and commits disabled travellers to a specific time and train which, on the day, may not be the best option. If they use a mobility scooter, they also have to check whether all the trains that they are travelling on that day will take their scooter, because there is no consistent policy across train operators on what size and type, if any, of mobility scooters they will take.

Yet the Department for Transport appears to agree with private railway operators that limiting disabled people to trains that they have pre-booked and stations or trains that are manned is acceptable, and are pushing for the extension of driver-operated only trains.[3] The Department and franchise holders are also trying to reduce station dwell times, even down to 30 seconds, which is simply not enough time to get out a ramp or allow for people who can only walk slowly. Such decisions are likely to be illegal, given the requirement that disabled people have access to public transport on an equal basis with non-disabled people, but that doesn't seem to carry much weight with the government and private companies.

The rail operator Govia Thameslink Railway (GTR) came under fire for issuing "grossly insulting" disability guidance to its staff.[4] This included not assisting disabled people to board a train if there was a possibility that this would delay the service. GTR said that they had a duty to their other passengers to avoid train delays. Alan Benson, chair of Transport for All, said that the leaked GTR policy "clearly establishes that the priority is to run trains on time, which is understandable given the fines incurred and the criticism GTR have faced over recent years. That this comes at the expense of passengers requiring assistance to overcome the barriers inherent in British railways is completely unacceptable."

Ann Bates, who is a former rail chair of the Disabled Persons Transport Advisory Committee, pointed out that this was the basic consequence of government policies that have forced train companies to cut staff and run more services with fewer delays. GTR has been subject to extensive strikes on its Southern line, and these strikes have spread to other train companies, as staff protest against the implementation of driver-only trains. The provision of a second member of staff to assist disabled passengers and resolve other on-board problems is vital for safe and accessible travel, but it is losing out to profit margins and government policies.

Ms Bates has been told that she could not travel on a train for which she had booked assistance, because the staff at her boarding station could not contact the destination station. Getting a taxi instead is not a reasonable adjustment for disabled people. There is a large shortage of accessible taxis, with most operators not allowing accessible taxis to be pre-booked; and as Ann says, "Why would I get a taxi to join the same traffic queue I had paid to avoid?" Ann has been in discussion with the Equality and Human Rights Commission, and at the time of writing has said that she understands the EHRC to be considering legal action against the government.

When considering the accessibility of buses, the Lords Committee reported that "on the whole, in larger towns and cities the bus services for disabled people are usually adequate, in smaller towns they are variable, and in the countryside they are with few exceptions inadequate." But this is to assume that a bus that is ostensibly accessible is being driven by a driver who will use the bus in a way that maintains the accessibility. Many wheelchair users, for example, report being denied access by bus drivers despite the provision of a ramp and a wheelchair space. Sometimes this is because a pram is taking up the wheelchair space. Although in law they must give way to wheelchair users, parents with shopping and sleeping children do not always want to have to fold up a pram and give way.

In 2000, the *Public Service Vehicle Accessibility Guidelines* made provision for every non-compliant bus to be withdrawn from service by the start of 2016 for single decker buses, and 2017 for double decker buses. As buses are generally replaced every 15 years, this allowed companies to replace inaccessible buses as and when they reached the end of their serviceable life, rather than scrapping them before then. Unfortunately, this was not met, and the Driver and Vehicle Standard Agency has had to take enforcement action against operators who are still using non-compliant buses. Bus operators have known of these deadlines for 15 years, but have neglected to use the time provided to update all of their fleets.

In 2012, when the Department for Transport consulted on whether to exempt bus and coach staff from training on disability access (an EU regulation from 1 March 2013), it received nine responses in favour of the exemption and 196 against. The Department decided to exempt staff from such training, in order to allow UK businesses to remain competitive with EU businesses operating in countries that had also allowed an exemption.[5] Thus private profit was put before the needs of disabled citizens.

Blind or deaf people struggle with transport services that do not provide adequate audio and visual information of services, and in particular of changes in services. Deaf people report missing trains because they do not hear an audio announcement of a change in platform; blind people of not getting off at the correct bus stop because the driver forgot to notify them. It is important for disabled people that staff are consistently ready and available to help, and are able to proactively offer help. It is equally important that public transport reliably uses a combination of visual and auditory announcements, to cater for all disabilities. The £600,000 provided for improving digital access to public transport for disabled people may help with this, although it is a small figure compared with the £47mn taken out of the Access for All budget.

Public spaces

Fiona, who is blind, often has difficulty getting around in public spaces. She can't have a guide dog, because she has no way of giving it the rest, relaxation and free exercise that it would need. She uses a white stick to identify unexpected objects or uneven surfaces on pavements, but this isn't perfect. It is easy to miss obstacles, particularly where much of the blockage is not at ground level – cars parked on pavements, for example, are only detected if the white cane happens to catch a tyre in passing, and wing mirrors can catch blind people out. In unfamiliar places, Fiona needs someone to be with her, and even in familiar places she needs other members of public to be around; she cannot go out on her own to places that are quiet.

One example of her difficulties was the main crossing point to get from her accommodation at university, on one side of a busy road, to the lecture halls on the other. The crossing point had an island in the middle, allowing Fiona to cross one lane at a time – if she could hear that the traffic noise was clear on her side, even if it wasn't clear on the other side. But the island was close to a bend in the road on one side, and the summit of a rise on the other. Fiona was unable to hear cars until they had come around the bend, or over the hill. This left her very little time to determine if there was a gap large enough for her to cross safely, in time to make use of it.

Often Fiona would walk further down the road, away from noise-dampening features and away from the traffic island. When a gap came, she would run for it. It wasn't safe, but it was much more reliable.

Fiona crossed that road twice a day, every day that she was at university. In all that time, she received only three offers of help. Sometimes she would hear someone walking past, and call to them for help – but they walked on. Perhaps they didn't hear her over the traffic.

Adding to blind people's difficulties, some town centres have become 'shared spaces', where vehicles have not been banned but instead now share the same paved surface as pedestrians. Pavements and kerbs are removed, taking any road/pavement distinction with them. The idea is that both drivers and pedestrians will behave more responsibly, and therefore safety will be improved. Vehicles in these areas are supposed to travel at much lower speeds, reducing the consequences of a collision, but this is not much consolation to people who cannot see well. The difficulty experienced at major road crossings – of being reliant on being able to hear cars, and not being able to hear well enough in certain areas – is made only worse in a busy town centre where pedestrians, bicycles and vehicles all mix together.

These shared spaces remove the national consistency that is so important for people with certain impairments. Tactile paving at road crossing points are a prime example of this; they tell blind people not just that there is a crossing point there, but what kind of crossing point it is. The creation of shared spaces removes this consistency and makes the public environment less accessible. The shared space created in Reading, by switching off traffic signals, came under significant criticism for making the area unsafe for people with visual impairments.[6] In London, vehicle speeds along Exhibition Road were reported to have initially decreased to 20mph when it started to be turned into a shared space in 2011,[7] but they have since increased to 27mph in 2018.[8] It is possible that what made the initial difference was not the fact

14. DISABILITY AND ACCESS

that it was a shared space, but simply that it was different to before – and people pay more attention in less familiar situations. Shared spaces generally were condemned as unsafe and exclusionary in Lord Holme's report, *Accidents by Design*.[9]

Many other town centres are becoming pedestrianised, banning the use of vehicles within them. Although this is done with the intention of improving the environment within towns, it reduces access for people with mobility problems. Disabled parking bays are removed, taxi ranks moved further away and bus stops relocated. At the same time, benches and public toilets are being removed, turning towns into what has been described as "standing-room-only."

Those who would normally use mobility scooters provided by ShopMobility charities can no longer get dropped off close enough to ShopMobility to hire a scooter. People with mobility problems are rendered unable to get to the town centres, and even if they did manage it, they are unable to remain without places to rest. Mobility problems can exacerbate any bladder or bowel problem by making it harder to reach a toilet in time; removing public toilets makes this even worse. Thus town centres are now systematically excluding people with mobility problems.

People with mobility problems face barriers from steps, kerbs, shop layouts, broken pavements and blocked pathways. There may not be enough space to manoeuvre a wheelchair down shop aisles and round corners, or between lamp posts and a kerb edge; where space is inadequate for wheelchairs, people with assistance dogs can also struggle. It is very rare for a pavement to be smooth tarmac; many are paved or even cobbled, or the tarmac is stony and coarse; pavements can also be littered with loose gravel, branches and rubbish. Tree roots create humps and cracks that can be impossible for a standard wheelchair to get over, and risk tripping people with limited vision or mobility. And few places are perfectly flat; even in flatter areas, pavements slope down to the road so that water drains naturally off the service, but this makes manoeuvring wheelchairs more difficult, as they constantly turn towards the road.

Crossing roads can be very difficult. There often is not a dropped kerb on both sides of the road, or one or both kerbs are so poorly made that there is still a substantial and time-consuming step to negotiate. At the same time, blind people need a physical barrier between the road and pavement to help them determine which is which; car driveways typically have a partially dropped kerb rather than tactile paving, but this makes wheelchair access more difficult, especially if no suitable wheelchair crossing places have been provided at adequate intervals along a road. In unfamiliar places, wheelchair users may find themselves backtracking several hundred metres just to cross a road.

Of course, much of this discussion of difficulties with wheelchair access assumes that a disabled person does, in fact, have a wheelchair.[10] Yet one in five disabled children wait longer than the four month target for a wheelchair from the NHS. On average, one quarter of adults referred to the NHS wheelchair service don't get any aids at all, rising in some areas to three quarters. Even where a wheelchair or other aid is offered, it is typically at the cheaper, most basic end, requiring hundreds or even thousands of pounds to make it suitable for the user. Cheaper or ill-fitting wheelchairs can cause pressure sores that cost thousands of pounds to fix. If a disabled person turns down a basic, unsuitable chair then a small voucher towards a suitable wheelchair may be offered, or nothing at all. Disabled people are increasingly dependent upon crowdfunding to purchase the wheelchairs they need if they are to get around.

A lack of toilets is another major issue. Councils are not given funding to provide public toilets, and nor are they legally required to provide any, making toilets prime targets for cuts from struggling local councils. There are even fewer fully accessible toilets, equipped with hoists for people unable to transfer themselves to a toilet. This leaves 250,000 people unable to relieve themselves when away from their own home. Public toilet provision is becoming a matter of charity, with Unilever (Domestos) now funding a campaign in the UK to increase access to toilets by asking local businesses to make their toilets available to the general public.

Fi is a mother of two who runs the Minicore Project, a charity for people who, like her, have minicore myopathy, a rare muscle-wasting disease.[11] She can't transfer herself from a wheelchair to a toilet, and is dependent upon hoists. But there are so few toilets equipped with hoists that Fi has to assume that she is unable to use a toilet outside of her own home. In order to be able to leave her home, Fi has had to drastically reduce her water intake – to 1 ½ child-size cups per day. To survive on this little, Fi uses chewing gum and other tricks to increase saliva production. It took her years to train her body to manage on so little.

But our kidneys and bladder are not designed to cope with so little water. It means that waste products become highly concentrated and remain in the bladder for longer periods, as do unwanted bacteria. Fi has had back-to-back urinary tract infections for over ten years. She is constantly feverish, fatigued and weak and has developed resistance to most antibiotics.

Fi now uses adult nappies. On one occasion, at hospital, a delay in getting home meant she sat in her used nappy for five hours. Yet Fi isn't incontinent. It's just that the government won't save her health by providing accessible toilets. She is one of many who are 'socially incontinent'.

Fi now has to have surgery to insert a catheter, which will mean that she can use standard accessible toilets that don't have a hoist. But catheters come with health risks, including UTIs – which Fi already has – and bladder cramps as the bladder tries to expel the foreign object. Often it is necessary to take ongoing medication to prevent the bladder expelling the catheter, and the catheters themselves have to be changed every 4-12 weeks. Fi's weakened immune system combined with her muscle-wasting disease means that surgery is risky and she could end up in intensive care. Other women who have had the surgery report horrific pain, as they like Fi cannot have general anaesthetics.

Fi's condition doesn't require her to have a catheter, or adult nappies, or to drink next to no water. Medically, the surgery should not be necessary. But it is made necessary because the government will not pay for fully accessible public toilets. The financial cost of operations, catheters and antibiotics is nothing compared to the human cost of untold misery. Yet both are entirely avoidable.

Other barriers

Many other barriers present themselves. A lack of Braille, Easy Read and Large Print forms of written communications hinder those with visual impairments, learning difficulties or for whom – like many of those deaf from birth – English is not their first language. The government itself falls down on this. Letters from the DWP say that large print and Braille options are available – but without providing large print and Braille on that letter itself to give notice of the option to ask for such a letter, blind people are left unable to read important communications. Websites can be difficult to navigate, and don't always point clearly to an accessible version even where one has been created. Even things like spell-check functions for online job applications are not often provided, although it would assist applicants with dyslexia, visual impairments and learning difficulties to apply on an equal footing with other candidates.

There is a lack of British Sign Language (BSL) interpreters, including cuts to Access to Work that mean BSL interpreters are no longer covered for deaf workers. BSL is an indigenous minority language in the UK, and a particularly important one as it is unavoidably the main language for many deaf people. BSL users have called for a BSL Act, which they hope would increase the provision of BSL interpreters and support the use of BSL. In particular, it is important that deaf children are taught by teachers fluent in BSL. In Scotland, 92% of teachers of deaf children are not fluent in BSL, and in England 10% of specialist deaf teachers have been lost since 2014.[12] In evidence given to the Lord's Committee, it was noted that there is also "considerable unmet need for BSL interpreters in health services, in education and in employment."

Yet society does not have to be so persistently inaccessible. In the USA, all cinemas, TV programmes and theatres provide subtitles or sign language interpretation. Businesses routinely provide sign language interpreters at the time and date requested by a deaf person, rather than making the deaf person wait longer for an appointment and come in at a time chosen by the business. In Chilmark in Martha's Vineyard and Bengkala in Bali, communities arose where every person was fluent in sign language, hearing or not. And when Gay Pride held an event in Manchester (UK), a BSL interpreter was on stage throughout the entire event.

When the House of Lords Select Committee asked witnesses about the provision of reasonable adjustments, they were told of problems across "almost every part of society". The House of Lords reported that they were told about:

> "...problems in gaining reasonable adjustments from employers and education providers, on buses and trains, and in taxis, shops, restaurants and hospitals. We were told of sports grounds and other entertainment venues that failed to make necessary adjustments. Problems were reported in the criminal and civil justice system and with bodies charged with enabling disabled people to access their rights.

> "We heard of employers responding to requests for reasonable adjustment by making an employee redundant and of 'disabled people being offered a termination package as a first response to a grievance being raised in respect of a reasonable adjustment.' We were told that pubs and restaurants sometimes used their disabled toilets as storage

14. DISABILITY AND ACCESS

facilities, while cleanliness was often a problem at sports venues. Attitude is Everything, a charity working to improve disabled people's access to live music, told us that festival organisers and those responsible for entertainment venues lacked 'creative thinking' on adjustments.

"Andrew and Michele Brenton described the practical and attitudinal barriers they faced when seeking to secure reasonable adjustments at a university. The British Deaf Association cited the refusal of schools to provide BSL interpreters for deaf parents. Mencap told us of how the Confidential Inquiry into Premature Deaths of People with Learning Disabilities had found many examples of where reasonable adjustments should have been made and were not, 'thereby disadvantaging people with learning disabilities at crucial stages of the care pathway'.

"The RNIB and many others cited problems with receiving information in inaccessible formats."

In giving evidence to the Select Committee, Fazilet Hadi said of the government that:

"This is not rocket science. They should have been doing it since 1999 and they are still not doing it. We have inaccessible websites, inaccessible streetscapes, inaccessible services, and government really should be leading the way. They should be role models for this stuff and they are not."

Lord Low, in the same Committee enquiry, explained that:

"There is powerful evidence of the serious impact of barriers to everyday living faced by disabled people as a consequence of the inaccessibility of vital products such as digital television, radio and 'white goods' because they are not often designed with the needs of disabled people in mind. Clearly, the voluntary approach supported by standards has not worked. What is needed is legislation requiring a consistent approach to promoting inclusive design by manufacturers."

The available data supports the oral evidence given to the Lords:

"The most recent evidence, from the Office for Disability Issues' Life Opportunities Survey, confirms that this remains the case. The Survey found that 16% of adults with impairments experienced barriers to *education and training, 57% experienced barriers to employment (compared with 26% of those without impairments), 75% experienced barriers to using transport (compared with 60%), 44% of households with at least one person with an impairment experienced barriers to economic life and living standards (compared with 29%) and 82% experienced barriers in leisure, social and cultural activities (compared with 78%)."*

Disabled people can struggle to access the countryside. It is considered, though data is limited, that less than 1% of countryside is fully accessible. For many footpaths it may not be practical to make them wheelchair accessible whilst still protecting the native wildlife, or the terrain may be unviable. Others, however, already have suitable footpaths such as paving slabs or well-maintained dirt tracks, and are only inaccessible because the choice of gates onto the footpath blocks wheelchairs or mobility scooters. Kissing gates, for example, may not be long enough for a mobility scooter. In these situations, a suitable (larger) gate is usually possible, but it hasn't been provided.

Other parts of the UK heritage are also inaccessible, due to their protected status. Listed buildings, as with any building, are required to obtain planning consent to make any structural alterations, but their listed status can mean that planning authorities refuse consent where there is concern regarding the historic features of the building. Historic England, previously part of English Heritage, is trying to change this by providing examples of how to make a building accessible whilst still preserving its historic features.[13] However, it is all too easy for companies to simply cite the listed status of a building as a reason not to make it accessible, even though this is not legally correct unless steps have been taken to explore and, if possible, act upon all available options.

Education and children

Education for children with Special Educational Needs or Disabilities (SEND) is crumbling, as schools' budgets are cut. Between 2014/15 and 2016/17, schools lost £2.8bn in funding and, despite government announcements of more money, 91% of schools are facing real-terms cuts.[14] Secondary schools have lost 15,000 staff, which again despite government claims have tended to hit the poorest areas hardest. Many children with SEND are not in school full-time, including 24% who aren't in school at all.[15] The majority do not get enough support.

14. DISABILITY AND ACCESS

One teacher reports:[16]

"There are days I go home and cry after school. I am failing my children... I have nine special educational needs and disabilities (SEND) children in my class... Due to school cuts I no longer have a Teaching Assistant (TA), who left last year and hasn't been replaced. This means that my ASD student is now left to cry in classes as he is academically four years behind his peers and cannot cope socially or emotionally. This means that I have to make a decision, a decision that no teacher should ever face. I have to decide whether I support my ASD student or support everyone else. Do I leave him to cry, putting his already fragile emotional well-being at risk or do I support the rest of my students who need me to extend and support their learning?"

In October 2017, Ofsted published the first of a series of reports into the education of children with special educational needs and disabilities (SEND).[17] This is part of a five year project, looking at 30 councils each year. The 2017 report covers the first 30 councils to be assessed. Ofsted found that the government's 2014 *Code of Practice* had not led to an improvement in education for children with SEND. Deaf children, for example, typically achieve a grade or more below their non-deaf peers at GCSE, whilst only 20% of children with SEND achieve five or more A*-C grades at GCSE, including English and maths, compared to 64% of non-SEND children.[18]

SEND children are not getting the support they need. Exclusion rates for SEND children are substantially higher than for non-SEND children, including unofficial – and illegal – exclusions in which children are sent home. Nearly all local areas investigated in 2017 had engaged in this practice. Access to therapy is poor with long waiting lists and limited contact hours, particularly in regard to the Child and Adolescent Mental Health Service, as services are overstretched because of underfunding. Many parents had no confidence in the ability of mainstream schools to meet their child's need, due to concerns over the quality of training of teachers and the ability of teachers to meet specific needs in a more general school. Special schools still tend to provide better quality education and support than mainstream schools, despite the efforts to end segregation.[19]

Further problems are created by the lack of funding for child protection services. Children England wrote that:[20]

> "Whilst it's our councils which make sure we have the right local services and professionals to keep children safe from harm, we trust central government to ensure those vital services are properly funded, wherever children need them, by distributing our taxes fairly."

Once the government has stopped giving any funding to local councils (which the government plans to occur in 2020), funding for essential children's services will be "left to the rise and fall of local economies." 89% of directors of children's services say that they are increasingly struggling to fulfil their statutory duties to children.[21] Services are having to become more tightly focused on those already in, or very close to, crisis with support given only for the immediate needs and not the wider concerns. Consequently, more children and families end up reaching crisis level, because the support is not provided at an early stage. The suffering this brings is entirely avoidable, and has no justification.

There have been some positive changes. The co-location of education, health and care in early years services means that effective and holistic support is often implemented, particularly for children with more severe needs or disabilities. However, these three services move further apart as a child progresses through education and into adulthood, making it ever-more difficult to pick up problems that may have been less obvious at a young age. And where home-visiting services have been lost, this hampers the successful transition of nursery children with SEND to primary school.

Parents find themselves forced to pay for education to make up what the state lacks. We saw this for Danni, when her parents had to make the choice of leaving their daughter uneducated or educate her themselves. But home education is expensive, as one parent has to give up work to be at home with the children. In contrast, Fiona did receive the help she needed – at primary and secondary school. But at sixth-form, one teacher repeatedly failed to hand the subject material to Fiona's assistant in advance of the lesson, making it very difficult for her to keep up with the lessons. Fiona's parents were forced to engage a private tutor for that subject, to cover the inadequacy of the state, as the alternative was to allow their daughter to fail one of her A-levels with all the attendant restrictions of future opportunity that that would have entailed.

University can be worse. Fiona was totally unsupported at university, despite being a straight-A student. She failed her second year, unable to take up the lecture material without assistance, and left the university.

14. DISABILITY AND ACCESS

A young woman who should have been a university graduate and given support and assistance to move into the open workplace was failed, leaving her restricted to washing plates in a cafe. And Danni has spent more than ten years earning her degree. If there were student loans – or even grants – for the Open University or for disabled students, Danni could have achieved more in less time and with less effort and cost to her health.

Improving access

Although there has been substantial improvement since the 1970s, when disabled people were predominantly living in institutions or trapped in their own homes, we still have a long way to go before disabled people can access the public environment as easily as non-disabled people do. Society may no longer frown upon the sight of a disabled person in public, but society does not provide a fully accessible environment and therefore still sees fewer disabled people than it should.

There are a variety of options for making the environment and education services more accessible to sick and disabled people, but they require political will and investment. The current government has spent more time downgrading requirements on public service providers than it has on enforcing compliance with the regulations that remain. The consequence is that, whilst the environment could be made accessible for all sick and disabled people on the presumption that it is needed, instead it is generally inaccessible and only when sick and disabled people protest enough is change made. Private profit – the incomes of company directors and shareholders – are protected at the cost of disabled people.

NOTES FOR CHAPTER 14

1. **House of Lords Select Committee on the Equality Act 2010 and Disability** (2016) The Equality Act 2010: the impact on disabled people Report of session 2015-16 LONDON. Quotes and data used in this Chapter are predominantly from this report unless otherwise specified

2. **Pring J** (28/06/2018) Minister lauds £600000 for rail access... after her department confirms £47 million in cuts. DISABILITY NEWS SERVICE.

3. **The Association of British Commuters** (25/07/2018) Exposed: Disabled access cover up at the Department for Transport TONBRIDGE

4. **Pring J and quotes therein** (24/05/2018) Equality watchdog 'considering legal action against government' over rail access failures. DISABILITY NEWS SERVICE
5. **Department for Transport July** (2012) Summary of Responses to the Government's consultation on EU Regulation 181/2011 on bus and coach passenger rights LONDON
6. **Royal National Institute for the Blind** (14/06/2016) Reading shared space scheme a real turn off. LONDON
7. **McGuirk J** (11/11/2011) A farewell to pavements LONDON: THE GUARDIAN
8. **Transport Network** (20/02/2019) Lord warns 'deadly' street design is increasing vehicle speeds LONDON
9. **Holmes C** (2015) Accidents by design: The Holmes report on 'shared space' in the United Kingdom
10. **Dugan E and Phillips T** (01/08/2017) How your chances of getting an NHS wheelchair vary wildly depending on where you live. NEW YORK: BUZZFEED
11. **Ryan F** (06/08/2018) 'It's horrifically painful': the disabled women forced into unnecessary surgery. LONDON: THE GUARDIAN
12. **National Deaf Children's Society** (15/05/18) New data shows councils cutting £4million of support for deaf children LONDON
13. **Historic England** (2015) Easy access to historic buildings SWINDON. **Historic England** (2015) Easy access to historic landscapes SWINDON
14. **National Education Union** (2017) Schools forced to cut teachers and teaching assistants posts to make ends meet LONDON
15. **National Education Union** (2017) Special education needs children being failed by education system LONDON
16. **Parker E** (03/05/2018) SEND crisis: A teacher's perspective. LONDON: NATIONAL EDUCATION UNION
17. **Ofsted** (2017) Local area SEND inspections: one year on. LONDON: OFSTED AND CARE QUALITY COMMISSION
18. **Equality and Human Rights Commission** (2017) Being disabled in Britain: a journey less equal LONDON
19. **Ofsted** (2018) The Annual Report of Her Majesty's Chief Inspector of Education, Children's Services and Skills 2017/18 LONDON
20. **Children England** (2017) Don't take child protection for granted LONDON
21. **All-Party Parliamentary Group for children** (2017) No good options: report of the inquiry into children's social care in England LONDON

15

Disability and poverty

We have considered in the previous chapters how the benefits system has been cut back since 2010 and the impact that this has on sick and disabled people, as well as on poor people generally. We have also considered the accessibility of the general environment and of people's homes, and the impact that this has on their ability to join in social activity. Many sick and disabled people struggle to navigate both their own homes and the outdoors, and with cuts to both income-replacement and extra-cost benefits, they also lack the finances to compensate for these difficulties by buying in additional support or using more expensive services such as taxis.

In this chapter we look more generally at the link between disability and poverty. The inability of many sick and disabled people to lift themselves out of poverty other than through the support of their government means that changes in government policy have a major impact on them. Social security is the difference between being accepted citizens of the UK, or being isolated and unable to fulfil basic needs.

Destitution and deprivation

Measures of severe poverty show that, after falling from 1997 to 2002, a substantial rise took place between 2008 and 2009, after which severe poverty has levelled out at 2-2.5% of the population (1.3-1.7mn people). Research carried out by the Joseph Rowntree Foundation (JRF) think-tank suggests that these people are likely to meet public consensus on what counts as destitution.[1] JRF used forums and surveys to reach an "expert-informed, publicly-endorsed" definition of destitution. Based on this work,

JRF estimate that 1.25mn people who are in contact with third-sector crisis services are destitute. This is a strictly conservative measure, as it excludes people who are not receiving such crisis services or are only in contact with statutory providers.

The JRF research defined destitution as "people who cannot afford to buy the absolute essentials that we all need to eat, stay warm and dry, and keep clean." To count as destitute, a person had to have been unable to purchase at least two of six basic essentials in the previous month.[2] The members of public who were consulted felt that people dependent upon charity to meet their needs should also count as destitute, so JRF additionally estimated a financial threshold below which a person would be destitute. This amounted to £70 per week after housing costs for a single person, a threshold below which many UC, JSA and ESA WRAG recipients will fall after using their £73.10 per week benefit to top up housing benefit and council tax. A lone parent with one child would be counted destitute if they had less than £90 per week after housing – leaving a sum of £20 each week for the care of their child. Many households in severe poverty experience periods of destitution, and the fact that destitution is not a one-off experience and that food-bank users often need repeat vouchers shows that charitable support is not an adequate response to poverty in the UK.

It is the situation of many who are subject to benefit delays, including some who have just been moved on to Universal Credit. It can also be the situation of people referred for a sanction, because the money stops as soon as a sanction referral is made, even though the decision maker, when the case gets to him some weeks later, may decide that the misdemeanour didn't merit a sanction. For sick and disabled people, destitution can occur when they have been refused ESA but can't honestly sign on for JSA as fit for work. Although an ESA refusal can be appealed, a person has to first ask the DWP to reconsider, during which time they do not receive any income if they have not signed on for JSA. There is no time limit on how long the DWP gives itself for carrying out a reconsideration. These sick and disabled people, who are unable to work or find suitable work, are being made destitute by one of the richest countries in the world.

When this poverty of income is combined with what we know about housing and deprivation, it is clear that many people in the UK including many of the long-term sick and disabled are living in sub-standard conditions. We saw in Chapter 13 that much of the private rental sector, especially that which is affordable and available to benefit recipients, is non-decent:

15. DISABILITY AND POVERTY

over-crowded; damp and mouldy; excessively costly to heat; in urgent need of repairs; rented from rogue landlords. The social sector is hugely over-subscribed and people may be forced to move away from the social networks from which they received much needed support, as well as many miles from their jobs and their children's schools.

Areas with high concentrations of poor people tend to be areas where the schools, healthcare and employment prospects are also of lower quality and quantity. The result is that most poor people are not merely poor; they are also deprived. Chronically sick and disabled people can end up trapped in areas where the healthcare is sub-par and waiting lists are long (doctors tending to go, if possible, where work is less heavy and better paid); where jobs are low relative to demand and those that are available tend to be the low-quality jobs that worsen health and fail to release people from poverty; and where housing is not only not adapted to needs but is also cold, damp, and poorly maintained.[3] It is no wonder that poor people are not escaping poverty.

People living in poverty are not simply struggling for money whilst living an otherwise decent life in a decent job with a decent home and decent access to healthcare. Instead, they are substantially deprived, living in cold and unsafe homes, without access to decent jobs or timely healthcare, and unlikely to escape their poverty and deprivation through their own efforts. If they do, they generally then move to a better area, leaving those who don't or can't to live in an increasingly ghettoised, deprived and under-performing area.

> **Box 13. Poverty in the UK**
>
> Proportion of households unable to afford:
>
> heating to keep a home adequately warm: **3% in 1999 increased to 9% in 2012**;
>
> a damp-free home: **7% to 10%**;
>
> to be able to replace/repair broken electrical goods: **12% to 26%**;
>
> two meals a day: **1% to 3%**;
>
> meat/fish/vegetarian equivalent daily: **2% to 5%**;
>
> fresh fruit/vegetables daily: **5% to 7%**;
>
> celebrations on special occasions: **2% to 4%**;
>
> enough bedrooms for children: **3% to 9%** of children.

Poverty and work

The government says that it wants work to be the way out of poverty for everyone. It frequently states that work is the best route out of poverty, and that this is a key reason for reducing the financial value of state benefits – putting people into deeper poverty whilst out of work means that there is a bigger gap between in-work and out-of-work income. The government hopes that this will incentivise people to go into work, but of course what it is doing is making people so poor and the benefit system so miserable that people are desperate to take any work – however few hours, however insecure, however pressured and unhealthy, however far away; anything that gets them away from the punitive, invasive and impoverishing benefits system. Often this work is only marginally better, by virtue of being paid work not benefits; it is typically insecure, short-term and damaging to health. It certainly does not provide a way out of poverty.

For chronically sick and disabled people, even when they do work it is usually at lower hourly wages, with fewer hours worked each week (which increases the weekly pay gap) and less likelihood of progressing in work (leading to a larger lifetime pay gap). Sick and disabled people are more likely to be in low-paid work and to work part-time than are non-disabled people. Working yourself out of poverty is difficult if you can't leave part-time entry-level jobs; it is even harder if you can barely work at all.

Arguably it is income, not work, that is the key to social inclusion; after all, "income is of fundamental importance to participation in the everyday life of the community."[4] And it is necessary to recognise that not everyone can work; for some, a paid job may be "very difficult or virtually impossible", "require a disproportionate personal effort", or "require more resources than a society can or wants to devote."[5] Countries should promote income security and adequacy for those with disabilities including chronic disabling illness, so that these people are not "denied the means to live decently because of disabilities that restrict their earning potential." Old-age pensioners get 93% of their Minimum Income Standard (MIS; a consensus-based definition of the minimum income for social inclusion), including social participation, met through means-tested state benefits; working-age people should not be denied the same just because the cause of their long-term worklessness is different.[6] All people need a decent income, not just the old and the healthy.

The government says that it wants everyone to "enjoy the independence, security and good health that being in work can bring."[7] It must recognise

15. DISABILITY AND POVERTY

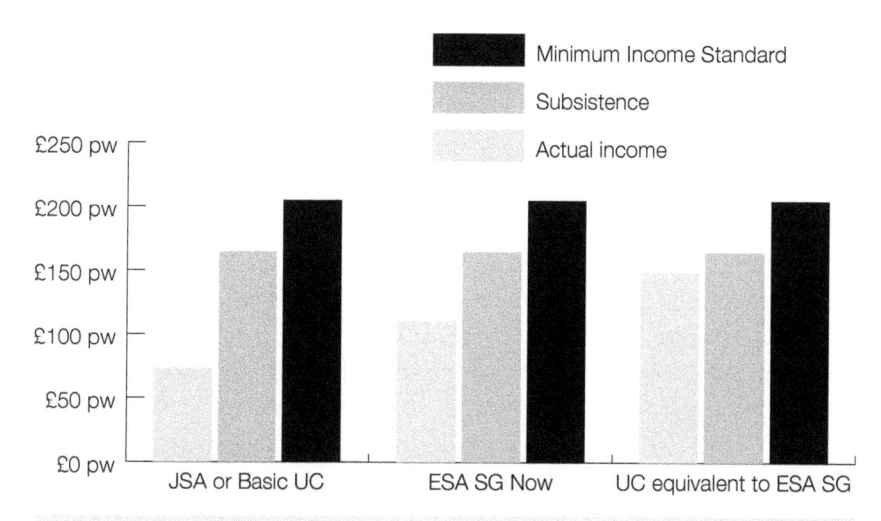

Figure 9. The inadequacy of Universal Credit

On Universal Credit the incomes of disabled people are far lower than the level set by the Minimum Income Standard and are even below defined subsistence levels.

that for people with limited ability due to chronic illness or disability, paid work will not give them the independence, security or good health that a decent, secure and well-paid job gives to a healthy person. A person who cannot work, who struggles to work or who is made ill through work needs a different way of getting independence, security and good health. That way is the provision of adequate and secure income-replacement benefits, extra-costs benefits and healthcare from the government. Saying that the government wants to give sick and disabled people "the chance to be all they want to be" whilst removing their independence, security and health is both unjust and unkind. And it is failing to provide sick and disabled people with the very thing that the government claims to want above all else – equal opportunity to thrive.

Poverty and disability

JRF have also done work to establish what is the Minimum Income Standard that a person needs in order to cover both necessities (long-term subsistence) and the costs of adequate social participation for a single person.[8] The group concluded that a minimum of £197 per week, excluding rent and council tax, was necessary for a basic standard of living and social inclusion in 2018. Even taking out the weekly alcohol budget, the 'eating out' portion of the food budget and the entire social participation budget, leaves long-term subsistence needs at £156.62 per week, which is more than even the sickest people can get through UC or ESA (Figure 9). Moreover this assumes that council tax and rent are fully covered by their associated benefits, which they are not. If the average contribution to rent and council tax made by benefit recipients is added on to long-term subsistence costs, then the basic no-frills minimum income is £164.50 per week. These shortfalls will only get worse as housing benefits fall even further behind rent.

This means that according to normal, reasonable people, UC for people too sick or disabled for either work or work-related activity isn't enough to cover the long-term subsistence needs of an individual. There is no social inclusion in this budget. No gifts for nieces and nephews at Christmas or birthdays. No hobbies, pets, sports, TV, Netflix or eating out. No religious, social or cultural participation. All that is covered is the very basics – simple food; utilities bills; hygiene; basic personal and household goods to replace those worn out or broken; public transport (no car); internet (no computer) and a smartphone (no landline).[9]

And for people on JSA, ESA WRAG or their UC equivalents, things are even worse (Figure 9).

The JRF research includes calculating the cost of fully meeting nutritional needs. But for people in destitution or struggling to meet their basic needs, nutrient-rich food is too expensive.[10] If your choice is between one cabbage or one loaf of bread plus two tins of spaghetti hoops, the cabbage is not going to win: you'll die of malnourishment before you die of malnutrition. For the price of a second cabbage, you could have your electric heater on for 1.5 hours. When you don't have enough money, switching to nutrient-poor food is inevitable. Unfortunately, cheaper versions of the same item commonly also come with higher salt, fat and calorie counts.

As the JRF report shows, people in poverty report distressing stories of what it means to lack enough money:

> "Well obviously I do get into a bit of debt sometimes because if I need to go and borrow some money so I can put a bit more electric or something on, or get some more heating or anything, then the first thing you do when you get your money is pay it back so therefore you're short again."

15. DISABILITY AND POVERTY

"Back last year... I was struggling. I've never done drink or drugs, I've never done that, but when it comes to food, electric and all that lot, it gets hard... I had to wait for a year to be assessed [for a Work Capability Assessment]."

"I'm constantly in the middle of a mental breakdown."

"Your body's crying out for food and all that and of course, you start getting hit with depression."

"I was on ESA, I've got depression and that, and they stopped my money because I couldn't make the appointment... I've gone without food, without clothes, I've slept rough...when I've had no money."

"It destroyed me because I've always been able to go out and buy clothing for myself, for my son. I used to always be able to treat my son to things but I can't and that kills me."

"I'm a diabetic so I'm supposed to eat like four or five small meals a day and sometimes I don't eat for three days... I'm actually on bread and a couple of tins of beans, but by about Sunday I'll have nothing, I'll have to wait until Wednesday."

"... A good example the other day, I got a very angry and a very upset, and quite rightly, phone call from my ex, my little one's mum. He apparently has an itchy rash. She said, "I've got no money until tomorrow." I didn't have a penny. I couldn't provide basic medicine, calamine lotion was all she was after, I couldn't even provide that for my ill child. That is some depressing stuff."

"I used to be on average 9 stone 7; I'm now just under 8 stone... all the stress and everything. The doctor weighed me. He said that's malnutrition."

"Milk for your tea. It costs about 50p for a pint of milk but if you haven't got 50p, you haven't got 50p. It's those little things that make being in this situation a bit more bearable, that little luxury. I know a cup of tea isn't a luxury but it's those certain little things that make your day a little bit more bearable."

For someone considered to be able to engage in work-related activity, the gap between their income and what they need to live healthily is appalling. If they spent the full £45.78 that a nutritionally complete diet costs, plus the £4.56 rent and £3.30 council tax top-up, they would have less than £20 per week for hygiene, heating, electricity, water, internet and phone. As well as needing internet and a phone to keep in contact with the DWP and comply with conditionality, they are likely to also need to travel to Jobcentre or other premises where they are required to attend for work-related activity. No savings are laid by to replace broken goods. There is nothing with which to purchase warm or weather-proof clothing when old ones are worn out.

If in fact their rent gap is higher, as is increasingly likely – Shelter estimates gaps as high as £50 per week by 2020/21 – then the impossibility of such lifestyles should be evident to all.[11]

Yet the majority of people in WRAG, as well as in the ESA Support Group, will not only be on benefits for a prolonged period, but may never become well enough to work. Many have not just permanent conditions, but deteriorating ones, yet are treated as though they can expect to return to work. This is their lifetime income. These people are excluded from society through the triple barriers of being unable to participate in the labour market due to chronic illness or disability; struggling with social participation for the same reasons; and having an inadequate income that means they can't afford the adjustments that would make some participation possible.

In other countries, these people are often transferred to a sickness pension, particularly if they are already nearing the end of their working life. In the UK, ESA SG performs a similar role, but without the security or adequacy that is provided by old-age pensions, because ESA or the equivalent UC awards are constantly reassessed. Pensions recognise that people who cannot work still need and have the right to participate in society. Social isolation has a substantial negative impact on health, and for the government to leave people isolated on the grounds that they do not wish to ask better-off people to contribute more tax is to say that sick and disabled people are worth less than those able to earn large sums. The ESA SG, if not also WRAG, should be set at a rate that is adequate to meet social inclusion; ESA WRAG at the very least should cover long-term subsistence costs.

Not only is the likelihood of being in poverty greater for disabled than non-disabled people, disabled people experience additional costs that further deepen their poverty. As Walker and Walker noted, people with disabilities "require compensation to meet those [additional] needs and overcome any disadvantage associated with them, quite apart from the need for income maintenance." This is the purpose of extra-cost benefits, which we have seen already didn't meet need even before being replaced with a reduced benefit. And social care is increasingly being cut back, meaning that disabled people have to fund social care themselves out of money that was given to them for other purposes.

15. DISABILITY AND POVERTY

The government has consistently said that it is supporting the 'most needy' and has used this as a justification, or at least a mitigation, for its decision to cut support across the board for 'needy' people. But the government is not protecting the 'most needy'. In fact, the more needy someone is, the more cuts they have faced. Across the population as a whole, households with no disabled people have lost £1000 a year; those with a disabled adult have lost £2500 a year; whilst those with a disabled adult and a disabled child have lost £5500 per year through government cuts.[12] People in poverty have lost an average of £2700 per year since 2010, whilst disabled people in poverty have lost an average of £4600 and the most disabled people, those who receive social care, have lost £6350.[13] The result is that the most severely disabled have borne cuts more than 6 times the size of that faced by the average citizen – despite needing the highest incomes to meet their needs, and being the most likely to be in poverty in the first place. As the EHRC said, "The Government can't claim to be working for everyone if its policies actually make the most disadvantaged people in society financially worse off."[14]

> **Box 14. Austerity's impact on poverty**
>
> Households that include a disabled person are more likely to be in relative poverty (19% vs 14%).
>
> Disabled people are increasingly more likely than non-disabled people to live in poverty.
>
> Disabled people are more likely to live in deprived areas and in poor housing.
>
> More than half of disabled people have no savings, compared to 1 in 10 of the general population.
>
> In the 55-64 age group, the gap in disabled vs non-disabled private pension wealth is £125,000.
>
> For only the second time since records started in 1987, UK households have seen their average income fall below their outgoings. The last time this happened was in 1988, with a shortfall of £0.3 billion. The shortfall in 2017 was over £24 billion.

The government is not looking after its needy citizens, whether they are the most needy or not. All sick and disabled people are being failed by this government, as none are getting the level of support that they need. The government is failing both to provide the opportunity to work for those who can, and an adequate alternative income for those who can't work. Because of the government's failure in other parts of the welfare state (housing, education, jobs, healthcare, social care), there is now "an overwhelming moral case to raise people out of poverty by raising welfare benefit levels."[15] Governments should be concerned with how they can grow the economy to support the people at the bottom, not with cutting government expenditure with the vague goal of reaching a reduced State.

Whose fault?

Poverty is closely linked with ill-health, as both a cause and consequence of illness. People who are too sick to work, or who can work only limited hours, necessarily end up on low incomes if they do not have an alternative source of income. People who are on low incomes undergo excessive strain and distress in managing their income, going without not just the niceties of life but also the necessities. It is cognitively challenging to manage on a small budget, because of the care and attention required for every single purchase including being prepared for future purchases. It is emotionally draining to refuse, again and again, to treat one's self to even the smallest pleasure. It is stressful to be continually aware of the limits of one's income, the current and future demands on it, and the uncertainty of your ability to meet those demands.

The emotional distress has negative impacts on both mental and physical health. Lacking adequate food harms the body, as does insufficient sleep. When under prolonged stress, the body switches over into a state where it seeks to consume more food and lay down more fat, particularly around the midriff. The immune system is compromised, leaving people more vulnerable to infection, and heart rate and blood pressure both increase. Depression sets in, as does generalised anxiety, caused by the heightened cortisol levels. Resilience is reduced.

Poverty doesn't just make people stressed and unwell; it also reduces their brain power.[16] Mullainathan and Shafir call this the "scarcity tax" because it occurs whenever a person is scarce of something, not just when money is scarce. Their studies have shown how lacking enough time, social interaction or food (when dieting) all reduce brain power by redirecting attention to the thing that is lacking. This leaves less computing power for other necessary, desirable or beneficial tasks. Financial poverty, however, is worse, because there are no holidays from poverty.

15. DISABILITY AND POVERTY

The brains of people who are struggling financially are unavoidably attracted to ideas or things associated with money. It happens below the level of conscious awareness or control, directing the person's attention to matters relating to money. The consequence is that less brain power is available for everyday life and work, like a computer running multiple programs at once. People cannot think as clearly; they make more mistakes and misjudgements, and struggle more with complex problems. The financial stress of being in poverty can reduce IQ by 13-14 points; enough to take someone from average to borderline deficient.

Poverty also reduces executive control and will-power, making it harder for people to act for the long-term good if it means short-term harm, or to resist short-term good that brings long-term harm. Unlike muscle, will-power does not increase the more we use it; in fact, it depletes. Poor people, constantly having to refrain from buying the things they want and often also the things they need, cannot maintain that level of will-power for everything. Rich people cannot either, it's just that they are much less likely to need to, or to notice the effects if they fail. For sick and disabled people, so much will power goes into managing their illness – doing necessary (or mandated) things that they aren't up to doing, or refraining from things they want to do because they know it will make their illness worse (or conflicts with government mandated actions) – that even less willpower is left for ordinary life decisions.

For some, the importance of maintaining mental health through small 'treats' – like sweet food or a TV licence, the poor person's equivalent of a meal out and a trip to the theatre – can end up feeling more important than physical health. Or for a parent whose child is always missing out, dependent upon hand-me-downs and never able to have a friend over for tea, buying the more expensive branded trainers for once is more a case of kind parenting than it is of irresponsibility. These decisions contribute to our media stories of poor people making 'bad' spending choices.[17] But people in poverty, with debilitating chronic illness or multiple disadvantages, have little to hope for and therefore little to save for. They don't have enough income to save for things that would improve their life in any meaningful timeframe. The only option that is viable is to attempt to make the here-and-now more bearable. For better-off people, this is called self-cherishing. For poor people, it is another reason to be abused for their poverty.

It is not that poor people are feckless, irresponsible or incapable of handling money. In fact, poor people have a much more accurate appreciation of the value of money than do the better-off. The poor don't need lessons in budgeting. They already know how to budget, down to the last penny, and they know that decent, secure work is the best source of financial security. Their problem is not a failure to budget or reckless lack of responsibility, but that they don't have access to decent work, let alone to an adequate income.

The heavy conditionality in the benefits system exacerbates the impact of poverty. Shafique writes:[18]

> "If so much of people's cognitive capacity is taken up by navigating the absurd complexities and requirements of the welfare system - on top of the everyday pressures of hardship - how can we realistically expect people to simultaneously plan for the long term, invest in their skills, and progress through work? It is the stability of affluence that creates an environment for 'building character' and achieving success, not the other way around."

If you don't have enough money to get by, you will find yourself constantly tired, hungry and stressed. Your physical health will be compromised; your mental health worn down and your brainpower depleted. It is inevitable that relationships suffer, marriages breakdown and children miss out. But if your income increases – if the government introduces tax credits, for example, or you are given an unconditional personal budget – then your life also improves: parents spend more money on clothes, books and fruit and vegetables for their children;[19] homeless adults identify their own routes off the streets and into training;[20] less money is spent on drugs, alcohol and other temptation goods.[21] Poverty is not only unnecessary as an encouragement to work, but is an active barrier – and one that is entirely soluble.

Social mobility

Politics since 1979 has placed a particular emphasis on individual responsibility, equality of opportunity and the freedom to succeed, in contrast to equality of outcome. The ideal is that, to whomever a child is born, this has no impact on their success and wealth as adults. Poor children are not held back or excluded from better paid or higher status jobs. Rich children are not protected against the consequences of either laziness or lower ability. Where people end up is based upon their abilities and their willingness to work hard, not on their background. What matters is that everyone has the

15. DISABILITY AND POVERTY

opportunity to succeed, so that where they are naturally talented and want to work and learn, they have the chance to do so.

The extent to which this happens is shown in the measure of a country's social mobility. Social mobility means that people can move freely up and down the income scale. The children of rich parents are allowed to fail as much as the children of poor parents are given the opportunities to succeed.

Sadly what we see in the UK is that our social mobility lags behind almost all other developed countries. Income inequality – when the incomes of the top 1% are included – is substantially higher now than in the 1960s and 70s, having risen rapidly in the 1980s, followed by a slight upward trend since the 1990s. The policies of small state and deregulation which the government has followed since the end of the 1970s has not resulted in the social mobility and equality of opportunity that we were promised. Other developed countries manage to provide opportunities for poor children and adults to excel, so there is no reason to believe that the UK cannot or that it would suffer if the government improved the education, training and employment opportunities available to poor people.

The Social Mobility Commission reports that, "from the early years through to universities, there is an entrenched and unbroken correlation between social class and educational success."[22] High quality childcare puts children nearly eight months ahead of their peers at age five, a difference that only increases as they progress through the education system, whilst a good nursery can all-but eradicate the differences that would otherwise be seen in outcomes between children from poorer versus richer backgrounds. But instead what we see in the UK is that children from poorer backgrounds are being failed in a way that is not consistent with any assumptions of the distribution of IQ across the income groups.

The quality of public sector childcare is significantly higher than in the private, voluntary or independent sector, yet the availability of public sector childcare has been falling for over 30 years. The 2017 Government's free 30-hours of childcare for working parents is a myth: the government is not paying nurseries fully for the cost of childcare, meaning that nurseries are having to either close, decline to provide free hours or increase other fees to get the money that they need. Nor are the 30 hours available every week: they only apply during school term times. The most necessary childcare, for children of poor parents and whose parents work irregular, unpredictable or atypical hours, is the least available, and these parents could not afford it if it were. The government's childcare policies will disproportionately benefit higher earners, as childcare services have been forced to make cutbacks in the services that they provide.

The Social Mobility Commission concluded in 2016 that:

"Children who happen to grow up in a social mobility cold-spot area have their potential capped by the lack of opportunities available there. Comparing the outcomes and opportunities of children growing up in different areas of England exposes a divided nation where a child's future is compromised before they have a chance to prove what they are capable of."

Exacerbating this problem, post-secondary education and training available to young adults is poorly matched to the skills required and job opportunities available in the labour market. For those whose abilities are better suited to skilled trades and manufacturing jobs than in the knowledge sector, the opportunities to develop these skills are limited and often of low quality. Most apprenticeships offer only "low-skill qualifications in lower-pay sectors where there is little opportunity for progression," whilst the higher-yield apprenticeships are more likely to be taken up by young adults from more affluent backgrounds, who have the social capital and academic qualifications to secure places on the better training schemes. Thus, these opportunities fail to reach the people who most need them. Without the government or employers providing training or career opportunities, poor people are stuck. They cannot afford to invest in themselves, and no-one else is offering to do so.

Education, however, is not enough. There must also be a range of jobs available, including jobs which match a person's innate skills and trained abilities; and there must be the housing and transport links to enable a person to get to jobs. Joking references to 'get on y' bike' don't apply when the manufacturing and trade jobs to which people did once cycle are no longer available, let alone within a reasonable cycling distance. The UK economy is heavily oriented towards finance and services, not skilled trades, which means that people who would have thrived in manufacturing industries are instead left with low-skill, low-pay, career-less jobs. People cannot get jobs that don't exist; if the government does not ensure full employment, then it is inevitable that some will miss out through no fault of their own. This is against the principle of equal opportunity, as well as being against basic human rights.

If a person is sick or disabled then their opportunities plummet even further. Their choice of living accommodation is hugely restricted, because the vast majority is not accessible. If a disabled person doesn't live near accessible transport – and the London Underground and many suburban and rural train stations are inaccessible – then they can't get to work, can't socialise, can't go shopping. Lack of adjustments at work or in education and training keeps them from getting and sustaining decent work. The high pressure of modern workplace excludes chronically ill people, whose bodies simply cannot take it. For all that the current government says that "a disability or health condition [chronic illness] should not dictate the path a person is able to take in life", the fact is that such illnesses or disabilities do dictate future paths.[23]

The price of austerity

The Right Reverend Paul Bayes, Bishop of Liverpool, wrote in the foreword to Liverpool Council's cumulative impact assessment that:[24]

> "A measure of a true and just society is our attitude to the poorest and the most vulnerable in our society. This report provides a statistical analysis of that measure and it makes hard reading. It does not surprise me that the brunt of cutbacks and difficulties are shouldered by those in poverty, the long-term sick and the disabled, nor that people face double and triple whammies as the different cuts strike them over and over.
>
> "It does not surprise me; but it angers me. It angers me that we allow this to happen repeatedly to our sisters and brothers, to our children, to our neighbours. It angers me that our hard-working local politicians are forced to make heart-breaking, difficult decisions over where best to spend their very limited resources. It angers me that central government seems not to recognise both the injustice and impracticality of their funding regime."

The government hasn't considered how multiple cuts interact with one another, or how a cut in one area impacts on the need for another – such as cuts to social care resulting in increased need for healthcare. By neglecting to carry out such impact assessments, the government is able to present spending cuts as savings. In fact what happens is that poor people pay the price, but the government does not notice as it does not 'see' these people. It does not account for the cost of living in poverty, in a deprived and under-resourced area, in inadequate housing, alternating between the health damage of bad jobs and that coming from the government's benefits regime. The government does not account for the cost of physical and mental illness caused by living in these conditions, nor the lost revenue from failing to provide for adults or their children to engage in productive careers. Nor does it incorporate the future costs caused by failing to invest in preventative action or early care. In fact, despite – or because of – spending cuts, government spending has increased whilst the lives of poor and disabled people have got worse.

Disabled people are the most dependent upon healthcare, social care, social security and wider public provision of services. Without the government stepping in to provide directly what disabled people – who often cannot work, or work much – need, the outcome is unavoidable deprivation. Disabled people in poverty do not have the option of buying in the services the government no longer provides, or purchasing the support that they need to participate; few have the opportunity of getting a better (or even any) job to increase their income. Whenever the government cuts its provision, it is the poor who are affected the most; and the disabled are disproportionately likely to be part of the poor.

The New Statesman has run a number of articles on what they call Britain's crumbling and decaying public realm. The litany of what has been lost is long. In healthcare alone, there is the NHS' unprecedented cancellations of non-emergency operations in January 2018; the rising need for healthcare at the same time that doctors and nurses are leaving and GP surgeries are closing; and the ever-growing gap between poor and rich as GPs continue to flock to wealthy regions and abandon the unprofitable, unsustainable poor. The loss of Sure Start centres, libraries, green areas, children's play equipment and swimming baths all result in the loss of community space and places for children to exercise through play. Some headteachers are forced to ask parents to supply what the school cannot; others find that they are supplying food and laundry services to children whose parents are destitute. Child protection services are increasingly unable to protect against harm, instead finding themselves reacting to harm that has already occurred: serious investigations into concerns of significant harm have increased from 77,000 to 200,000 since 2008; and the number of children on Child Protection plans has increased from 31 per 10,000 children to 58.[25]

Even without reading the news, the middle class are discovering what austerity means through their pot-holed roads, long waits for GP appointments and reductions in bin collections. Walk through any major city and it is clear that homelessness has risen substantially. Walk in the countryside

15. DISABILITY AND POVERTY

and you can see what happens when councils no longer have the resources to maintain footpaths, clear invasive and troublesome weeds or remove litter. All across the country, the government's failure to pay for even a basic level of service is starting to show.

Writing in the *New York Times*, American journalist Peter Goodman explains what has happened in the UK:[26]

> "Conservative Party leaders initially sold budget cuts as a virtue, ushering in what they called the Big Society. Diminish the role of a bloated government bureaucracy, they contended, and grass-roots organisations, charities and private companies would step to the fore, reviving communities and delivering public services more efficiently.
>
> "To a degree, a spirit of voluntarism materialised. At public libraries, volunteers now outnumber paid staff. In struggling communities, residents have formed food banks while distributing hand-me-down school uniforms. But to many in Britain, this is akin to setting your house on fire and then revelling in the community spirit as neighbours come running to help extinguish the blaze."

Money is to the economy like oil to a machine. Let it run dry, and the machine breaks.

NOTES FOR CHAPTER 15

1. **Fitzpatrick S, Bramley G, Sosenko J, Blenkinsopp J, Johnsen S, Littlewood M, Netto G and Watts B** (2017) Destitution in the UK. YORK: JOSEPH ROWNTREE FOUNDATION

2. These six are: **shelter** (have slept rough for one or more nights); **food** (have had fewer than two meals a day for two or more days); **heating** their home (have been unable to do this for five or more days); **lighting** their home (have been unable to do this for five or more days); **clothing and footwear** (appropriate for weather); **basic toiletries** (soap, shampoo, toothpaste, toothbrush)

3. Hart J (1971) The inverse care law THE LANCET VOL 297 ISS, 7696, PP. 405-412 DOI:10.1016/S0140-6736(71)92410-X

4. **Walker A and Walker L (1991) Disability and financial need – the failure of the social security system.** In Dalley G (ed) Disability and social policy. LONDON: POLICY STUDIES INSTITUTE

5. **OECD (2003) Transforming disability into ability** PARIS

6. **Davis A, Hirsch D, Padley M and Shepherd C (2018) A minimum income standard for the UK 2008-2018: continuity and change.** YORK: JOSEPH ROWNTREE FOUNDATION.

7. **DWP and Department for Health** (2016) Improving lives: the work, health and disability Green Paper LONDON
8. **Davis A, Hirsch D, Padley M and Shepherd C (2018)** A minimum income standard for the UK 2008-2018: continuity and change. YORK: JOSEPH ROWNTREE FOUNDATION. The allocated food budget for a single person was £49.29, but this included money for eating out as a leisure activity. In 2016 a nutritionally complete diet without excess calories was calculated to cost £41.93 per week (Scarborough et al 2016), and in 2018 a different study reported the cost as £45.78 per week (Jones et al 2018).
Scarborough P et al (2016) Eatwell Guide: modelling the dietary and cost implications of incorporating new sugar and fibre guidelines. BRITISH MEDICAL JOURNAL OPEN VOL 6 ISS. 12, PP. E013182 DOI:10.1136/BMJOPEN-2016-013182.
Jones NR, Tong TY and Monsivais P (2018) Meeting UK dietary recommendations is associated with higher estimated consumer food costs: an analysis using the National Diet and Nutrition Survey and consumer expenditure data, 2008-2012. PUBLIC HEALTH NUTRITION VOL 21 ISS. 5, PP. 948–956. DOI: 10.1017/S1368980017003275.
9. These may not be strictly considered 'necessities' by some. But for people living off benefits, access to internet and a phone is essential for communication with the DWP and participation in the conditions of benefit.
10. **CAP write** "Indeed, for the price of one cabbage from Tesco (79p), you could buy a loaf of budget range bread (36p) and 2 tins of Everyday Value spaghetti hoops (21p each) – several meals, carb-heavy and filling, but with next to no nutritional value. Similarly, for less than the price of one loose pepper (55p) you could buy a 1kg bag of budget range white rice (45p) that could last you a week or more." **Christians Against Poverty** (2018) The true cost of poverty. BRADFORD
Heating costs taken from confusedaboutenergy.co.uk page on Heating Costs, updated 16/10/2017, which gives the cost of electric bar heaters, fan heaters, oil-filled radiators and convection heaters as 48.9p per hour.
11. **Shelter** (2018) Shelter briefing: ending the freeze on Local Housing. LONDON
12. **Portes J, Aubergine Analysis and King's College London** (2017) Distributional results for the impact of tax and welfare reforms between 2010-17, modelled in the 2021/22 tax year: Interim findings November 2017. LONDON: EQUALITY AND HUMAN RIGHTS COMMISSION
13. **Duffy S (2014)** Counting the cuts: what the government doesn't want the public to know SHEFFIELD CENTRE FOR WELFARE REFORM
14. **Isaac D as cited in Butler B** (17/11/2017) Women and disabled people hit hardest by years of austerity, report confirms LONDON: THE GUARDIAN
15. **Shildrick T, MacDonald R, Webster C and Garthwaite K** (2012) Poverty and insecurity: life in low-pay no-pay Britain. BRISTOL: POLICY PRESS
16. **Mullainathan S and Shafir E** 2013 Scarcity: why having too little means so much LONDON: ALLEN LANE
17. **Brown M** (27/06/2017) If you're asking 'What real poor person could be at Glastonbury?' you've never been poor. LONDON: INEWS

15. DISABILITY AND POVERTY

18. **Shafique A** (08/06/2018) The marshmallow test and the crisis in society. LONDON: RSA
19. **Haushofer J and Shapiro J** (2013) Policy brief: impacts of unconditional cash transfers PRINCETON
20. **Hough J and Rice B** (2010) Providing personalised support to rough sleepers: an evaluation of the City of London pilot. YORK: JOSEPH ROWNTREE FOUNDATION
21. **Evans DK and Popova A** (2017) Cash transfers and temptation goods. ECONOMIC DEVELOPMENT AND CULTURAL CHANGE VOL 65 ISS. 2, PP. 189-221
22. **Social Mobility Commission** (2016) State of the nation 2016: social mobility in Great Britain LONDON
23. **DWP** (n 7)
24. **Bayes P** (2017) Foreword to Liverpool City Council 2017 Welfare reform cumulative impact analysis. 2016 interim report: February 2017 LIVERPOOL: LIVERPOOL CITY COUNCIL
25. **Holt A** (06/11/2018) Child protection services near crisis as demand rises. LONDON: BBC NEWS. **Association of Directors of Children's Services** (2018) Safeguarding pressures Stage 6 Research Report. LONDON
26. **Goodman PS** (28/05/2018) In Britain austerity is changing everything. NEW YORK: THE NEW YORK TIMES

16

A breach of rights

In this book we have considered the question of how the UK treats its sick and disabled citizens, from a spectrum of breaking our human rights (the UN view) through to being a world leader (the government view). We have looked at a lot of evidence from varying angles.

The government view

The post-2010 government believe that they have carried out tough but fair economic and social policies. They believe that the country was in too much public debt after the 2007/08 financial crisis; that this was in large part due to Labour's failure to keep public spending below tax receipts; and that to continue spending more than came in through tax would badly harm the country. The government also believed that high benefit receipt represented widespread individual moral failing, rather than a structural economic failing.

The prescription was to cut public spending, with a particular focus on the social security system as being, in the Government's view, both economically and morally wrong. The expectation was that the economy would quickly recover due to spending cuts whilst more people would get work due to social security cuts. Tax revenues would rise, benefit spending would fall, the government would achieve a budget surplus, and public debt would fall. The confidence of private business in the UK economy would be strengthened, leading to more private investment and rising wealth and welfare for all.

16. A BREACH OF RIGHTS

The data

The anticipated outcomes of spending cuts have not occurred. Instead, the economy has largely stalled. Occasional quarters of higher growth, whilst greeted with praise by politicians and journalists, are not sustained over the longer term. Substantial harm has occurred, public services cannot keep up and public infrastructure is literally crumbling.

The austerity measures have not worked because, as the data shows, austerity is not the right response to recession.

Because the government creates money by public spending and cancels it by tax, government debt represents simply the total savings in the private sector. As Chapter 8 discussed, government spending and taxation can be compared to the issuing, cancellation and collection of stamps. The government on average has to print more stamps than are used to send post, because some stamps end up in collection books. Similarly, the government has to spend more than it gets in tax, because some money ends up in people's savings. The deficit simply represents the amount of money saved in a given spending period, whilst the debt is the sum total of private savings.

Without money, useful work that needs doing can't be matched up with people who want to do some work, and we end up with the current bizarre situation where the government pays people to look for work that doesn't exist, whilst at the same time vital and beneficial tasks (particularly those public services that local councils provide) go undone. To keep the economy going, governments need to spend more than they receive in tax; they need to target this spending at areas where the private sector falls down; and they need to use taxes to prevent high inflation. When done properly, the government can ensure adequate incomes and full employment in decent jobs for all its citizens. It could even make it possible for citizens to work fewer hours – such as a four-day working week – and still ensure that the lowest paid have enough to live off.

The deregulation and shrinking of government spending that we were told would result in improved wealth for all has instead resulted in the very top sucking ever-more wealth to themselves whilst economically oppressing the workers on whom their wealth depends. The result is a sick-work culture: UK citizens hold strong attachments to work, even when their only experience of work is of toxic jobs; sickness presenteeism costs more to the economy than sickness absence; people who take time off or leave work due to illness are demonised and stigmatised, which unsurprisingly creates distress and depression; and all the time employers are allowed to impose harmful working conditions upon staff in the flawed belief that such practices will (indirectly) improve these workers' quality of life.

High benefit expenditure represents not a failure of culture, but a failure of the government to provide a morally just economy. It shows that the government has failed to ensure enough jobs at high enough wages for all families to have a decent income without recourse to the means-tested components of the benefits system. It shows that the government is neither investing directly in the education and training of its citizens, nor ensuring that they have the income to source such training for themselves. It demonstrates a failure of housing policy, to provide pleasant housing at no more than 1/3rd of a household's income. And it suggests a failure of the health, social care and occupational therapy systems to help people maintain an ability to work for as long as reasonably possible.

If the government had increased its public spending to compensate for the fall in private spending, the economy would have improved and benefit expenditure would naturally have fallen as fewer people needed it. Instead, the government has attempted to artificially shrink benefits by cutting how much it will pay and to how many individuals. Because this could not and did not result in an improved economy, these people were pushed into deeper poverty without any improvement in their chances of getting out of poverty through paid work, and indeed making it harder for them to get work due to less money to spend on job-seeking and employability-enhancing behaviours.

The cuts that ensued have been the largest in the UK's history, shrinking the state to historic lows. For sick and disabled people, who are disproportionately dependent upon public spending and the least able to mitigate cuts by getting (more) paid employment, the government's response to the 2007/08 financial crisis and recession has been particularly cruel. Already having to cope with illness, disability, inaccessible buildings, inadequate transport and the extra costs associated with managing their disability, the government made things worse by reducing how much financial and in-kind support these people could receive. Cuts to ESA/UC, DLA/PIP, social care and the Independent Living Fund, Access to Work, Disabled Students' Allowance, housing benefits and more have all made it much harder for disabled people to buy what they need for a decent standard of living even before adding in the costs of disability and contributions to social care. The result, not unsurprisingly, is increased illness, poverty and distress instead

16. A BREACH OF RIGHTS

of the security, healthcare and opportunity that the government should be providing.

Many sick or disabled people don't have the option or ability to take up paid work, either because illness limits their abilities or because state support to provide accessible work is not available. Even the most generous income-replacement benefits are inadequate for a minimum standard of living, and many people receive so little that they are put into destitution. The only housing that benefit recipients can afford is in the bottom 30% or less of the rental market where many are unfit for purpose. The sick and disabled are in a particularly bad position, because so few properties are accessible, leaving many trapped in just a couple of rooms. At the same time, the poorest sick and disabled people – those placed in JSA or ESA WRAG – are forced into activity that harms their health and drives them further away from being able to work. The consequence is an additional 200 suicides per year.

Cuts to local government have negatively impacted schools, child protection services, libraries, public swimming pools, waste collection, health and safety standards and other neighbourhood services. Social care is collapsing, with privately-contracted providers handing back their contracts to local councils because they can no longer afford to provide care, and the numbers of social care recipients little more than half what they were in 2009 – when population growth means they should be higher. Coupled with inaccessible homes, many disabled people are left treated less well than dogs – which at least get to go out of their home once or even twice a day and are not expected to foul themselves.

Prolonged underfunding of the NHS means that waiting times are getting longer, rationing of certain treatments is increasing and hospitals are missing A&E targets. In January 2018, non-emergency operations had to be postponed for a month in order to cope with the mismatch between the need for healthcare and the available staff. The unprecedented cancellation and relatively mild start to 2018 still didn't prevent excess deaths of 30,000 people compared to previous years. There literally aren't the staff and finances to cope.

Summary of austerity's outcomes

A selection of figures from the rest of this book helps to show just how much harm has been caused:

- A change in regulations in January 2016 meant that more people were told they were fit for work (44%, up from 35%), and fewer that they could not work and would not have to undergo conditionality (38%, down from 54%). This means that many sick and disabled people now get less money and are required to engage in more activity – activity which is often unsuitable and, combined with the threat or imposition of sanctions, causes health to get worse.
- ESA is associated with around 200 additional suicides per year and 90,000 additional cases of mental illness.
- The ESA SG falls short of what is needed for subsistence living in the long-term by £10/week. It covers only 57% of the income necessary for social inclusion.
- ESA WRAG covers 62% of the income necessary to cover long-term subsistence living and only covers 38% of the income needed to participate in society. This is borderline destitution, and many people will, after using their income-replacement benefit to top-up their rent and council tax benefits, be left unable to cover all of their needs.
- At least 1.25 million people were in destitution in 2015. In the years running up to 2010, severe poverty was at 1% of the population (vs 2-2.5% now), and destitution was even lower.
- 1 in 4 people can't afford to repair or replace broken electrical equipment, making healthy eating more challenging. 1 in 20 can't afford daily protein; 1 in 28 can't manage daily fresh fruit or vegetables, and 1 in 33 can't manage more than two meals a day.
- Around 800,000 adults received social care in 2018, compared to 1.7-1.8mn in 2009.
- 29% of households receive housing benefit, but: housing benefit covers less than 30% of properties; 28% of private rentals are inadequate; and only 20% of landlords are willing to let to benefit recipients. The proportion of affordable properties and willing landlords has fallen because of benefit cuts. The absolute number of inadequate private rental properties is increasing.
- It is believed that over 2mn people live in houses that actively damage their health.

16. A BREACH OF RIGHTS

- Disabled adults have lost £2500/year in support since 2010. Disabled adults who were already in poverty have lost £4600/year, with the most severely disabled losing £6350.
- The UK has experienced the worst economic recovery on record, even worse than that after the Great Depression. The UK did not lose as much GDP per capita as in the 1920s – 7% vs 10% – but ten years later, output is only 3% above pre-crash levels compared to more than 10% ten years after the Great Depression crash.

Government resources

Breaching human rights doesn't so much mean failing to provide full human rights for all citizens (no countries are expected to have reached that point yet) as meaning that a country has gone backwards in providing access to human rights. It more specifically means that a country has gone backwards without firstly ensuring that it is using all the resources available to it to protect human rights; secondly ensuring that poorer citizens are given the greatest and if possible complete protection against the impact of any rights-related cuts; and thirdly ensuring that any cuts against poor people are only temporary and are reversed as soon as possible.

The 'maximum resources' requirement means that a government must have fully explored and used all measures possible to increase its revenue, including through raising taxes, collecting more of the taxes that are due, closing tax avoidance loopholes, closing tax breaks to large corporations such as private schools, pursuing tax evaders, creating money (quantitative easing) and borrowing. In contrast, the UK Government has reduced tax on corporations and better-off individuals and has also cut the number of HMRC staff, making it harder for it to tackle tax avoidance and evasion or collect all of the tax due. It has studiously refused to borrow to invest, despite record low interest rates and demand for the security of government bonds. More importantly, because the UK is not dependent upon either borrowing or taxation to fund necessary public services, nor is it constrained by either of these factors. Consequently, the UK has unequivocally and without justification failed to utilise all of its resources to protect and enhance the rights and living standards of the poor.

The spending cuts, by being focused on welfare, have necessarily hit the poorest people hardest because these are the people who most depend upon welfare. Again and again, the government put private business and the better-off public ahead of its poor, sick and disabled citizens. Constant references to 'taxpayers money' and 'sustainability' spread the illusion that what the government was doing was right and fair, when in fact it was redistributing the costs of the financial crisis from those who caused it to those who couldn't afford it.

As well as being disproportionate, the spending cuts are demonstrably not temporary. So far from seeking to reverse cuts, many were only brought in in 2017 (such as cuts to PIP and ESA), whilst others are year-on-year cuts scheduled to continue until 2020. Nowhere in the government is there any indication of any intention to calculate the true cost of living, of housing and of the extra costs experienced by sick and disabled people, nor any intention to guarantee to raise benefits to these levels in order to protect and provide for the poorest and most vulnerable people in society.

The government's justifications for its cuts do not hold up. Economically, austerity as a response to recession has been neither necessary nor appropriate. Rather, it is government investment in an economy that rescues it from recession and restores it to the economic growth that is needed to repay any debt. Morally, there is no case for cutting state benefits in order to correct poor individuals' attitudes and behaviour: poor people retain strong commitments to work despite negative experiences. Sick and disabled people don't have bad or ill-informed attitudes that need correcting. Rather, what they have is chronic illness or disability which needs supporting.

The cuts to public spending were therefore neither proportionate, temporary or necessary, and nor did the government fulfil its obligation to its citizens to utilise the maximum resources available to it.

A breach of rights

The government has laid out a number of arguments in justification of it cuts to sick and disabled people's support, variously arguing that: cuts aren't affecting disabled people; it is necessary that government spending be reduced substantially; limited resources need to be retargeted; and cutting social security is morally right to correct workless people's deviant attitudes and behaviour.

None of these stand up to scrutiny. Government cuts are substantially harming sick and disabled people, leaving many destitute and trapped in their own homes and preventing them from being able to access, and afford to access, society as full and equal citizens. The government has cut both

16. A BREACH OF RIGHTS

disability-specific and general benefits, and in the case of the Bedroom Tax the government specifically refused to exempt disabled people on the grounds that this would exempt too many people from that cut.

The government did not have to make cuts: austerity not only doesn't help the economy, it actively harms it by removing vital finance and demand. Instead, the government should have used its ability to collect taxes to fund redistribution and investment that protects and helps the poor, thus stimulating and revitalising the economy at the same time as not only protecting the poor from harm but actually enabling them to do better.

Because the government could, and should, have increased its financial resources, it was not necessary to 'retarget' any benefits. Instead, the government could have directed additional money towards those sick and disabled people who were not receiving as much support as they need. In particular, it could substantially increase the funding for social care and the NHS, increase sickness benefits and especially the current ESA WRAG and UC equivalent, increase funding for support for sick and disabled people to work, and increase funding for extra-cost benefits. The government could also invest in a large, accessible house-building programme, for both affordable home ownership and the social rent sector; this would have the dual advantage of reducing the housing benefit bill and growing the economy.

Finally, we have seen that the narrative of a dependency culture in the UK is unsupported. It is not simply that there is a lack of evidence, but that the evidence shows a strong commitment to work even amongst people who are too ill to work or whose only experience of work is of low paid, dead end jobs. What is needed is a renewed labour market in which all jobs are decent, secure and adequately paid, and a renewed commitment from the government to full employment. Until then, it is particularly unjust that benefits be cut; the government is simply penalising poor people for the consequences of government policy.

The post-2010 Governments have caused substantial harm to sick and disabled people's health, living standards and social inclusion. It has done so without any moral or economic justification, and has signally failed to uphold one of governments' most fundamental reasons to exist: to ensure and improve the access to basic rights of its most vulnerable citizens. Sick and disabled people in the UK today are treated as second-class citizens, and until this situation is rectified the UK Government will continue to be violating international law by its ongoing breach of disabled people's rights.

17

Epilogue: Moving forward

A rights-based approach

The initial welfare state was based on the idea of contribution: working men paid in what they could, and in return they, their wives and their children were protected from income loss during periods of unemployment, and the widowed and disabled also received support. People who hadn't paid in couldn't get any support unless they were in severe need.

But this approach quickly proved problematic. There were simply too many people in need who, for whatever reason, hadn't had the opportunity to contribute by signing over some of their earnings to the State. There were more single parents, more civilian disabled, more women in work, more pensioners and fewer jobs-for-life than were initially planned for. Supplementary benefit provided on a case-by-case basis proved to be administratively costly, intrusive, inconsistent and inadequate for need.

Contribution-based benefits aren't means-tested and initially weren't time-limited, meaning that at least amongst those who had been able to pay the required amount of National Insurance there were equal pay-outs when needed. But successive governments, seeking to save money, down-graded the contributions-based benefits. A jobseeker can now only claim benefits on the grounds of his or her NI contributions for 6 months, and a person assessed as unfit for work but fit for work related activity for 12 months. And those contributions must have occurred in the previous two tax years, which risks penalising people who don't sign-on immediately after job-loss. The consequence is that people who have more savings, who tend also to be those who have enjoyed higher incomes and paid more in NI, receive less benefit in return if they become ill or otherwise unemployed for more than a few months. This undermines the principle of contribution-based benefits as well as reducing national support for the social security system, which increasingly is seen as paid for by the better-off whilst benefiting only the poor.

Contribution-based benefits face another major problem: they don't begin to measure the fullness of our contributions to society. As consumers, we create demand for the jobs that other people then fulfil; as family, friends and neighbours we meet the social needs of one another; some of us directly create jobs when we need carers, childminders, cleaners and gardeners. Our income doesn't reflect this, and nor does it reflect the value of our job to society. Remove all the cleaners and waste collectors, and a country grinds to a halt. Remove the politicians, bankers and company directors, and frankly we largely get along just fine.

The adult at home raising children is forming the character and confidence of the next generation of adults. The young person seeking work has a lifetime of potential contributions still ahead. The volunteer who can't find a job is contributing to the meeting of needs that aren't met by the State. The disabled person unable to work is contributing love, friendship and support to a host of other people. All these and many other ways in which we live, interact and participate are forms of contribution which the narrow National Insurance-based definition does not account for. Contribution-based benefits don't work when the measure of contribution is one that not everyone can meet, and that excludes many of the ways in which we do contribute.

The United Nations Conventions and Human Rights Declarations make clear that everyone, regardless of their ability to support themselves, has the right to a standard of living that meets not just their physical needs but their social and cultural needs as well. Support should not therefore be based upon a narrow financial definition of contribution, because support is a basic human right. More than that: it is national governments that are responsible for ensuring that all of their citizens have access and opportunity to what they need for a decent life.

Add in to this the desire to achieve equality of opportunity, which requires State intervention to maintain, and a rights-based approach becomes increasingly sensible. Ensuring that everyone has equal opportunity means investing in people who cannot invest in themselves, whether because they are young, sick, caring for others, unable to find work or any other reason. Children cannot become successful adults if they do not receive a high-quality education from an early age. Adults cannot work if there are not enough decent jobs to go around, or they cannot live near those jobs, or childcare or transport is prohibitively expensive. Sick people cannot seek treatment, thus allowing a recovery and return to work, if healthcare is to be paid for at the point of use. In so many ways, if the State wants equality of opportunity, it must provide for it directly wherever the market cannot or is not.

Underlying mechanisms

The details can vary, but every citizen should be able to know that their basic core of rights will be met and that their government is striving to ensure that all rights for all of its citizens will one day, and as soon as possible, be fulfilled. Governments that are not doing this are at fault. Governments therefore should not just implement policies that they think will work based on ideas that they think are true, but must check that their policies are having the intended effect. Governments are too powerful to hide behind the excuse that they thought they were doing the right thing.

In theory, the general mechanism or approach for providing access to basic rights doesn't matter. The point is that everyone does have access to their full human rights, not how it is provided. If every citizen has their rights fulfilled, then there is no oppression or injustice or breach of rights to complain about.

But in practice, we do know that the mechanism matters. This is because some political approaches, however much their proponents wish or believe them to work, just don't work. In the course of this book, we have seen how living standards and equality improved greatly under the post-war welfare state. By the 1970s, there was no longer a housing shortage. There was much less poverty, and the poverty that remained was being talked about in terms of disadvantage rather than deprivation and destitution. It was relative rather than absolute. Full employment was enjoyed by all, supported by a national education system. Inequality had dramatically fallen. Death rates had fallen with the discovery of penicillin and the introduction of a healthcare system that the poor could also access. The welfare state, despite various failings and inadequacies, was highly successful.

17. EPILOGUE: MOVING FORWARD

But under the 1980s ideology of a small state, inequality rapidly shot up. The dominant political position, in which government leaves space for the private sector to fulfil people's needs, has not worked because the private sector cannot fill in where people's basic rights and needs are not commensurate with their income. Whilst proponents of this position argue that they support it because they want to see equality of opportunity, in fact this is not what happens. Instead, social mobility has fallen, inequality has grown, the economy has stagnated and both the numbers of people in poverty and the depth of poverty those people experience has increased. Since 2010, the government's commitment to pulling back the state has caused deterioration and failure in pretty much every area of life – education, child services, social care, healthcare, housing, jobs, income, roads, public transport, libraries, sure-start centres, parks, public toilets, waste collection, recycling, police, justice, prisons... the list goes on.

Policies of small state don't work. They are based on false premises of laziness amongst the poor, disabled and disadvantaged, when in reality the easy majority of people very much want to support themselves through paid work. Small State policies rely on beliefs about how the public sector impacts the private sector that are the opposite of reality, and consequently stymie the economy and frustrate individual ambition at the same time as their advocates claim that policy is implemented in order to strengthen the economy and reward personal effort. Strong public sectors create the environment for private sectors to thrive, but small public sectors shrink the economy and thus shrivel the private sector as well.

In many ways and for many reasons the government cannot simply allow the market to rule. The market will always fail those with less money and less power. In the absence of regulation, businesses will maximise their profits by pushing as many of their costs as possible onto other people. Zero-hour contracts, insecure jobs, low pay, hard working conditions, few rights, high pressure, constraints on rest and refreshment and toilet breaks – all push the costs of production onto workers for the sake of consumers and bosses. Greenhouse gas emissions, mini earthquakes, water pollution, soil degradation, loss of habitat and wildlife decline push the costs of production onto local residents and future generations. In the absence of regulation, free markets will lead to exploitation.

And some things just can't be provided by the private sector. The cost of buses and broadband and postal services in rural areas exceed the number of people available to pay for them. Street lighting and security benefit everyone but the only way to make everyone pay is to collect a toll or tax. Healthcare and education at the point of use typically exceeds the individual's ability to pay, yet a sick and uneducated labour force limits everyone's ability to thrive. Housing providers maximise their profit by restricting the supply of houses, but this runs counter to the right to a decent home for everyone.

The rules of the economic game have been set to allow employers to pay people less than they need for the cost of life, whilst directing increasingly vast sums of money at people whose predominant contribution to productivity is to start off with more money and assets than others. The fruits of labour go to the owners of capital rather than the ones doing the front-line and ground-level work. Success is increasingly the preserve of the lucky few, the ones who happened in a moment of serendipity to break through, whilst equally talented and able people never make it. Inequality distorts the economy and the country, giving wealth to people who don't need it and depriving those who do; leading to investment in lawyers and petty patent disputes rather than genuine learning and development.

The rules of the economic game need to be changed. Governments need to block exploitation and ensure that business success is shared amongst all who produced it, not just the top. They need to ensure that the costs of cheap goods are borne by the company owners, directors and shareholders, and not by the staff members creating and delivering the goods. They need to ensure that any destruction or pollution of the environment is paid for by the companies involved, rather than by the local residents and future generations. They need to protect the poor's right to freedom, rest and leisure; to family life, health and wellbeing; and to participation in society and culture. And they need to make sure that the rewards of technological innovation are spread across all citizens, and don't merely accrue to a few vastly wealthy individuals.

The CHORUS principles

A new settlement needs to be created based upon the responsibilities of the state and the rights and responsibilities of the citizens. The approach has a responsibility to ensure that all of its citizens can meet their core rights to essential food, primary healthcare, basic housing and shelter, and basic education. But the State cannot stop there, because human rights are not met only by the bare minimum but by working to achieve dignity and full and free development of personality for all citizens.

17. EPILOGUE: MOVING FORWARD

Because the free market approach does not work, and the private sector cannot provide for those with insufficient money, the state must take responsibility for investing in everyone through a holistic state. Through this holistic state provision, we can ensure opportunity for all on an equal basis. There is no equality of opportunity wherever people are left in poverty; children and deprived adults go without access to decent education; or there are pockets of deprivation where the housing is poor, jobs are sparse and high-strain, and healthcare is under-resourced. The state needs to re-commit to holistic welfare, in which the need for social security is taken as an indicator that more money needs to be invested into other parts of welfare: housing, jobs, education, healthcare and social care.

In return for this state responsibility – for core rights and holistic state provision designed to ensure opportunity for all – citizens must recognise their responsibility towards the state that has invested in them and has created the circumstances necessary for them to thrive. The citizen must live in a peaceful and harmonious way, not infringing upon the rights of others; provide for themselves and their children as far as they are able; and pay taxes as required by the state. The better-off must recognise the contribution that a secure and stable state with a healthy, skilled and thriving workforce makes to their own success, and be willing to see the rewards of business success shared across all of their staff. Such a reciprocal contract between state and citizen creates a community of people mutually willing to support one another during times of need, avoiding the division of inequality and us/them politics.

The holistic welfare state should be universal and equal. No-one should be means-tested out on the grounds of assets or savings or, for all except income-replacement benefits, on the grounds of income. No-one should receive more or less because of their age, their income prior to unemployment, the cause of their income loss or how much they are considered to have contributed to the state. The holistic welfare state should be available as of right to all citizens, without means-test or National Insurance-type restrictions which introduce costly administration and create an us/them distinction between those who can and can't access state provision.

The state should also seek to share the rewards of scientific and technological advancement across all of society. No one person can ever claim to be the sole inventor or creator of anything. All invention and advancement rests upon the work of people who have gone before, from plastic and machine-woven cotton to microchips and semi-conductors. And mass-production of any good relies upon a whole suite of people: cleaners; delivery drivers; factory workers; administrators and logistic co-ordinators; the public sector that keeps roads usable, the workforce healthy and the country generally secure and stable. Even without recognising the large role that government funding plays in research and development, there are good reasons to share success across the whole country rather than give it to a few select people.

> **Box 15. CHORUS principles**
>
> The **CHORUS** principles for a new settlement between citizen and state:
>
> **CORE RIGHTS** - the State ensures that no citizen goes without essential food, basic housing, primary healthcare and a basic education.
>
> **HOLISTIC** - the state builds upon these core rights to invest in all of its citizens through full and well-resourced education, healthcare, provision for disability and carers, decent affordable housing, full employment in decent jobs and income protection through social security.
>
> **OPPORTUNITY** - the aim of the state's investment in its citizens is to create and maintain equality of opportunity.
>
> **RECIPROCITY** - citizens recognise their responsibility to live peaceably, pay tax and, as far as able, provide for themselves. States recognise their responsibility to ensure that core rights are met, peace and justice is maintained, and that there is opportunity on an equal basis for all.
>
> **UNIVERSAL** - every citizen has access to state provision of income (whether jobs or social security), housing, education and healthcare. No-one is restricted due to a lack of national insurance or related contributions; age; previous employment; previous income; or savings. Only income replacement benefits are means-tested on the basis of income.
>
> **SHARED REWARDS** - all of society should benefit from scientific and technological advancement.

The first five pillars of the holistic welfare state

In the principles for a new settlement, the state is committed to meeting everyone's basic needs and ensuring equality of opportunity through the holistic provision of education, housing, jobs, income protection and

17. EPILOGUE: MOVING FORWARD

healthcare. Everyone can get the same support out from the state when they need it, and everyone has the opportunity to make the most of their lives. Without such a commitment from the state, it is inevitable that many will be unable to do well despite the hard work and striving that is so necessary to survival at the bottom of the UK's labour market. These five make up five pillars of a holistic welfare state. They are similar to the UN core rights and the five pillars of the original welfare state, which suggests that they are key components of any just and fair society.

For our children to be able to thrive and make the most of their natural interests and abilities, we need to ensure that they enjoy an education that gives them a range of skills. In justice, we cannot promote the happiness and job satisfaction of only those individuals who like the service-oriented industry that we currently have. Children and adults with interests in the trades and creative industries have just as much right to a job that they are inherently suited to and interested in. The education system should equip all children with a range of skills outside of the academic, ensuring that all children have a truly free choice of where they work as adults. In this way, employers have a range of qualified candidates to choose from, and the economy operates on a higher skill level and stronger footing.

We also need to ensure that we have enough houses for everyone. The cost of housing is simply unreachable for young or poor people, but we cannot make people wait until they have half a lifetime's (middle-class) earnings before we house them. People who cannot afford private rent or a mortgage still need somewhere decent to live. The market can't, and won't, fill this gap, because the market has to make a profit. Therefore the state must recognise that it has a role in the market by contributing those goods and services which are basic rights but which the poorer people in society cannot afford.

To address poverty, we need to ensure that there are enough jobs to go around and that those jobs pay an adequate wage. If the government wishes to help employers by permitting low wages, then it may do so – but only if it protects employees from this government largesse by topping up their income through the benefits system. It cannot morally follow the current strategy of benefiting employers at the cost of employees, for the government does not exist for the benefit of companies but for the benefit of its citizens, and particularly those on lower incomes. Additionally, because of the vicissitudes of life and variations in performance of the economy, even a state aiming for full employment needs to ensure access to a subsistence income for jobseekers.

To ensure that jobs provide an adequate wage and are available in sufficient number, the government must re-commit to sustaining full employment. Again, it is not morally acceptable for the government to protect companies and higher-worth individuals by causing poorer people to lose access to work. Let the government ensure that the poor are okay, and the rich will look after themselves. This necessarily means strengthening rather than weakening workers' rights, including the role and authority of trade unions. This doesn't mean making trade unions into tyrants, but redressing the current imbalance in favour of the owners against the workers.

In the ideal system where everyone can earn enough to support themselves, benefits need only be subsistence-plus. That is, they need only cover a little more than the basic necessities, thus accounting for unexpected costs and the cost of job search, as well as human dignity. But this only works if unemployment is genuinely short-lasting. Given that long-term unemployment and inability to work will always remain, there needs to be a system for properly supporting the long-term unemployed. It may be that a government prefers to explore directly employing long-term unemployed people on full-time, living-wage contracts rather than pay unemployment benefits adequate for social inclusion. But for people with long-term inability to work, whether carers or the sick or disabled, benefits must cover social inclusion just as we expect them to for old-age pensioners.

Finally, there must be access to healthcare. This is both a human right and a piece of basic economic sense. Sick workers can't work as much or as well as healthy people, and the failure to cure or control contagious disease can undermine a workforce. The NHS is rightly a source of national pride and international envy, worthy of protection and proper investment.

And employers must not create working conditions that are damaging to health. Whilst many modern businesses seem to have forgotten or overlooked the importance of health, this has not always been the case. Henry Ford, amongst others, championed the five-day, 40-hour working week because productivity was higher when the same people worked shorter hours; nearly 100 years later, we have the opportunity to move to a four-day week. Too much work, whether long hours or fast pace or both, wears people out and renders them less productive. We can improve the productivity of our workforce, and the wellbeing of our workers, by allowing people to work at a sustainable pace for sustainable hours.

UBI and job guarantees

The UN declarations make it clear that if paid work does not pay enough for an adequate standard of life – where that includes not merely access to basic physical necessities, but also the ability to enjoy rest and family, social and cultural life – then it is incumbent upon the state to provide the rest directly.

One recurrent idea for this is Universal Basic Income (UBI). This is a fixed sum of money, paid to every adult citizen, without means-test, taxation or conditions. Other aspects vary: there might be a sum paid to children but put into a trust fund for them, or a sum for children might be paid to the parent(s); the level of the UBI might be just enough for short-term subsistence needs, long-term subsistence needs or to reach the minimum income standard needed for equal social participation, or it might be some random amount agreed upon politically. However, if it is insufficient to keep citizens from at least destitution if not some measure of deprivation then it is failing its primary purpose, which is a guaranteed protection against poverty at a time when jobs are increasingly insecure.

Critics argue that it would be prohibitively expensive, and query why a state would pay money to someone who doesn't need it; proponents point out that any money given to the better-off in a UBI system would be withdrawn very easily through an adjustment of tax rates relative to the non-UBI system. Indeed, the removal of means-tested benefits and concomitant rollover into the tax system is one reason why some right-wing economists and politicians advocate for UBI: it vastly simplifies the benefits and tax system, and consequently reduces the high administrative costs of our current system.

UBI has the potential to be transformative. When individuals are given small, repeated payments (large lump sums tend to be less well used) then they respond positively: they take up study that will allow them to go into a more productive career; they are enabled to spend more time with family and in socially useful activity; they develop hobbies into worthy artistic endeavours. Overall, individual wellbeing, personal development and productivity improve.

Where things become less certain is what happens to wages: will people work for lower wages because they can now accept less per hour and still get the same total income? Or will they refuse low wages because they can just about get by without, thus forcing employers to pay more? When wages increased during the 20th Century, economists largely expected that people would work less: they could now do fewer hours for the same income. But instead, people worked more: the cost of not working an additional hour was higher. People worked more, earned more, and had less leisure time in which to actually enjoy what they had earned.

There is also a question over whether UBI would ever be sufficiently politically acceptable, and whether it would transform or polarise social attitudes. On the left, UBI is promoted because it has the potential to free the poor from the exploitative working conditions imposed by the rich and from the trend for machines to replace people whilst leaving the displaced workers unable to afford to retrain into new industries. UBI is seen as a way for the state to confirm the value and rights of every individual, whoever they are, and whatever work they do. But would society as a whole learn to see UBI this way, or would many see it as an expensive policy that encourages idleness, and which is vulnerable to attack and attrition from the right?

On the other hand, if the state fulfilled its duty to ensure full employment in healthy jobs that lead to successful careers, a UBI would no longer be needed on the grounds of a labour-market failure. It is this current market of insecure, toxic jobs, an excessively punitive and inadequate social security system and the unequal sharing of success that makes UBI seem so necessary.

An alternative approach that would simultaneously address the punitive benefits system and toxic jobs market is a Jobs Guarantee. This would mean that, instead of offering unemployment benefit to people who can and want to work, the state would instead offer a job.

Compared to the current benefits system, a Jobs Guarantee makes a lot of sense. The state is already paying people to 'work' at searching for work, for full-time hours but substantially less than minimum wage pay. But this helps no-one: not the state, as job-seeking does nothing to strengthen the economy; not the individual, who spends their days on repetitive and largely futile job-search; not the community, which sees many members endlessly seeking work whilst important and beneficial tasks go undone; not the economy, because there are available workers and unfulfilled demand, yet the two aren't matched together. It doesn't make sense that money is being paid, people are seeking work and work is going undone all at the same time. Why not instead, for the same money, pay people to work? For £170 – Jobseeker's Allowance plus average housing benefit – a person could be doing 17 hours of useful work each week for £10 per hour.

To prevent abuse by private companies, the jobs available should be determined upon by the local community; the cost of administration could be met by incorporating those roles into the guaranteed jobs too. A range of tasks could be available: basic tasks that don't require training or demanding working conditions (e.g. litter picking; painting); tasks that can involve on-the-job training and lead to a career (conservation and landscaping; librarians; road maintenance); or tasks that provide social services to the community (social clubs; exercise clubs; community cafés). The Jobs Guarantee should be paid at the living wage and per hour worked, thus allowing people to choose how many hours to work according to what they need. The jobs must meet the UN human rights criteria of just and favourable pay and working conditions, as indeed should all public sector jobs; governments simply have no excuse for failing on this.

A Jobs Guarantee fulfils the principle of reciprocity. Currently, there is an expectation that those who are able to work and wish to receive state support during unemployment must be actively looking for work in return. But to ensure that this is happening, the state has to control what looking for work means and monitor the behaviour of all benefit recipients. Nor does the state commit to ensuring that there is enough work for all who want to work. The result is that, whilst no-one can receive unemployment benefit without at least doing something work-related, people are prevented from doing things that are actually worthwhile. In contrast, a Jobs Guarantee means that all who want work can be in work, which is where they want to be, and are doing something socially and economically useful with their time, which is what the state wants them to be doing. The Jobs Guarantee fulfils both sides of the reciprocity contract: individuals provide for themselves when they can, and the state ensures that they can.

A Jobs Guarantee fulfils multiple criteria. It improves the labour market by guaranteeing a decent job for everyone, so that private employers have to improve their jobs in order to attract staff. It creates and maintains skills, thus making people who otherwise would have been unemployed more attractive to private employers. It provides everyone who can and wants to work with the dignity of work, rather than the stigma of unemployment and the benefits system. It keeps people out of poverty. And it improves and strengthens the local community.

The sixth pillar: disability and carers

There is a need for the state to recognise that the ideal settlement between citizen and state is not possible for everyone. If the state has fulfilled its role in the provision of health and social care, decent jobs, training children in a range of skills and ensuring that housing is decent and near to jobs, then the typical citizen will be able to fulfil his or her part through providing for him or herself and paying taxes. But not everyone is able to provide for themselves despite the external opportunity to do so. For people with chronic illness or disability, as well as for carers and lone parents, the ability to work, either at all or enough to earn a liveable income, is often unrealistic.

The original welfare state was concerned with disease, but advances in healthcare mean that the primary medical problem now is not disease but disability. Conditions that previously would have caused death no longer do so, but many people are not fully cured and instead are left with lingering problems. Ironically, more healthcare can mean more disability, not less. And with an ageing population, the number of people living with disability is only going to increase.

A new settlement between state and citizen needs to recognise the necessity of catering for those who cannot engage in the basic settlement. The state has additional responsibilities to these people, to meet their needs directly rather than just through the provision of opportunity.

Sick and disabled people need a new sickness benefit with a new assessment. The assessment should be expert-based, perhaps by accepting sick notes from GPs or other doctors as the proof of health problems whilst appointing occupational therapists to discuss and work with people to establish what, if any, work is possible and what support would be needed. We must recognise that for many sick and disabled people a 'sickness pension' is indeed needed, at a level adequate for a decent life and with much greater security than the current system of frequent assessment. Those who may be able to work need a guarantee that the state will provide the support that they need to make work possible, which may mean ensuring that the Jobs Guarantee is available to all disabled people through the provision of all necessary support – including not just in-work support but transport, personal care and assistance at home.

Society needs to drastically improve its accessibility to sick and disabled people, with no more exemptions. If the government thinks that a company cannot afford it, then it is for the government to provide the access instead, not to make sick and disabled people pay the cost through lack of access. Extra-costs benefits need to actually look at the extra costs that sick and disabled people have, including higher utilities bills and domestic tasks such as shopping and cleaning. They must carry out a valid assessment of need, and match benefit to the cost of meeting that need.

Social care needs to be centrally funded in a similar system to the NHS, rather than being constricted by local councils' budgets and varying from place to place. Social care must not be capped, because a cap means that an individual's support depends upon how many other people are in need, rather than simply being about what he or she needs. Similarly, the NHS needs to be properly funded and invested in, based on a realistic appraisal of what society needs and what it costs to provide that.

If we were to prioritise sick and disabled people, the whole of society would improve with it. Bad work – the low paid, low skilled, low autonomy, insecure, high pressure jobs dominating the bottom of the labour market – would be eliminated, because these jobs make healthy people sick and make sick and disabled people worse. Housing would be of good quality, accessible and close to jobs, schools, green places and public amenities, because this is what it must be if disabled people are to be able to get out of their homes and access society. Public transport would be frequent, prompt and pleasant, with plenty of room for all passengers. Education, by having to find ways to give quality teaching to children who can't access standard methods or who can't learn specific tasks, would be forced to meet the needs of those who learn in different ways, or who have different abilities, from the current academic-focused approach.

People unable to work, or unable to work enough, are still people. They are still worthy and deserving. They still deserve their basic rights. It isn't okay to say that we don't need to support the workless because they can relieve their poverty by getting work. Those who are too sick or disabled to work, those who are devoting some of their work-capacity to caring for others and those who are looking for work are all restricted from work by circumstances outside their control, whether that is disability, the needs of others or the simple fact that if there aren't as many hours of work available as there are hours of available labour, some people will spend longer looking for work than they would like.

Two futures

There are two ways forward from here. One is to continue as we are, as a country that prioritises private profit over individual need. In this scenario, the welfare state continues to be grossly underfunded. People who are too sick to work are forced to try to work because the alternative is starvation. The support that disabled people need to access decent, sustainable work isn't there. The effort required to work takes everything else away from them. They won't be able to sustain a relationship, bring up children, care for elderly parents, attend religious observances, or take part in community activity, because they will have put everything they have into paid work.

And even then, they won't earn enough to support themselves, and they won't be able to maintain a clean and healthy home. The pressure to work when not well will put stress and strain upon already sick people, making their health worse as they worry about their work capacity and engage in work at times when they should be resting. And the socially useful contributions that chronically sick people can make without harm to themselves will be cut off from them. They won't have the energy to greet their partner with a smile and a kiss; to hug the child who has failed her exam; to be there for the friend who has been diagnosed with cancer. They won't be able to share their experience-based knowledge with others who have the same illness, or put in a few hours of voluntary work as and when possible. They won't be able to maintain the flowerbed that supports the bees that farmers need to pollinate their crops. They won't be able to spend a week doing the laundry or sorting the recycling so that it's one less job for their partners to do after work. They won't be able to take pride in plaiting their daughter's hair each morning or in repairing her football kit, nor commiserate or celebrate with their son depending on his musical prowess.

These are small, but they are part of the many ways in which each one of us contributes to society outside of paid work. They are the ways that those too sick or disabled to work can contribute. They allow a person the freedom to engage in only what they are capable of, when they are capable of it. They allow a person to be socially useful and part of society, no matter how ill or how far from the labour market. They allow sick and disabled people to make some of the most valuable contributions of all – of family and friendship. But in the current scenario of continuing as we are, none of this will be possible.

In the other scenario, the state commits to giving sick and disabled people their right to a decent life. Chronically sick people are freed from the stress of insecurity and poverty, and are enabled by an adequate income to participate in and contribute to society. Some even find that their health improves enough to enable them to take on some work. Disabled people receive comprehensive, occupational therapy-based support to find, obtain and maintain work that matches their skills and abilities. They can love their partners and bring up their children without the arguments and distress

17. EPILOGUE: MOVING FORWARD

caused by not having enough. Society is made accessible so that sick and disabled people can participate, and with accessibility being the norm social attitudes also start to change, seeing disabled people not as burdens but as valued individuals. Those who can't work will still be valued for the contributions that they do make, simply by being alive and in relationships.

There is no requirement that the UK follow the first scenario rather than the second. Inequality is neither inevitable nor ingrained. But to change all this, we need to recognise that poverty still exists, and that even without a return to destitution there would still be a need to challenge deprivation and disadvantage. It isn't enough for a country to satisfy itself that all of its citizens have some income plus access to basic healthcare, education and housing. Society through the state has to continue to improve the lives of its poorer citizens so that they have equal access to quality healthcare, education and housing; can access the same cultural, social and artistic pastimes; and benefit equally from technological and scientific advancement. If the state truly wants equality of opportunity, then it must become a true welfare state.

Sick and disabled people do not have to be second-class citizens. But until citizens come before companies and people before profit, the sick and disabled will continue to be the least and the last.

About the Author

Stef Benstead is an independent researcher in disability and social policy. She has worked with Ekklesia and the Spartacus Network and is currently working with the Chronic Illness Inclusion Project and Church Action on Poverty.

Stef has a 1st from the University of Cambridge but had to leave a PhD at the same university after becoming severely ill with the genetic connective tissue disorder, Ehlers-Danlos Syndrome.

Since leaving her PhD, Stef has been using her interest in research to investigate the welfare system, particularly for people with chronic illness and disability, to show not just where and why it is going wrong but how to do things better.

Acknowledgements

Huge thanks to my editor, Simon Duffy, who has taken a lot of time out of his very over-crowded life to shape and improve this book beyond its first conception, and pushed me to achieve a higher standard than I at times would have settled for. The book is much better for his efforts and exhortation.

Lightning Source UK Ltd.
Milton Keynes UK
UKHW041555190421
382249UK00003B/1012